WW II LETTERS
TO MY GIRL BACK HOME
From Nigeria, Arabia and Turkey

By

Allan Robert Humbert

© 2002 by Allan Robert Humbert. All rights reserved.

No part of this book may be reproduced, stored in a retrieval system, or transmitted by any means, electronic, mechanical, photocopying, recording, or otherwise, without written permission from the author.

ISBN: 1-4033-3647-4 (e-book)
ISBN: 1-4033-3648-2 (Paperback)

This book is printed on acid free paper.

1stBooks – rev. 12/09/02

Acknowledgments

I am indebted to the following for their help on the book: Frank and Rosemary Martin, Helen Blackman Fritz, my family—Mozelle, Richard and Kathryn—and finally the many others who offered helpful suggestions over the past several years.

Dedication

To Mozelle
The Girl I Waited For

Daily our ranks grow thinner. We who once sprang at a single bound to the top of a double bunk now find ourselves mildly embarrassed when a cafeteria waitress asks us if we need help with our tray. Sometimes, in the quiet of a long night, we think back. And we remember...

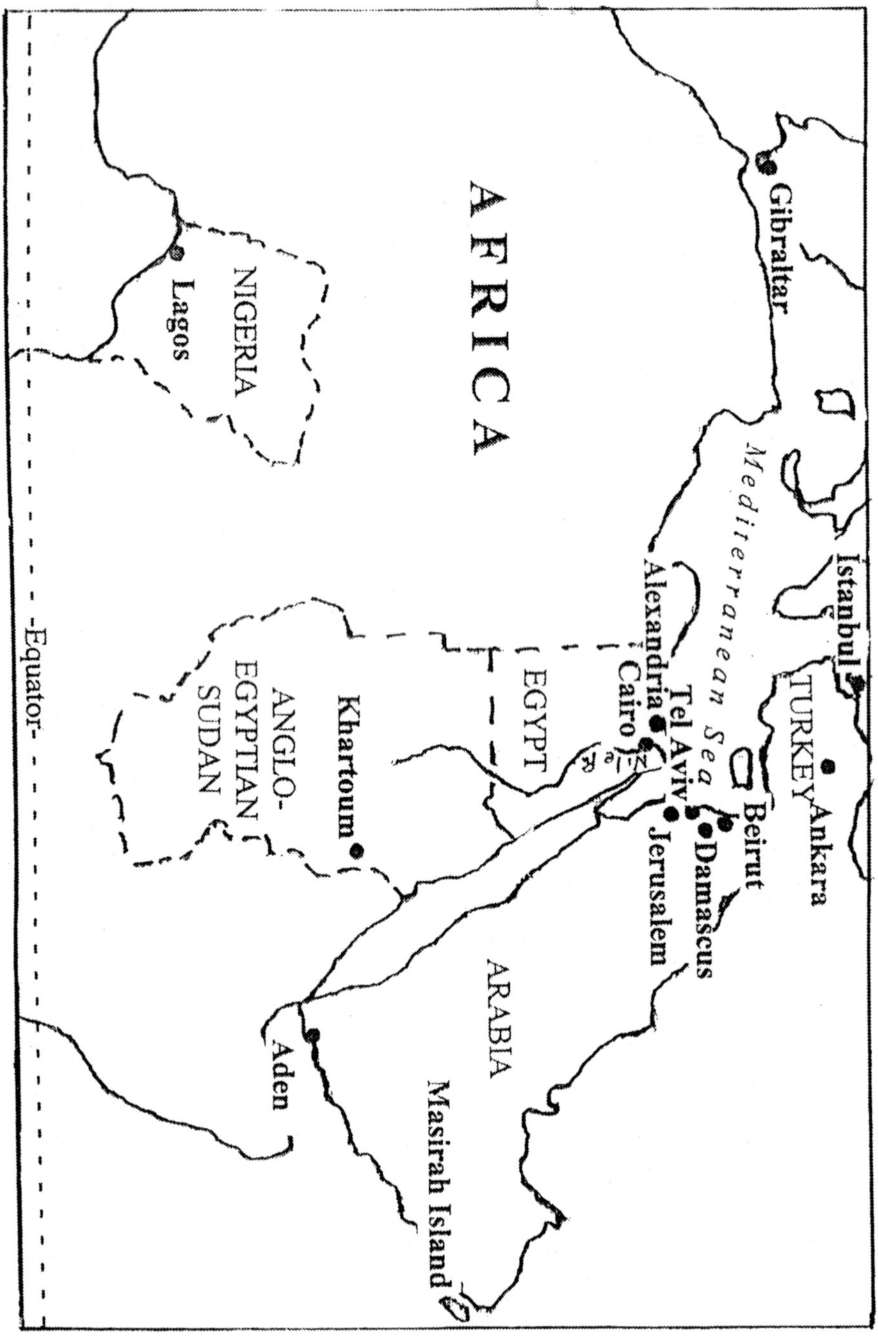
AFRICA
Gibraltar
Mediterranean Sea
Istanbul
TURKEY
Ankara
Beirut
Damascus
Tel Aviv
Jerusalem
Alexandria
Cairo
EGYPT
NIGERIA
Lagos
Khartoum
ANGLO-EGYPTIAN SUDAN
ARABIA
Aden
Masirah Island
Equator

Contents

PART ONE *Voyage and Arrival*

CHAPTER **PAGE**

1 On the High Seas 1944 1
2 Egypt and the Sudan 1944 14

PART TWO *In the US 1938-1942*

3 Muncie, Indiana 1938 21
4 College 26
5 Looming Military Service 30

PART THREE *US Service 1942-1944*

6   Bring Enough Clothes for Three Days 37
7   Troop Train—On to Basic Training 41
8   Chanute Field Weather School 1942 44
9   Tallahassee Weather Observer 47
10 Weather Forecasting School 52
11 Seymour Johnson Field, North Carolina 1944 57
12 Camp Patrick Henry, Virginia, March 1944 69

PHOTOGRAPHS

PART FOUR *Nigeria, Arabia and Turkey*

13 Lagos, Nigeria, May to July 1944 87
14 Lagos, Nigeria, August to October 1944 110
15 Masirah Island, Arabia, October 1944 to March 1945 .. 126
16 Palestine Furlough, March 1945 152
17 Masirah Island, Arabia, March to May 1945 172
18 Ankara, Turkey, June to September 1945 199
19 Ankara, Turkey, June to September 1945 234

PART FIVE   *Over and Out*

20 Homeward Bound 266
    Epilogue 2002 281

: *WWII LETTERS TO MY GIRL BACK HOME*
From Nigeria, Arabia and Turkey

Chapter 1

ON THE HIGH SEAS 1944

Our group of Air Force weathermen left Camp Patrick Henry, Virginia, on a showery April day, laden like donkeys with pack, blankets and equipment. A band escorted us to the train and we stepped directly from the train onto the ship.

Slowly the Liberty ship steamed away from the dock through the dirty brown water. When compared to our recent grim instructions for surviving (theoretically!) while swimming away from a torpedoed ship in burning fuel oil, our departure seemed strangely uneventful. The SS Ralph Izzard was carrying, among other war materials, crates of fighter planes bound for Murmansk. We 87 weathermen were incidental. The government was determined that each ship be loaded to capacity, regardless of whether it transported ammunition, servicemen or mules.

Having been assigned quarters, we were free to wander about the vessel, so long as we stayed out of restricted areas. Those of us who had never been aboard an oceangoing ship found the Ralph Izzard fascinating. American know-how was producing ships at a faster rate than any maritime construction the world had ever known, 426,533 tons in 1940 increasing to 10,142,776 tons in 1944, 23 times as many, with over 2,700 Liberties produced during the war.

Some 441 feet long, 57 feet wide and displacing 14,000 tons, the Ralph Izzard was able to reliably haul cargo anywhere in the world. Driven by a sturdy 2,500 horsepower steam engine, the ship had a speed of 11 knots. With capacity for 50,000 gallons of fuel oil, and plenty of provisions for weeks at sea, the vessel was a self-contained floating village. We felt confident that it would take us to our destination—not that we knew where we were going.

Sixteen long wartime months had passed since I had been drafted. Time enough had elapsed to have become a trained weather observer, to have experienced army life in four states of the US, and most importantly to have found the right girl. We saved our letters from each other.

Fifty-odd years later, as I reread them, I see a couple of young people, idealistic, optimistic and high-spirited. Millions of other soldiers had their stories, too. However, I was lucky to have been sent to so many unusual places, and I'm glad we still have all the letters written at that time, describing not only events and places, but how we felt about it all.

An occasional page has a word cut out, where an army censor deleted military information unintentionally divulged. Because we did our best not to write anything which would have value if the letters fell into enemy hands, the dates and locations of some events are lacking. Moreover, we soldiers pretty well kept any fears or misgivings about the voyage to ourselves. There was no need to alarm those back home. Also, if some of the sentiment seems a bit cloying, our feelings were sincere.

On April 14, I wrote:

I've not been the least bit seasick. Lots of the guys have, but only about half the group.

This is really a nice set-up, little or no work, having the run of the ship, nothing to do for a long time but read and relax. So far, I've had no difficulty occupying my time. We have three delicious meals daily—even better than those of my former camp, and we are so lazy that we resent even the intrusion of mealtime into our peace and quiet.

Last night I went out on the deck and looked at the sea and sky. There's nothing like it. One of the strangest sights is the phosphorescence of the water. It glows like a luminous watch when the waves break, due to many tiny animals being disturbed.

WWII LETTERS TO MY GIRL BACK HOME
From Nigeria, Arabia and Turkey

Yesterday the water was green, but today it was blue as a picture—absolutely different from any water I ever saw. Sometimes I think we're gaining money from the government. Cruises like ours would cost hundreds of dollars in peacetime.

April 15
Atlantic Ocean

Lazy, lazy day; nothing to do but read a bit, think and relax. We eat and sleep and grow beards—at least some of the guys do. However, I prefer to shave. Classes in French and Arabic are beginning, and I'm enrolled in both, but we go too fast.

Yesterday the PX opened and I bought some candy and a little bit of junk.

We have more fun spreading rumors. Of course nobody believes them, but here are a few: "The captain of the ship is now on his first voyage. He has fits. The Von Tirpitz (German battleship) is sailing in our convoy. Men are secretly being thrown overboard at night; Subs are chasing us. The ship's guns won't fire. All the ammunition on board is in the form of blanks ..." Actually we know that all this is a joke; probably the rumors wouldn't exist if they were true. But they are fun.

April 16, 1944
The Broad Atlantic

Sunday—just nine weeks ago tonight we were enjoying our last date for a long time. Now, out here on the ocean, any romance must be on paper, and there are no letters from you for inspiration.

Situations such as ours put a lot more emphasis on old-fashioned faith than those in peacetime. In a way, the entire problem deals in faith—being in a war because we believe in something strongly enough to fight for it—the faith of the people over there that we are on our way to render help, and our faith in the people back home. By now you have just about received my last letter written in the States, and for many weeks you will be without mail, hoping that one comes along soon. Yet I know that each night

Allan Robert Humbert

you will be writing me, just as I am writing you, and that sooner or later we will be together to stay.

There were church services on deck today, consisting mainly of singing. The boys had the right spirit, even if the tunes were lacking a little. Songs about the sea were very real. For instance, "Let the Lower Lights Be Burning." The ocean has an irresistible power that compels respect from all persons, especially at night. But by the time you're reading this, the only voyage facing me will be the one returning when the war is over, say in a couple of years.

From more letters:

April 18
Same Old Sea

Food here is so good that people are beginning to complain about having so much of it! Tonight we had steak—I was lucky enough to get seconds, and both pieces were delicious. We are taking yellow Atabrine pills for malaria daily, although nobody has seen any mosquitoes.

I enjoy these stormy days, even if the inside of the ship is hot and crowded, because the size and action of the waves is greater. I like to play a little game, standing by the rail, and watching them roll in till one is ready to break over the deck before I jump back. Only once did I get wet.

Still another game is my effort to sleep on deck. Twice I tried this, only to be ignominiously forced to go inside. But I'm going to try it again tonight.

April 19
Same Old Ocean

As for sleeping out, I tried it again last night. Jonner, Hartig, Cristo and I made our bunks topside on deck, as had been planned. Using every trick I could think of, I made a bed which was waterproof. It was covered with canvas all over, like a sleeping bag, except for the seam in the center underneath. I lay down, not sleeping. The wind was quite high and a thunderstorm was coming up, but I decided to lie there and see the storm through. So I did, but got soaked through the seam in the home-made sleeping bag. About 11:30 p.m. I came in, soaking wet and barefooted, looking like a drowned rat. Tonight it's cooler, so I'll sleep below.

This little dining hall is as lively as the Tally Ho (a favorite hangout of Ball State students) ever was. A phonograph is going full blast; card games are everywhere; people are writing letters; some are shooting craps at another table, and dozens are reading.

The Atlantic seems quite chummy now. A rainy day makes the visibility lower, keeping you from seeing more than a small area of the ocean. The result is a cozy illusion that the horizon is only a few miles distant, entirely different from the reality of being far at sea.

As our voyage continued, we sensed from the general direction of travel that the ship was heading for the European Theater of Operations. So far as we could tell, enemy submarines were nowhere to be seen. Nevertheless, it didn't take a lot of imagination to visualize a torpedo crashing into our quarters at night. Perhaps we would even see the infernal thing lying there for a few seconds before blowing us to bits.

Everyone took security measures very seriously. We had lifeboat drills and kept our life jackets close at hand. Each jacket was fitted with a one-celled flashlight having a red lens, in case we had to be rescued from the ocean in the dark. Some of us went even further, keeping a belt at hand with items which might be vital in case of disaster, such as a rope, whistle and knife.

The Ralph Izzard was fitted with heavy canvas blackout curtains over the doors, from which not a ray of light escaped. Smoking at night on the deck was forbidden, and we sailed with the ship in darkness. The vessel had watertight compartments which could be sealed from one another in case a compartment was flooded.

Liberty ships were defended by an Armed Guard contingent. Not really navy personnel, the Armed Guard were more or less employees and were paid more than the navy men, a fact resented by the sailors with whom I talked.

The ship's weapons consisted of a 3-inch gun in the bow and a 5-inch gun in the stern, plus six 20-millimeter machine guns, two on the deck a few feet forward of the 5-inch one, and four on the deck, located on platforms raised several feet above it. Guns are distinguished by the diameter of the projectile. The inner diameter of a 5-inch gun is five inches, while that of a 20 mm machine gun is 20 millimeters, about 4/5 inch. This armament was fully capable of shooting down attacking planes, and similar large guns had on occasion even sunk submarines which had surfaced.

From a letter of April 20, 1944:

Censorship being as it is, I can't write about the activity right now...(Author's note: I have no written record of the exact dates on which the following events occurred, although I remember them vividly. Because the events mentioned were military information which we were forbidden to divulge, I wrote nothing more in this letter. But on June 20, after our voyage had ended, I got permission to explain what had happened.)

On June 20, 1944, two months later, I wrote:

I've asked our lieutenant whether it is now all right to tell about some of the excitement that occurred on the boat. He gave permission, and the account follows:
We were all given the opportunity to volunteer for duty on the boat's gun crews. You know how well I like anything mechanical; in fact, my very first wish on boarding the ship was to shoot one of the 20's.
One day I was writing you, sitting calmly in the galley, when suddenly began the alarm, Clang! Clang! Clang! Clang!, a bell that would wake the dead. So I dropped my pen, jumped over the table, and zipped upstairs like something out of a Walt Disney cartoon movie. Our assigned position was away up on the bridge, so I had to climb one ladder and two stairways to get there, but I managed OK, and was the first one on the bridge.

WWII LETTERS TO MY GIRL BACK HOME
From Nigeria, Arabia and Turkey

Then to work—jerk the cover off the gun, open the ammunition boxes—by this time the gunner and my assistant were there—help the guy cock the gun, slip a magazine in place, and wait. Nothing ever happened on any of the alerts, but we wouldn't have been brokenhearted if it had. War is a bad business, but part of it is fun.

Our job as ammunition carriers was to help members of the Armed Guard load the can-like magazines for the 20-mm gun with cartridges from the ship's magazine, and then dash back up on deck carrying the loaded 'cans' to the gunners above. On one occasion, while a fellow and I were in the magazine doing so, the crewman had a tray filled with cartridges. Suddenly the ship lurched, causing him to drop live 20 mm gun cartridges all over the floor. Luckily none of them detonated.

Then one bright day, our commander, after a long talk with the commodore, got permission to have target practice. So the ship pulled out of the convoy and all the guns were fired. At the 20's, the gunner and one assistant got to shoot half a magazine. Punch and I matched coins, and I won. So by and by, I had the thrill of being strapped to the gun, pulling the trigger and feeling the gun vibrate like an old Ford, while red-hot tracer bullets whizzed up into the sky.

Every other bullet was a tracer, and at each shot the gun recoiled, shaking me as if I were a rat being shaken by a dog. You could see the brilliant trajectory as if it were a stream from some hellish fire hose. In serious use, the gunner could just aim the red stream at the target. The sound of the gun was a sort of POOM! POOM! POOM! POOM!

Other gunners were also getting practice. Immediately behind us, at the rear of the ship, the Armed Guard was firing the 5-inch gun. Men would load the shell into the back of the gun and lock it into place, while it was aimed and fired by the gunner. At the instant of the explosion, we would feel the hot flash on our face from the burning powder. The report arrived a fraction of a second later, since sound travels more slowly than light. Men joked that the cost of one shell was about the same as the price of a war bond—$18.75. US savings bonds were being sold to finance the war.

From a letter of June 23, 1944:

Allan Robert Humbert

Concerning excitement en route, the truth is that we had little. There were lots of alerts, but these were mostly practice. However, we did hear the firing of heavy coastal gun batteries, and there were depth charges dropped. One charge was dropped close enough to our ship that we could see the spout of water that arose. Depth charges jar the ship as though a giant iron hammer had suddenly struck the side. Intended for destroying submarines, depth charges are lobbed over the side of the ship, exploding at a pre-set depth. One night at least three dozen were dropped. And of course people got rather excited.

Another time, in the Mediterranean, we saw a DE (Destroyer Escort) a few miles away, steaming around the convoy belching black smoke. They were putting down a smoke screen to hide the convoy from the enemy.

Although well aware of our danger, we felt a sense of gratitude to the US Navy who were constantly on guard to protect us.

Once gunnery practice was finished, the ship returned to normal. The average convoy crossing was without incident. U-boats by 1944 were being hunted down and destroyed so they were less of a threat than before. However, as late as 1945, they were still sinking ships.

Storms which we encountered at sea seemed far more threatening than did the enemy. Almost everyone living on land is accustomed to watching branches bending in the wind, sheets of rain being driven by it, and angry-looking clouds flying across the sky. But when a storm at sea occurs, and all you have for survival is a fragile ship that is rolling in the vast ocean a thousand miles from land, you feel downright frightened.

The whistling wind and the sound of waves pounding against the steel sides of the ship remind you that nature is still in command. You look outward from the deck—assuming it's even safe to be on deck at all—where once was the horizon are now huge green and gray hills of heaving water. One moment, and you're looking upward at the top of a crest, and the next, down into a valley where you can see the underside of the ship. Anything that isn't tied down may be washed overboard by the crashing waves. Even if you're inside at the meal table, your dishes will be sliding back and forth upon it, stopped from falling to the floor only by special guard strips attached to the edge of the table. You sense why sailors are superstitious, and only hope that the men and women who built your ship did a good job.

Still, in a few hours, the wind subsides, the sun comes out, and the same ocean seems blue and inviting.

Continuing letters:

April 21, 1944
Atlantic Ocean

Tomorrow there will be a mail collection, and although it will be quite a while before any is actually sent, it seems nice that the subject is coming up.

Today we opened the Red Cross kits that we were given. Each consists of a handy little bag containing stationery, a pencil, package of cigarettes, sewing kit, paperback (mine: <u>The Case of the Howling Dog</u>), Life Savers, playing cards, soap and soap box. Moral: Give to the Red Cross.

April 22, 1944
Same Old Ocean

Another day passes on our "pleasure cruise." Tomorrow, though, we who have been long free of work detail get KP. Nothing difficult; we work only a few hours at a time. This will be our first detail, so I shouldn't complain.

I wish you could see how blue the water is. It's almost a royal blue, though not quite. Maybe you'd call it an "unbelievable blue"—at any rate I wouldn't have believed that water could have such a color. It seems to be begging for someone to swim in it.

Our energy constantly dwindles, or at least our ambition. We have perpetual spring fever, and the only effort we exert is to eat. We feel fine; the weather is beautiful but we simply lack all ambition. I feel like the man in Thompson's <u>Castle of Indolence</u>—

Allan Robert Humbert

"a pleasant land of drowsy-head it was, of dreams that pass before the half-shut eye."

April 23, 1944
Atlantic Ocean

Today was my first turn at detail aboard ship. I had KP upstairs. There was very little to do—I hardly worked a couple of hours, being allowed off for church in the morning. The evening meal consisted of cold cuts; there were very few pots and pans to wash, so I finished in plenty of time to watch the sun go down.

While on KP, I received a strange request from a colored* fellow who works in the galley. He, upon returning to the states, will visit his sister. She will invite him to a Sunday evening meeting at a Baptist church where he will be asked to make a talk, and I'm supposed to write the talk. Everything happens to me!

*At the time this was written, the term "colored" did not carry the opprobrious connotation that it does today. It was, in fact, the usual way to designate a black person and meant no disrespect. To me it seems dishonest to rewrite these letters in the interest of ethnic correctness.

April 24, 1944
High Seas

This should be close to payday again, but on the ocean one doesn't get paid, so we'll just have to wait.

We are becoming junior astronomers. By the time we reach our destination, we shall know most of the common constellations. I always think of you when looking at the stars—how we used to do the same thing. We miss civilization just now. I would cheerfully pay several times the regular cost just to see a good movie again. And even that pleasure would not compare with being with you.

One day a weatherman burst into the dining hall and yelled "Land! Land!" We ran up on deck and saw the distant shoreline, dotted with red cottage roofs in the sunshine. Soon we were sailing through the Strait of Gibraltar into the Mediterranean Sea with the famous rock itself on our left. My letter of May 1 was true enough, but it neglected to mention the dangers which the ship faced, now in reach of planes from enemy bases in Europe.

May 1, 1944

This afternoon while lying on deck getting a sun tan, I thought, "It'll be a long time before I can get tanned so cheaply. The government is compelled to give us almost a vacation."

May 4, 1944

...Since writing you last night I have finished two books and begun another. The first was Bruce Barton's <u>The Book Nobody Knows</u>.
It's nice to think that in only a week or so I'll be getting mail and you'll be hearing from me once more. It's been a whole month now since I heard a line from anybody anywhere, and for all I know, Indiana may have blown away.
However, we do get news from BBC, and aren't too far behind on current events. A couple of guys have been detailed to listen to the ship's radio daily and write up the news.

One of the great ironies of war is the unequal sacrifices demanded of soldiers. Some men deliberately seek out dangerous assignments. I have talked to macho individuals who looked forward to personal hand-to-hand combat as a sort of ultimate contest. Others, hundreds of miles from any real danger, have become mental cases purely from fear. Many, of course, were placed in combat units through no choice of their own. I think most of us regarded fighting as something we might have to accept, but not necessarily seek out.

While we weathermen were having an easy time of it, there was a troop transport ship loaded with infantrymen within a few hundred yards of us. Through binoculars, we could see them on deck. They were magnificent physical specimens, heavily muscled, stripped to the waist, heads shaven. Daily they engaged in vigorous calisthenics. We, on the other hand, were lounging contentedly and reading books.

When the convoy sailed south of Italy, the infantry ship curved northward toward the beaches of Anzio, where intense battles awaited them, while we steamed eastward. Seldom had the expression, "There, but for the grace of God, go I" seemed more appropriate.

Our ship continued without incident to Port Said on the north coast of Egypt. We could see blimps floating over the port, held by cables. Any German bomber attempting a bombing run would find itself entangled in the cables of these barrage balloons.

We sailed through the Suez Canal connecting the Mediterranean with the Red Sea, a distance of 158 miles. Part of the canal passes through a natural lake. The man-made section is lined with beautiful white ceramic tile. Drawn by electrically powered locomotives, the SS Ralph Izzard glided southward with incredible smoothness. Here and there along the canal we could see British outposts manned by soldiers.

My last letter of the voyage:

Well, we're docked. This has been a beautiful day and it's very nice to be landed. A bunch of natives came on board last night with pocketbooks, beads, and bracelets to sell. They aren't the least bit dumb. Instead of "Lo, the poor native," it will be "Lo, the poor soldier!"

Altogether we have been quite busy, getting packed, hunting up missing stuff, etc. People are getting tired of the boat, though doubtless they'll get much tireder of the place we go. This is the flattest country I've ever seen.

Maybe this afternoon we will be able to go ashore, getting this mail on its way to you.

Before the month ended, we learned of our assignment to the 19th Weather Squadron with headquarters in Cairo, Egypt. We lived in pyramid tents on the undulating sands of the Sahara Desert. We were to be on what the army described as "detached service." Small groups of perhaps 15-30 would operate weather stations on bases which spread across Africa, Arabia and elsewhere in the Middle East. Subject to control of base commanders, we would be mostly on our own. The army seemed to be in no hurry to put us to work. There was time to read, do sightseeing and become accustomed to this ancient land of the Pharaohs.

Days were blazing hot and nights cool and mysterious with the sky filled with the most stars I have ever seen. Lying on the army cot, I reflected on the past months which had brought me to Egypt and wondered what would be next.

Allan Robert Humbert

Chapter 2

EGYPT AND THE SUDAN 1944

Egypt
May 1944

From my letter of May 11:

Some day in the future when I balance my books to see whether the army has been a gain or loss, one item will stand out to make up for the many months I've spent to no purpose. That item is our trip to Cairo, sponsored by the American Red Cross, that splendid and vital organization.

Our transportation consisted of GI trucks. They possess the general characteristics of all GI trucks, particularly durability. Our view, standing in the rear, was totally unobstructed, and what a view it was!

Cairo is a peculiar combination of contrasts. The people are almost all Moslem. All men wear the red "fez" which looks exactly like the hat of an organ grinder's monkey. Some wear clothes like ours, but the common garment is what looks like a long dirty nightgown. Few women were to be seen; rather few were veiled.

There are the cutest little donkeys—I wanted to buy one (They cost only about 20 bucks. Camels are higher priced; they cost a hundred dollars or so.) Socony-Vacuum is the predominant company and the "kerosene trucks" are little carts pulled by donkeys. These hard-working donkeys pull almost anything. I saw men riding them, and I'll swear that the men were better able to carry the donkey than the donkey the man. Tomorrow I'll tell you more about the trip.

May, 1944

This has been a swell day. The best thing of all was a GI show and movie here (Note: Camp Russell B. Huckstep). The band was really super—played all the songs we like including "Paper Doll," "Begin the Beguine," "You'll Never Know," and "Stardust." Although a military outfit, the band dressed in spic and span white coats and black trousers. The movie was "Bedtime Story" starring Loretta Young and Fredric March. I would have paid plenty to see the show, had it been necessary, but it was free.

May 12, 1944

Getting back to Cairo, it really is a study in contrasts. We saw many people who must have been in actual hunger. Fresh food is fairly common, and looks good. However, we have been warned that it is safest to eat and drink nothing but GI food and beverages. (You know I'm Scotch, anyway, and could never see the justification for passing up army chow to pay hard-earned cash for the same item in a restaurant.) Sanitary conditions in the East are rather well known. No comprehensive plan exists to improve the country's health. A complicating factor is the indifferent attitude of the average Moslem. Since his ancestors have managed in the old way for centuries, he figures he can, too. He has a point there; a native can live in conditions that would kill a foreigner.

...After passing through the city, we visited the Great Pyramid, plus the smaller ones and tombs beside it. We had our picture taken with the pyramid in the background. By and by, you'll get the photo. The pyramids are certainly big, although the Sphinx isn't so large. An encyclopedia can tell you more about their history than I. However, they were quite impressive, especially considering how few mechanical devices were available to help in their construction. Great blocks of stone were put in place. Even today such work

Allan Robert Humbert

would be amazing. Naturally, we went inside a tomb, which was cool and dark. The stone sparkles in the rays of the flashlight.

On the same trip, some of us paid to ride a camel. It is said that a camel is the only creature on earth that smells worse than an Arab. In fairness to the natives, though, it must be stated that water was scarce and soap was expensive. If some of us had to make the choice between ultra cleanliness and hunger, perhaps we wouldn't be so clean ourselves. Temperamental beasts, angry camels have been known to turn and spit their repulsive green cud into the face of the rider. Riding one is something like riding a mobile stepladder. Once you have mounted, the camel straightens its forelegs to the first joint, which elevates you somewhat; then he straightens the first joint of his rear legs, which raises you further. Then the last joint of the forelegs is extended, and finally the last joint of the rear legs, hoisting you high into the air. In spite of their shortcomings, good camels are highly prized and useful animals.

Continuing:

The greatest sight of the entire trip was the great Mohammedan mosque, the Citadel. It surpasses anything America has in design and elegance. Built in 1807, it has workmanship that we can hardly imagine. The mosque is made of gleaming alabaster, which looks like ivory. Tourists entering must put on sandals, while the Moslem must remove his shoes and wash his hands and feet. There are at least three domes, one being five stories high. The domes are richly painted, and there is an immense amount of gold leaf in sight. Above one door is a solid gold plate that cost 35,000 Egyptian pounds.

For a small charge, the electric lights are lighted, making the domes more beautiful than ever. An immense crystal chandelier dwarfs the one in the US Capitol.

More shopping and sightseeing continued on the 13th. A nice Englishwoman from the Red Cross took us to the native bazaar. We found a mixture of oriental-looking goods that had little appeal, and really exquisite porcelains priced at $200 and up. I bought dictionaries, a French-English one and an English-French. In a pinch, such dictionaries could help one communicate by simply looking up the French equivalent of the English words you wanted, then writing them down on a card and handing it to the person who spoke French. He, in turn, would do the same thing with the French, and though cumbersome, some communication was possible. At the American PX, I bought handkerchiefs, a tropical helmet, sergeant's stripes and a blue bathing suit.

The Red Cross stationery I was using on May 16 was headed:

AMERICAN RED CROSS
Able Bodied Welfare

Except for having photo IDs made, I'd little to do but shop. Stores would probably be scarce in distant posts where we might be stationed, so we tried to prepare as best we could.

Besides a bracelet, I bought still another item—a swagger stick which doubles as a blackjack. There are parts of Cairo where you need one, too, and they are handy at all times as a sort of extra persuasion. The natives have been known to gang up on people, though not recently. I didn't think of carrying one till after seeing a colonel carrying one all over town. He said they were nice things to have. I decided to buy one for the going price of 7 ½ piastres. The native seller asked $1.50, so I went to the PX and bought it for 30 cents. Then, just for meanness, I took it around and showed it to the guy who had wanted $1.50, making him a little mad.

Oh yes, yesterday we took a trip out to Memphis (not Tenn.) We saw the great statue of Ramses II, a whole piece of granite lying prone on the ground. Also, we saw the 24 coffins for sacred bulls. The time needed to make all this staggers me. On the way out, I amused myself tossing cigarettes from the truck, watching the natives scramble for them.

There was one beautiful little Arab girl, only six years old. Upon noticing that we admired her, her father actually offered to sell her for only 50 pounds. The more I think of that, the more I wonder. I hope things never come to that in America. It would almost be worthwhile to buy the kid, send her to America and raise her correctly. Maybe everybody would be better off. As it is, she has only a few short years of beauty left till she looks like any other Arab woman, which is pretty bad. Still, she might be happier as she is. Taking responsibility for other people's lives is a grave step.

On May 22, I wrote:

Another day, another dollar. Remember how aggravated we used to be at Seymour Johnson Field, being made to take charge of work details to pick up papers? I can recall thinking, "Gee, I wish I were overseas; then there wouldn't be time for all this stuff." So I get overseas, and what happens? My first detail is to take a truck and driver and five Sudanese out on the Sahara Desert to pick up trash! Not a bad job, except in principle. In fact, we have things so nice here they could hardly be better. We had ice cream at dinner.

These Sudanese are like kids. They're black, and for my money, are Negroes, but actually there is a difference. They have typical Arab features. I had no difficulty getting along with them. Our non-com stripes seem to impress them; all we need to do is to keep a sober face and look wise. We aren't supposed to do the work; in fact, we were told not to. Still, it seemed silly, seeing a little matchstick on the desert, not picking it up myself, instead, calling over a guy to do it for me.

With such a kaleidoscope of experiences in a new and fascinating land, it was hard to realize I had been in Egypt less than three weeks. And when informed that changes in stations to which we were assigned usually involved traveling by way of Cairo, I was pleased.

Only four days later, I was writing from an air base a thousand miles south, Khartoum, in the Anglo-Egyptian Sudan.

May 26, 1944
The Sudan

No mail for the last couple of days, but mail seldom intercepts planes that are in flight.

We visited Luxor, Egypt, and saw all the old tombs that are around. For lodging, we had the Savoy Hotel, which furnishes three meals per day and one's room for 66 piastres ($2.64). The meals are OK, but not as good as those found in mess halls. The milk is obtained from goats; the bread is like a soggy dog biscuit, and omelets are served at every meal. Yet the place is ritzy, and last night we had finger bowls.

The country looks much better from the air than it does at close range. (In fact, the farther we were away, the better I liked it.) We noticed the native quarter where buildings were jammed so close together that they seemed to be touching each other. Also, we saw shallow circular bowls in the earth about 25 feet across, around which a man was driving a pair of donkeys. They were pulling a device which resembles disks such as farmers use, going continuously in a circle. This is their primitive method of threshing grain.

We also saw their arrangement for drawing water from the river. A large vertical wheel much like an old mill waterwheel extends down into the river. Jars are attached to the wheel, and as it is turned by a cow operating a gear, the jars are successively dipped into the river, raised and allowed to dump the water into the irrigation ditch. The cow walks continuously in a circle to operate the machinery.

We flew over a desert so bare and vacant that it might have been on the moon or on another planet. For mile after mile there was nothing but an irregular ocean of sand carved as if by a river, yet without a drop of water. Everything we saw was of one color, something like khaki, and there was no sign of a single living thing. Inside the plane it was cool, but as soon as we began to descend, it was hot again. The temperature outside at present is 109 degrees Fahrenheit. Yesterday the maximum was 115.4, but the air is so dry that the heat doesn't bother us much. Relative humidity is 10%.

Allan Robert Humbert

The Sudan
May 27, 1944

...I'm writing this while stretched out comfortably on a blanket lying on the floor of a plane, high over French Equatorial Africa. We've been joking about the famous quotation "War is hell." There is lots of room—here on the plane, more room in the sky, and plenty of space beneath us. Below is the desert; above are clouds; we live in a cool little world of our own. The motors make a steady roar, but that's OK. I can truthfully repeat that old saw, "having a wonderful time; wish you were here."

The food last night was wonderful, also. At the PX they had ice cream, coke, beer and even bobby pins. More fun!

* * * * *

Seven thousand miles westward lay Muncie, Indiana, where, for me, it had all begun...

Chapter 3

MUNCIE, INDIANA 1938

In September, 1938, my home town, Muncie, Indiana, was already a nationally known city. Ball Brothers fruit jars had been made there since the late 1880s. Delco batteries were in thousands of autos all over the US. Rivers across the land were spanned by bridges constructed by the Indiana Bridge Company. Many other companies also flourished.

Located in Delaware County about 50 miles northeast of Indianapolis, Muncie was the hub of manufacturing activity in east central Indiana. Its growth had been greatly stimulated by the discovery of natural gas. By 1888 there were 35 wells providing low-cost fuel which attracted industry from all over the US, especially manufacturers of glass and steel, which required a great deal of energy. Although the gas had dwindled by the early 1900s, it had given Muncie a great start. Muncie's development as a railway center continued.

Much that took place in Muncie was similar to urban development that occurred in many American cities. So much so, in fact that sociologists Robert and Helen Lynd had selected Muncie as the site for an exhaustive study to determine how increasing industrialization had changed the basic values of society. They lived in Muncie for a year. Their conclusions were published in a 1929 book, *Middletown: A Study in American Culture,* and in a 1937 sequel. These books were widely read not only by sociologists and university students, but by the general public, and firmly established Muncie in people's minds as the typical American city.

Allan Robert Humbert

    For our family, living some three miles north of town, prospects seemed encouraging. For me, they seemed as bright as the shiny sterling silver of my Eagle Scout badge, earned barely two years earlier. Little did we dream that world events were developing which would change our lives forever. Perhaps a brief glance at my family's situation will give the reader a sense of what life was like all over America, when World War II didn't even have a name ...

    My father was 40, my mother, 36; they seemed determined to create a population explosion, having six kids already with two more to come. On Saturday after supper we all rode to Muncie in Dad's 1928 Dodge sedan. I felt uncomfortable as the entire stair-stepped tribe paraded down the sidewalk: myself, 18, Dorothy, 16, Vera, 12, Helen, 7 and Barbara 4, led by the sturdy patriarch, Ivan, and his wife, Inez, who carried 8-month-old Rosemary. I would have preferred to stay home, but Dad had strong ideas about family togetherness and I knew better than to ask.

    Muncie's automotive-based economy was on an upswing; the Great Depression was over, but its lessons of fierce frugality remained. While the other kids went shopping by themselves on streets perfectly safe for everyone, my parents and I would purchase the weekly groceries. I accompanied them to help carry the sacks from the Doeding Coffee Company on Jackson Street. We savored the fresh-roasted coffee being ground while Mom thoughtfully conferred with Mr. Doeding on the price and quality of every item. He might spend 20 minutes dutifully assembling her order, from the time he wrapped the meat and tied the paper with a string until sacking up the final delicious extravagance, a bag of 10 cents-per-pound chocolates.

    Just before the stores closed at 9:00 p.m., Dad would stop at the Ideal Fruit Market to buy at bargain prices fruit certain to deteriorate by Monday when the store would reopen.

    We ate well. Sunday School and church were compulsory at our house and Sunday dinner was memorable. (In Indiana, you ate *dinner* at noon, and *supper* in the evening.) The menu might include smoked ham, rich brown gravy on bread and potatoes, plenty of other vegetables, milk, coffee for my parents but not for us, and for dessert, apple pie with ice cream, both dishes home-made. The ice cream was so rich that only the addition of "Rippey's Fomaline" to the liquid mixture kept it from becoming butter in the rotating can of Dad's freezer which he had motorized. He took pleasure in piling huge scoops onto pieces of pie as they were passed to him, using an immense spoon.

One reason dishes tasted so good in those days was the liberal use of eggs, butter and cream. People felt that such "natural" ingredients were bound to be healthful. We never heard of the word cholesterol. For those of us who grew much of our own food, cost wasn't a problem, either. Even the kittens in the barn got their share of milk, squirted fresh from the cow.

Despite the rich diet, few people were overweight. There was entirely too much physical work to do. Food production required considerable time and effort. Raising our own meat meant feeding cattle and hogs daily. Even though we had only a few cows, one hog and a few dozen chickens, they demanded constant care. If we wanted fried chicken, I had to catch one, kill it, and turn it over to Mom for plucking and cleaning before she fried it. Eggs had to be gathered—my sisters' job. The vegetable garden had to be fertilized, plowed, cultivated and harvested.

Lacking today's automatic central heating, most people burned coal. My father hauled ours from a coal yard in town to a pile in back of our house, and it was my job to carry it into the house, and to carry out the ashes. During mild weather the fire was allowed to go out, which necessitated bringing in kindling, not to mention chopping boards into kindling in the first place. Soot from the coal made it very difficult to keep white shirts and blouses nice, and the once-white buildings in town were a dirty gray.

Nevertheless, electric power was easing people's burdens, having reached my folks' place in the early 1930's. A visitor to our home in 1938 would have found a Frigidaire refrigerator, a Marion electric range, a washing machine, and Dad's special pride, a $200 Philco console radio, not to mention several smaller appliances.

Appliances were simpler then. Some were dangerous. Mom's electric range had bare heating coils exposed. Once I saw her thrown to the floor by an electric shock when she touched a pan she'd carelessly allowed to boil over onto the live coils.

Few appliances were totally automatic. The toaster would brown two slices of bread at a time, but only on one side. Then you had to manually flip them over. Still, a little ingenuity could work wonders.

Dad made his own clock radio. The small radio was located on a shelf near the bed. Next to it was a switch, and next to the switch, an ordinary wind-up alarm clock. He soldered an arm onto the winding key of the clock, positioned so as to flip the switch when the alarm would have sounded. He disconnected the bell. When the time came for the alarm to have gone off, the unwinding spring turned on the switch and the radio. Result: pleasant awakening music.

Few women worked outside the home. Just being a housewife was a full-time job. Monday was wash day. Despite having a washer that would agitate the clothes and an automatic wringer that would squeeze out the water, she had to heat the water and pour it into the washer. In addition, it was necessary to fill two tubs with cold water for rinsing, and to prepare starch for shirts, etc., bluing to brighten yellowed whites, and a pre-soaking in concentrated soap to take the grease out of dirty overalls. Every garment had to be washed and wrung out twice, and then hung out to dry on the outdoor clothes line. In winter the garments froze stiff.

Tuesday was ironing day. Mom took pride in sending her daughters to school in nicely pressed dresses; with no permanent-press fabrics, ironing took all day. She made most of their dresses. Although she was aided by an electric sewing machine, she had to buy the fabric, pattern and thread, then cut out and sew each dress.

In addition, there was mending, cooking, canning, child care, church activity, her home-ec club, and flower gardening plus feeding and nurturing a dog and up to seventeen cats. In her spare time, she did quite a bit of reading.

As the only other driver in the family besides my father, part of my responsibility was to take my sisters to various school functions. Dad had given me a black 1928 Dodge coupe for my 16th birthday, having paid $35 for it. The car was advertised as "The Fastest Four in America."

There were always one or two cows to milk each morning and evening, the yard to mow, and a large garden to be hoed. On weekends I worked as janitor of the Normal City Christian Church.

We lived on a small farm north of Muncie. A person traveling away from town would have noted on the east side of the road a huge sycamore tree on the property from which hung four swings. Some 30 yards north was a fine white barn standing in marked contrast to a small weathered house. Northward along the highway lay the unfinished excavation where the folks' new house was to have been located. They had built the barn just before the Depression and had planned to construct the house next.

I looked forward to the fun and challenge of becoming a freshman at Ball State Teachers College. Had I given the matter a thought, I might have remembered reading about the Japanese invasion of Manchuria in 1931 and the rise in Germany of a hoodlum group led by a radical named Adolph Hitler ...

Chapter 4

COLLEGE

Looking back at those long-ago days, Ball State seems like a romantic place. Compared to the large universities of today, it would scarcely have been noticed. But to a freshman coming from a county high school with only 23 in the graduating class it seemed impressive and bursting with opportunity.

Located in northwestern Muncie its tree-shaded campus was a place of quiet beauty with winding walks where excited, cheerful students could be seen hurrying to their next class.

Ball State Teachers College was a cozy realm of its own. Incoming freshmen found themselves caught up in a whirl of activities. Football and basketball games, marching bands, fraternities and sororities, men being required to wear funny-looking green caps that told everyone that our rank in the establishment was utterly beneath that of the upper classmen.

Lots of new friends and acquaintances. Idealistic young professors who were stimulating and yet demanding. More classwork than we could manage. Science labs which to us seemed ultimately complete. Convocation programs, sometimes with world-class speakers. Pep sessions in the gym with the Ball State band playing, resplendent in red-and white uniforms.

By the "anything goes" moral standards of some colleges today, Ball State might seem oppressive. As future teachers, we were expected not only to know our subject matter but to serve as examples to the students we would some day have in our classes. Ball State was not a religious institution; nevertheless we were expected to conduct ourselves as ladies and gentlemen; no smoking, no alcohol, no improper language. And if our own standards were lax, Deans Grace Dehority, Harry Howick and Ralph Noyer were there to keep us sober and on the straight and narrow path.

Not that we didn't have fun. There were dates, fraternity dances, ball games, parties, church events, discussion groups, academic clubs, the college newspaper, etc. Moreover, we commuters were allowed to have our car on campus, and the mobility was a definite social plus.

To save expense, I commuted to classes from home, eating sack lunches with my father, whose auto repair shop was only a few blocks from the campus. Without even a sign to identify it, his business was well known and patronized by a clientele which included hourly factory workers, gun cranks, top corporation executives, and even the president of the college himself, Dr. L. A. Pittenger. Most were isolationist and resolutely Republican. When Wendell Willkie ran against FDR, President Pittenger predicted that FDR would be beaten so badly that he would resemble the remains of a cat that Dr. Pittenger had dissected while a college student.

Dad would adjust his language to match that of the person with whom he was speaking. His English could be perfect in the presence of a professor, lapsing informally downward when talking with someone less educated. I never heard him swear.

He took pride in his work and was sometimes consulted by fellow mechanics who had confronted a tough technical problem beyond their expertise.

Woe to the individual who blew his horn in the alley back of the shop expecting instant curb service, instead of entering the shop and approaching in the properly respectful manner. Dad would blithely ignore the guy, who would sometimes depart in rage muttering imprecations while his rear wheels sprayed a cloud of cinders.

Meanwhile, people in many walks of life were becoming aware that events in Europe were continuing to deteriorate. The Munich Conference approved German acquisition of the Sudetenland. Hitler occupied the rest of Czechoslovakia. Insurgent forces completed the conquest of Spain and Mussolini invaded Albania. We Midwesterners felt that all of this was unfortunate but not really our problem. Europe had always had wars. Besides, for students, there was plenty to do at Ball State without worrying about conflicts thousands of miles away.

Because most Indiana high schools in the '30's and '40's had few students, township trustees had a real problem finding enough teachers qualified to teach the many subjects needed.

Some of us tried to make ourselves more employable by having several college majors rather than specializing in just one area. Also, it was more fun having exciting new courses to study rather than the sometimes dreary advanced ones in science and math.

One such course I took was journalism, under Professor Sharley B. DeMotte, who not only taught but was Director of Publicity for Ball State. She stressed accurate reporting, writing news so people would enjoy reading it, and more importantly for publicity purposes, writing in a way which would cause the reader to agree with the beliefs of the newswriter. She was a close student of world affairs, and we respected her opinions.

Anyone who has enjoyed the privilege of a college education knows that the friends and acquaintances one makes are as valuable as the subjects studied. In journalism activities, I got to know Howard Blackman of Kendallville, Indiana. Blond, somewhat below average height, with a slight brogue and an infectious smile, "Blackie" as he was called, starred in campus plays and was a member of the Spotlight dramatics club and attended our church. Although we were very busy we sometimes took drives around Muncie, and had long philosophical discussions.

Sometime during the 1940s, he and I were in the Ball State newsroom when Mrs. DeMotte said, "You realize, don't you, that the United States will have to get into the war." We were troubled by her remarks and never forgot them.

Events in Europe continued to worsen. The Nazis seemed invincible. By June, 1940, France had been conquered. Only the miracle of the Dunkirk evacuation saved the British Army to fight another day. The Battle of Britain which began on July 10 shocked and infuriated us. Throughout it all, the words of Winston Churchill rang out in defiance of Adolph Hitler and rallied support for the Allied cause. To this day, I can close my eyes and recall every intonation of the grand old warrior's voice, as he declared, "We shall never surrender ..."

He was the bulldog of the free world and not about to let a gang of Nazi guttersnipes conquer England.

Since high school I had been interested in weather, having designed and built a weather station for my room at home. It showed wind direction and velocity, temperature, rainfall and atmospheric pressure. I took a meteorology course at the college and became the official college weather observer. For several months prior to Pearl Harbor I broadcasted the local weather on Radio Station WLBC. One day I got on the air and predicted rain. An accommodating thunderstorm developed, and I walked out of the station in a downpour.

Despite my interest in the subject, I was later to learn that weather forecasting demanded a chess-like mind that I did not have.

Chapter 5

LOOMING MILITARY SERVICE

DECEMBER 7, 1941

We were at home on that fateful Sunday afternoon when news of the attack on Pearl Harbor was broadcast. We listened as the announcer told how Japanese planes had struck the naval base there sinking eight American battleships and destroying or heavily damaging many others. Two hundred planes were destroyed and facilities at other Pacific bases were hit.

When President Roosevelt on the following Monday asked for a declaration of war, his words echoed our sentiment, that the day would "live in infamy." Even at this writing, it is sad and upsetting to view the sunken remains of the battleship Arizona at the National Monument there and see oil slicks still rising from the rusting tanks below the water while the bones of American young men molder in the rusting hulk beneath us.

No longer was there any doubt. We were in the war for the duration. The entire nation geared up for the largest military effort in the country's history. Not that the US was totally unprepared. To his everlasting credit, President Roosevelt had already led the movement to provide aid to England, such as exchanging 50 over-age destroyers for our use of British bases. A huge shipbuilding program was under way. The Selective Service Act of 1940 was in place; men were being called into service daily. Young men all carried draft registration cards. Deferments from the draft became increasingly harder to obtain. Often we'd return to class on Monday morning and find empty chairs where students had sat the Friday before. Being at the close of my Junior year, I knew I'd be lucky to graduate before being drafted.

The mood at Ball State was subdued and serious. A few weeks before he graduated, my friend Howard Blackman and I visited his home near Kendallville. On a gloomy Sunday afternoon we drove out in the countryside to an abandoned cemetery. One tombstone caught our attention. It was that of a Union soldier of the Civil War. The stone had broken and lay there neglected. Some long-forgotten young man had died for his country. Now, not even his grave was honored. I photographed it, and even thought of a caption, "Reward of the Valiant." I remembered old Ben Franklin's statement, "There never was a good war nor a bad peace." We didn't talk much on our way back to the campus.

Rationing began, as well as price and rent controls. In January 1942, the government started rationing tires. Dad's concept of a drivable tire was one with at least some observable tread. He sold several he had, as required, receiving a check of 40 cents for the entire lot. He never cashed it. Other rationed items were autos, typewriters, bicycles, stoves, meat, coffee, sugar and fuel oil for home heating, as well as coal, in the Northwest. Most burdensome of all was gasoline rationing. The standard "A" card allowed only three gallons per week. This put a real crimp in auto travel.

One saw more and more men in uniform. Even fathers were being drafted. Those of us still in college sensed an attitude of public disapproval as if we were shirking our duty. War news became a matter of daily concern. Reports from soldiers already overseas, stories of heroism, and casualty listings brought the war ever closer. We realized that until the thing was over, our own lives were on "hold," and that winning the war was more important than were the lives or fortunes of any of us.

Social events themselves took on a wartime flavor. The last fraternity dance that I attended had a seafaring theme. On the dance floor was a huge mock-up of a battleship, complete with naval gun turrets.

THOSE EARLIER WARS

Many American men throughout our history have had acquaintance with armed conflict. For those who escaped personal involvement, there have been fathers, grandfathers or brothers who fought and who passed on stories of the excitement, adventure and horror that is war. Groups who oppose war because fighting isn't "nice" ignore the fact that there have always been wars whether both combatants wanted them or not. Nations which permit their defenses to fall below a safe level do so at their peril.

Stories of heroism abound. The young Athenians marching off to fight the Persians at Marathon against overwhelming odds—*singing*. Or Pickett's charge at Gettysburg—how the Confederates thought the Union artillery had run out of ammunition and charged across the open plain, only to be ripped to ribbons as the enemy guns opened up, grapeshot tearing great gaps in the ranks. Or Antietam, where the creek literally ran red with blood.

My father was in World War I. So were many other men of his age. He caught the 1918 flu which was so terrible that soldiers who had it literally tried to keep their families from knowing they had the disease. Worldwide, it killed some 30 million people. In some places, so many soldiers died that corpses were stacked up like cordwood until the frozen ground would thaw and allow them to be buried. Dad was too sick to shave. By the time he was well enough to do so, his beard was half an inch long and he weighed only 80 pounds, although he was five feet 10 inches tall.

I once talked to a veteran in Chicago who also had the flu at that time. An Australian officer, he treated himself by drinking orange juice and sleeping in his heavy army overcoat until the disease ended.

WWII LETTERS TO MY GIRL BACK HOME
From Nigeria, Arabia and Turkey

Our neighbor, Bill Fishback, had been in the American Expeditionary Force in World War I. During the fighting in France, a 75-mm artillery shell landed in the mud three feet from him. Luckily, it was a dud. He didn't get a scratch.

Knowing what the young guys might be up against, some veterans arranged to teach men who would soon be recruits the basics of marksmanship. Some said their salvation "over there" had been baseball, because in the days before weapons were in good supply, hand grenades were plentiful and the same skill it took to throw a baseball applied just as well to throwing hand grenades.

At Royerton High School, our principal Clifford French would hold an Armistice Day assembly program each November 11 to remind us of soldiers' sacrifices and to impress us with the realities of war. Veterans would speak; to us at the time they seemed incredibly mature. We would sing the old WWI songs such as "It's A Long Way to Tipperary," "Pack Up Your Troubles in Your Old Kit Bag," "There's A Long, Long Trail A-Winding," and others. Mr. French was a Navy man. A friend of his who became a high school principal once told me of a post-war experience he had. Newly returned from WWI, he found himself in a college class where a smug young professor was making snide remarks about the loose morals of servicemen. The recently-discharged veteran rose from his chair, lifted the professor by the collar, dropped him back in his seat and returned to his place in class. For the rest of the period, the class sat in dead silence while the professor trembled in white-faced fury. When the closing bell rang, the professor went straight to the administration. The case went before a committee, where the president of the college conducted a hearing. Upon hearing the facts, he said quietly, "Gentlemen, this case is closed."

As for the sights and sounds of combat, a professor of mine, Dr. Robert C. Scarf, of Ball State, told me after WWII of a veteran he knew who returned from WWI and asked *his* professor, who had fought in the Civil War, how long it would take to forget the carnage he had seen. He replied, "It took me twenty years."

Allan Robert Humbert

RANDOLPH FIELD, TEXAS 1942

Instead of the expected induction notice, it was a pleasant surprise to receive a letter notifying me of an appointment as Junior Instructor of Meteorology at Randolph Field, Texas. Little did I know that such civilian positions would last only 30 days before being taken over by commissioned officers and that physical limitations would preclude my acceptance in that group.

I set out for Randolph Field accompanied by a college classmate, John Finney. We drove Dad's venerable 1928 Dodge Victory Six sedan which was already laboring under 100,000 miles. I dropped John off in Louisiana and headed west toward Texas in unsettled weather. As I drove, the wind and rain grew stronger and stronger. The road seemed deserted. All the billboards were flattened. Trees bent horizontal in 75-mph winds. Occasionally I could feel the left-hand door panel of the car pushing against my knee due to the force of the wind. I had to keep steering into the wind to keep it from blowing the car off the highway. When I reached Randolph Field, I saw several soldiers standing out in the storm, two to a plane, each holding down a wing to keep the aircraft from blowing away. Unknowingly, I had driven through a hurricane. Still, to a 22-year-old, it was fun.

Although my stay in Texas was short, the surroundings and people were different from those in Indiana. The smell of natural gas permeating the air along the coast, climate so hot and humid that postage stamps stuck together, friendly Southwesterners like the Theo Kneupper family with whom I roomed in Converse, plus the dead seriousness of an Army Air Force base training pilots who would soon be in combat, all combined to make a memorable experience.

Randolph Field was a beautiful place. Situated some 20 miles northeast of San Antonio, with low, Spanish-style buildings, to me it resembled a luxury resort area. But the roar of engines from hot primary training planes quickly destroyed the illusion. I saw pilots come in too fast for a landing, causing the wheels of the plane to strike the ground with so much force that it would bounce 30 feet into the air.

Suddenly the job ended. The Army decided that henceforth all instructors were to be commissioned personnel rather than civilians. A minimum age requirement of 30 for such commissioning left me out in the cold. So it was back to Indiana. I notified my draft board and set off for home.

Still, it seemed like a good opportunity to visit the West. I decided to take a look at Boulder Dam. Only after approaching Boulder, Colorado, did I discover that the dam actually wasn't there but in Arizona. I headed east again, feeling that the draft board might take a dim view of my unauthorized absence.

I was discouraged. One night I had to drive down a lonely mountain road in a fog so dense that only by opening the car door and shining the flashlight on the pavement below could I see the road well enough to stay on it. Nearly broke, I stayed overnight in a motel where the rate was $1.00 per night. I paid in advance for a second night, with the understanding that I could get a refund if I didn't stay the second night. The motelkeeper refused to honor his promise, so I was out the dollar.

To make matters worse, my once-faithful Dodge developed a problem. The engine would run OK for a couple of miles, then abruptly lose power. One of the valves was sticking open. So I would have to stop the car, remove the spark plug, reach into the engine with a screwdriver and hammer down the valve. The engine would then run all right for another mile or so, and the whole maddening process would repeat.

As the car limped into Taos, New Mexico, I wondered what in the world to do. Finally I found a kindly mechanic who agreed to let me leave the car in the parking lot of his garage, and to serve as my technical consultant while I made the repair. He charged me only $5.00 and the car never faltered as I continued homeward.

From the endless yellow hills of New Mexico, eastward through the plains of Kansas and beyond, everything seemed still and lonely. With gas rationing in effect, only essential traffic was present, and the new national speed limit of 35 miles per hour slowed the pace of highway traffic to that of a leisurely Sunday afternoon.

The peaceful scenery was in marked contrast to events overseas. On September 16, the Germans were on the outskirts of Stalingrad.

Allan Robert Humbert

On November 8, British and American troops had landed in Morocco and Algeria. In the Pacific theater, by October 26 Japan's offensive against Guadalcanal had failed and by November 1, Americans there had begun a counteroffensive.

Soon I was back home in Muncie. Already most of my friends had been drafted. Husbands and fathers were not exempted. I awaited the inevitable notice of induction, thankful for having been allowed to complete college and looking forward with a certain sense of calm anticipation to military service.

WWII LETTERS TO MY GIRL BACK HOME
From Nigeria, Arabia and Turkey

Chapter 6

"BRING ENOUGH CLOTHES FOR THREE DAYS"

Early on a gloomy morning in November 1942, I was one of a group of 28 selectees from Delaware County who boarded a bus for Fort Benjamin Harrison at Indianapolis. Several mothers and girl friends of the prospective soldiers were crying as we left. I felt proud that my own mother remained in firm control of her emotions although she and Dad felt as bad as anyone else. The mood on the bus was quiet. Surprisingly soon we arrived at Fort Harrison, were fed and given physical examinations. Those who passed were sworn into the Army of the United States and sent home for two weeks leave.

We reported for active duty on November 20, 1942, beginning a process that would leave its mark on us throughout our lives. Our first bit of culture shock had occurred earlier as we stood naked in long lines while army doctors poked and prodded us as if we were so many pieces of meat. "Turn your head and cough!" Cold fingers had been thrust into our groins searching for hernias.

Physical standards were high early in the war. Candidates for pilot training, for instance, not only had to have sharp visual acuity, but also excellent depth perception. Failure to meet such standards could effectively bar one from qualifying for such service and the rank that might have accompanied it.

On the other hand, when demands for manpower increased as the war continued, standards were lowered. Some said that later, "If you could see lightning and hear thunder, you were in." Another version had it that two army doctors simultaneously looked into your ears, one into the right ear and the other into the left. If they didn't see each other's eye, you were accepted.

Coming straight from civilian life, most of us were accustomed to working in small groups with people much like ourselves. The army was different. Here there were all types, a broad cross-section of the public. The guy next to you might have been a farmer, lawyer, or ex-convict. He could be devoutly religious or a profanity-spouting hothead—or just another fellow like the ones you knew at home.

Privacy ceased to exist. Anything and everything you did was in the presence of others, from one or two people to hundreds.

The army quickly let us know who was in charge. Whether through encouragement, patient explanation or occasional sarcasm, we learned to cooperate as well as we could. When accosted by an officer because he failed to salute, and asked, "How long have you been in the army, soldier?", one new recruit replied, "All day, sir."

The problem of keeping people in line was just as common in other branches of the service. A seaman once declared to his chief petty officer, "You can't make me do that!" "No," was the reply, "but we can make you wish you had."

The officer-enlisted man relationship was a source of stress, especially to men unaccustomed to dealing with rigid authority. As one illiterate draftee lamented to me, "They act like they don't button their britches the way we do."

Nevertheless, the general attitude at the reception center was one of mutual respect. Everyone realized that winning the war was of the most critical importance, and citizens all over the land cooperated in a universal patriotic effort that people today scarcely comprehend. On the front page of the Muncie Star of November 8 a headline read: ENEMY LOSSES SET AT 5,188 IN SOLOMON ISLES, and the subhead, "American Losses Placed at About One Fifth of the Total." Compared to the plight of the guys overseas, our frustrations were trivial, and we knew it. We were too busy to get into trouble. Besides, in our short stay at Fort Harrison there simply wasn't time for animosities to develop. With everything from shots to lectures to uniform issuance to the classification process, it was all we could do to keep up.

WWII LETTERS TO MY GIRL BACK HOME
From Nigeria, Arabia and Turkey

We were issued clothing, including "fatigues" for everyday labor and "Class A" uniforms which were of high quality, and fit very well, thanks to careful measurements taken before we walked down long tables to pick them up. The room was permeated with the smell of moth balls. Shoes we received were brown and sturdy, sized somewhat larger than the ones we wore to Indianapolis. The army knew that frequent marching would in time cause our feet to grow somewhat larger, and issued shoes accordingly. Over the years, incessant polishing would cause the shoes to become softer and even more comfortable.

We were each provided with a large gray duffel bag for our possessions. As we moved frequently in the future to new posts, we would lug this bag everywhere, whether shivering in the cold or perspiring in tropical heat. We soon learned to travel light.

In the evening we used a rubber stamp to mark many clothing items with the first initial of our last name and the last four digits of our serial number. To me, this seemed ridiculous. Surely the army could afford to pay for an occasional lost sock! I was to learn later the grim reason for such marking. If we were some day to be blown to bits, our bodies could be identified from the shreds of clothing bearing these serial numbers. Of course our "dog tags" were the primary source of identification. There were two: one to stay with the corpse and one to be collected by the burial detail. The army thought of everything.

However, we seldom dwelt on such topics. We were ready for the classification process. I remember feeling ill during the tests. Most of us had some reaction to the shots. The classification tests indicated not only basic intelligence but also aptitude for various army jobs. Radiomen, for instance, needed the ability to distinguish and recall musical tones because learning Morse code was related to remembering musical scores. A person who could work easily with words and could type might be useful as a company clerk, etc.

Following tests, we were individually interviewed by the classification officer. At the interview we could explain our civilian work experience and state any service preferences we had. I told of my background in meteorology and was pleased to be assigned for training as a weather observer in the Army Air Force.

Allan Robert Humbert

The Army had an ingenious system for separating those who really knew something about a technical subject from those who were merely bluffing in hopes of getting an easy assignment. Each classification officer had a book with specialized questions related to particular fields. For instance, if you claimed some knowledge of weather, the officer might look in his book and ask, "What is a millibar?" If you knew the correct answer, your background was considered to be authentic.

One pleasant surprise of army life was the food. At a time when civilians were subject to rationing, we ate very well. For breakfast we'd sometimes be served enough bacon to have fed our entire family at home. Overseas situations might be different, but in the large US bases, the food was excellent.

In only a few hectic days, our classification was complete and we were on a train headed for basic training.

Chapter 7

TROOP TRAIN—ON TO BASIC TRAINING

We didn't know our destination. Already we were learning that the army kept careful control over information, especially that given to us soldiers. There were spies and saboteurs to worry about. From time to time newspapers carried stories about suspected acts of sabotage, and we were taught early on that even the most innocent-seeming information could cause loss of life if it fell into the wrong hands. Nevertheless, there was no hiding the fact that our train was moving steadily westward.

I remember that one character from Kentucky would, each time the train stopped, stand on the exit steps and bawl out, "LOOEY-ville." We traveled by coach, watching the scenery unfold by day and trying to sleep at night as the clickety-clack of the iron wheels went on endlessly, and the lonely whistle of the steam locomotive reminded us all that we were a long, long way from home.

Although we had occasional comfort stops, armed guards accompanied us in case we forgot to rejoin the group.

On November 26, 1942, we ate Thanksgiving dinner aboard the train. Men would file to the rear behind the dining car, fill their metal trays with turkey and all the fixings, then wend their way forward again to their seats. Ever the benevolent master, the army was determined that each soldier would receive a great meal, wartime, or not. We did.

A second set of railroad tracks ran parallel to those on which we traveled at perhaps 60 miles per hour. Occasionally we would meet an eastbound train on the other track. The lighted windows of their passenger cars would flash by in the twinkling of an eye.

For days the train sped on, across the prairies, through Nebraska and into Wyoming. At the higher elevations, the temperature was colder, and the streams which had flowed from the hillsides were congealed into ice. We crossed the Rockies and turned southward.

For the first time in my life, I realized the vastness of our nation. I wondered who in hell Adolph Hitler thought he was to believe he could defeat the United States of America.

By the end of November, we had arrived at a former Japanese relocation center near Fresno, California, where we were to receive basic training. At the time we didn't know how unfairly these innocent Japanese-Americans were being treated, as they were ruthlessly uprooted and arbitrarily moved from their homes in the interest of US security, even though most of them had been exemplary citizens.

Wearily we unloaded our heavy duffel bags from the baggage car and checked into camp, ready for basic training.

For most of us, basic training was simply the most grueling physical experience of our lives. The army believed that every soldier must be at least somewhat ready for combat and that the way to reach this readiness was to make basic training as demanding as possible. Lectures, drills, guard duty, weapons training, sanitation, military courtesy and the obstacle course combined to make life miserable.

Army obstacle courses consisted of assorted barriers which one had to go over, under, or through at top speed to reach the end of the course. Narrow logs spanning streams of cold water. More logs to be crawled under. Ropes from which to swing. A tall board fence to be gone over. Strangely enough, by running rapidly toward the fence one's momentum helped a person over the barrier. One consolation: at least we didn't face the prospect of having live bullets firing at us as we negotiated the course. Some infantry outfits did. There was a story of a fellow training in the desert with machine guns firing at about waist height. The unfortunate trainee encountered a rattlesnake, stood up, and was killed by the machine gun fire.

We didn't take guard duty seriously. Mostly we looked at it as an annoying way to ruin our sleep for 24 hours. Depending on the guard

WWII LETTERS TO MY GIRL BACK HOME
From Nigeria, Arabia and Turkey

assignment, you would be on duty for two hours and off for four. Not enough time to get any sleep before going back on duty.

To the command, "Halt! Who goes there?," one guy replied, "Donald Duck! Quack!Quack!Quack!Quack!" Later, in militarily more sensitive areas, we would learn that "Halt!" meant just that and trigger-happy guards just might shoot you if you didn't.

We learned to handle and fire weapons, not only how to shoot but how to take apart the guns and reassemble them with our eyes closed. I qualified with the .45 Colt pistol and in due time received a Sharpshooter's badge.

Our biggest gripe was the cold barracks. Only after one of the trainees literally died of pneumonia were we successful in getting oil burners installed in the frigid quarters.

A source of minor frustration was the street language which was so widely used. Particularly in basic training, the words and expressions were often obscene, vulgar and profane, running heavily toward mention of private body parts, secretions and functions seldom mentioned in polite society. I grew weary of such expressions as "PASS THE_____-_____BUTTER!"

Perhaps it was the total absence of women, or maybe just a way of striking back at a situation in which we were under almost total control from above, or maybe just the macho attitude of men wanting to show that they were as tough as anybody around, even if deep down we didn't really feel that way.

It was a relief later to be assigned to groups in which decent civilian speech was the norm.

Basic training was supposed to last four weeks. But not for me. One week after I arrived, they rubber-stamped my service record to the effect that I had completed the required time, even though I'd only been there a week. I received orders to report to Chanute Field, near Rantoul, Illinois, for training as a weather observer.

For a 22-year-old kid, moves such as this were an adventure. We were all under orders to read the bulletin board daily, and it was exciting to see your name listed, especially for an assignment that you had really hoped for.

If it seemed strange for the army to send one all the way to California, only to send the soldier back to Illinois, it must be remembered that troop movements were in terms of large numbers of men, rather than in terms of individuals.

Allan Robert Humbert

Chapter 8

CHANUTE FIELD WEATHER SCHOOL 1942

In the armed forces you seldom know what will happen next. For most civilians, one day may be much like another, and you yourself have considerable influence on what happens. But in the army, as a tiny cog in a vast machine, life can change quickly for good or ill without regard to your wishes. You get up in the morning, read the bulletin board, receive your orders and are on your way the next day.

In December, 1942, I was sent to Chanute Field, Illinois, for training as a weather observer. Overseas, Allies were pushing the Japanese in the Pacific back toward their homeland; Soviet troops were attacking the Italian Eighth Army. The US was gearing up for the war effort. Everyone had a job to do. Ours was to become weathermen, to make the observations which meteorologists could use to prepare forecasts on which effective flying depended.

To illustrate, the direction and velocity of winds aloft let pilots calculate the time needed to reach their targets. Cloud cover and visibility were important to know, both from the point of view of seeing the targets and that of avoiding enemy defenses. Even with today's sophisticated instruments, satellites and computers, weather forecasting is still far from an exact science, although it continues to improve.

Facilities at Chanute Field in 1943 were far superior to the spartan accommodations of the former Fresno fairgrounds from which I had come. Established in 1917 as a primary flight training center, Chanute Field was a well-developed air base, with heated barracks, paved streets, a state of the art kitchen, modern classrooms, and even a new movie theater on the base, not to mention huge hangars and air strips occupying many acres. It was named for Octave Chanute, pioneer student of aviation who advised the Wright brothers on technical matters.

It had the atmosphere of a small college. Intelligent, serious-minded students worked hard to complete their courses, aware not only that the war demanded it, but that their academic performance would be closely monitored and ruthlessly evaluated.

Classes met during mornings and afternoons. We learned to take instrument readings of air pressure, temperature, humidity, precipitation, surface winds and winds aloft as well as to judge cloud types, coverage, heights, and visibility. We also learned how to quickly plot this information on a blank map in a space for each station that could be covered by a dime. In addition, we learned to transmit the information by teletype. A course in basic meteorology aided our understanding of what we were doing.

The importance of our work to flying can be further illustrated by considering the problem of a pilot flying on instruments, unable to see the ground. We always transmitted the barometer reading—air pressure—as an altimeter setting. The greater the altitude of a plane, the lower the air pressure will be at that level. If the air pressure on the ground, is, say 29.8 inches (of mercury in the barometer), and the plane's altimeter is set for 29.8," the altimeter will read zero at ground level. Suppose the plane is flying in clouds and the pilot cannot see the ground. His altimeter, if set correctly, will tell him that he is at a safe altitude above the ground at that location. But if the weather observer has reported the wrong air pressure, say 30.0" instead, the pilot relying on the altimeter setting will think he is flying at a safe level when he is actually flying much lower. Thus, an incorrect altimeter setting can cause the death of a pilot.

Another example: Humidity of the air is reported as dew point, the temperature at which air in that particular parcel of air will condense out in the form of fog or a cloud. Suppose a pilot is flying through air which has a temperature of 45 degrees and a dew point of 35 degrees. He can fly safely without fear of fog forming which will keep him from seeing the ground. But supposing the weather observer has wrongly reported the dew point to be 35 degrees and it is actually 44 degrees. When the air cools only one degree, the pilot will find himself in a cloud, possibly with serious consequences.

All these subtleties made the job of weather personnel technically demanding and hard to learn, and while weathermen might never become combat heroes, planes could scarcely have flown without us.

In ten weeks, we had completed the course. Early in March, 1943, I received orders to report to Dale Mabry Field at Tallahassee, Florida.

WWII LETTERS TO MY GIRL BACK HOME
From Nigeria, Arabia and Turkey

Chapter 9

TALLAHASSEE WEATHER OBSERVER

Shortly after completing the course, I was on a train heading for Dale Mabry Field at Tallahassee, Florida. Traveling southward, the weather grew warmer mile by mile. In Illinois, winter prevailed, but by the time we reached Florida, spring was in full bloom. The dull brown of winter had given way to lush green grass and daffodils.

Tallahassee in 1943 was a pleasant southern city with a slightly rural flavor. Even downtown you could hear roosters crowing. Dale Mabry Field nearby was an advanced training center where P-51 pilots trained before heading overseas.

It was the job of the Fourth Weather Squadron to monitor the sometimes treacherous Florida conditions, providing up-to-the-minute weather reports.

I was quickly put to work. A few of the names I still remember are Henry LeFevre, H. O. Stanton, an observer named Pierson and a Lt Penney. The names of others escape me. The first instrument I was handed was a broom. It was my duty to keep the ubiquitous Florida sand at bay. Soon, however, another newer observer arrived, and I gladly passed the broom to him.

Most weather stations operated 24 hours per day, with each set of weathermen working an 8-hr. shift. Once each hour, we would check temperature and dew point, barometer reading, cloud type, height and coverage, precipitation, and visibility, as well as wind direction and velocity. If there was a significant change in conditions, we would send out a special report.

We also measured winds aloft, an interesting and ingenious operation performed by two observers, one inside and the other outside. The basic principle is that a specially-inflated balloon is released and followed by a theodolite, which is a telescope graduated so both the angle of elevation of the balloon and its direction from the station can be measured. This is done by the outside person. Suppose no wind is present, the balloon, rising at a known rate, will remain directly above the station, but if, at a certain level, it drifts south, a wind blowing from the north must have moved it in that direction. So all the inside person has to do is plot the positions above the ground of the balloon and he can trace wind directions for thousands of feet into the sky.

It was a fun process. For night readings, we attached a paper lantern having a lighted candle inside and observed it. The crosshairs inside the theodolite telescope were illuminated. As the balloon drifted farther and farther away, it would finally vanish among the stars.

To measure the height of the clouds when the sky was overcast, similar balloons were followed and the time it took for the balloon to vanish into the clouds was noted. For night measurements, some weather stations used powerful searchlights pointing vertically upward. These projected a spot on the base of the cloud layer. An observer at some distance from the light measured the angle from his location to the spot. Simple math would then reveal the height of the cloud layer above the station.

Weather reports were transmitted hourly to desired stations by teletype. Our station received reports from other stations by teletype also. The complete set of reports was used to make weather maps. All the data for each station was plotted on a map of the entire area, using simple symbols. Wind direction, for instance, was shown as a short line pointing into the wind and radiating out from the station dot like a hand on a clock. Wind velocity was indicated by barbs on the end of the direction line; the stronger the wind, the more barbs. Clouds and other phenomena were represented by little pictures resembling the object. For instance, a cumulus cloud consisted of a sort of half-circle flat on the bottom, which looked something like a cloud.

When the map was finished, the forecaster used the map to draw isobars, fronts, etc. needed to picture the weather clearly. Forecasts were normally made four times per day.

All in all, it was interesting work, and we took our responsibilities very seriously.

As for other aspects of military life, our attitude was one of grudging acceptance. Weathermen as a group were intelligent and well educated. Former teachers, lawyers, small business owners and many ex-students drafted from colleges and universities were among our ranks.

Our job situation didn't call for much teamwork or submission to bureaucratic army command. With only a couple of weather observers on duty on each shift, we escaped quite a bit of the military routine. We had our share of roll calls, calisthenics and formations to attend, but nowhere near what the "real" soldiers got.

Now and then we would march a few miles in formation, singing such songs as "Roll Out the Barrel." It was probably good for us. We needed the exercise. We were smart enough to stay out of trouble and were generally cooperative with authority. Lacking the onerous line-and-staff burden of outfits with large numbers of personnel, we really didn't suffer the interpersonal conflicts which were common in such commands.

Our attitude could be summarized by the opening words of an anonymous weatherman composer, sung to the French tune, "Vive l'Amour"

> "The Fourth Weather Squadron is marching today,
> Vive la compagnie.
> We march like the Infantry—
> In our own way.
> Viva la compagnie."

Nevertheless, we were an idealistic, high-spirited group. For off-duty relaxation we had a "dayroom," a simple one-room structure with tables, chairs, some reading material and a coke machine. Cokes were a nickel then, and getting change to use in the machine was a problem. Wondering just how honest the guys really were, I put 40 nickels in a bowl with a sign, "Change for coke machine." As time went by, dozens of airmen passed through that dayroom, many of them alone. Anyone could have helped himself to the coins without fear of being detected.

Two weeks later, I checked the contents of the bowl. Inside I found two one-dollar bills and a silver half-dollar.

Once our daily work was completed, we actually had quite a bit of free time, although still subject to military control. For relaxation there were sports for the athletically inclined, which most of us were not. Still, we found plenty to do. We never tired of watching P-51 Mustang fighter planes as they roared over the embankment at the end of the runway, their landing gears retracting beneath the plane for all the world like a kitten folding its paws before taking a nap. Only these kittens were driven by a 1675 horsepower engine and cruised at 275 miles per hour. We wrote long letters home and corresponded with friends in the service. Some of us read a lot. Occasionally we went to Tallahassee. As the weather got still warmer, we spent an occasional day at the beach basking in the warm Florida sun.

Once a friend and I were on a swimming date with two nice southern girls. I made the mistake of teasing them about the South having lost the Civil War. They got mad at us and went home.

It took a while to understand the southern point of view. Coming from Indiana, I felt that Indiana ways were the right ways. To me, the Civil War was a long-forgotten conflict of our great-grandfathers. But to the girls and to many other southerners it was still a source of resentment.

The reader should realize that many things have changed since 1943, and that we ex-servicemen have changed, too. We remember events from the perspective of somewhat naive youths in our early twenties. Florida seemed a long way from home. Sometimes we referred to ourselves as the AEF— "Americans Exiled in Florida." For a while at first, I felt vaguely uneasy at night, sleeping so near the edge of the US—afraid I might somehow fall off into the Gulf.

The South was not a place of racial equality. It would be 21 years before the passage of the Civil Rights Act. However, Muncie, Indiana, also had its share of ethnic and racial prejudice. Southerners seemed kinder and more sympathetic to the views and feelings of others than those of us from the North. They were more "laid-back" and courteous than we were. "Sir" and "Ma'am" just weren't in our everyday vocabulary. Even if regulations required that we address officers as "Sir," it didn't come naturally.

We gradually learned to accept the difference in viewpoint between our fellow southern soldiers and ourselves, and to avoid certain conversational subjects that we knew would only lead into arguments.

The summer of 1943 continued uneventfully at Dale Mabry Field. I had really grown to feel at home there. But in the army, things could change rapidly. Several of us had taken a qualifying exam for weather forecasting school and had practically forgotten about it. A few weeks later, I received word that I had passed and was ordered to Chanute Field. Reluctantly, I checked out, said goodbye to the guys and headed for the train station.

Chapter 10

WEATHER FORECASTING SCHOOL

Once more I was on a train, headed out of Tallahassee on the venerable Seaboard line. The weather was hot. When the train rounded a curve, we could see black coal smoke and cinders belching from the steam locomotive. Some of the cinders came through the open windows into my ears and onto my khaki uniform which had been clean that morning.

I boarded another train, this one bound for Rantoul, Illinois, and was soon back at Chanute Field, assigned to the Seventh Technical Training Squadron.

Chanute was even busier than before. One could hear aircraft engines roaring away on test stands day and night. For the first time, I saw headlights of huge bombers practicing night landings. The base seemed crowded and teeming with activity. In the noisy mess hall someone always seemed to be letting a glass milk bottle slide off the metal tray and crash onto the concrete floor below. Actually, considering the hundreds of soldiers who went through the line at every meal, a certain amount of breakage could be expected.

From time to time, word would reach us of war conditions around the world, either from soldiers recently arrived at Chanute, or through correspondence with other servicemen. One small group from Attu, Alaska, taught us the "Song of the Keebird," which went:

>"Singing the song of the Kee Bird,
>Kee, Kee, Kee-rist but it's cold!"

WWII LETTERS TO MY GIRL BACK HOME
From Nigeria, Arabia and Turkey

We heard of the 8th Air Force stationed in England who were taking many bloody casualties as they tried to pound the Nazis into submission. Sometimes the B-17s would land as wrecks barely able to return to their base before being junked. One of the first jobs to be done was to hose out the planes to get rid of the blood and gore inside. At first, crews from only a few bombers would be quartered in one barracks. At breakfast, every crew member from all the bombers leaving on a mission would be present. By the time of the evening meal, however, only a handful of men might be left, those from other planes which had returned safely, all the rest from the missing plane having been killed or captured. So the army stopped the practice of housing an entire bomber crew in a single barracks, choosing instead to scatter members among several barracks, so when a plane was missing, the loss would be less noticeable and not so bad for morale.

Meteorology is a tough subject. The army tried to cram a full college course into 16 short weeks and the instructors were more demanding than helpful. Weather, based fundamentally on the heating and cooling of air and water is interesting but ever challenging. For instance, a column of air may be thought of as consisting of a stack of elastic containers piled on top one another, much like cushions. The "cushions" at the bottom of the stack are compressed by all those above, so they are squeezed into a smaller volume. Thus, if some of the air at the bottom rises, it no longer has the weight of the other air compressing it. It therefore expands. But the air has just as much heat in it as before, only spread over a lower volume, so its temperature goes down. Air always contains moisture, so as it rises and expands, it becomes less able to hold moisture, and at a certain point, a cloud or fog will form in the formerly transparent parcel. If it rises still farther and cools more, precipitation may occur, which may be in the form of rain, sleet, or snow, depending. If winds into a certain region are converging inward from all sides, there is a continuous supply of moisture, and rain may last for many days…due to the rotation of the earth, an air mass tends to move from west to east, and also to curve to the right, something called the Coriolis force. (Mathematical formula: $2 \, mv \, \omega \sin \phi$!).

Nor is that all; weather processes interact with one another. Normally, when the sun goes down, the air cools, and on a clear night the lowest temperature will occur just at sunrise. But if there is a heavy cloud cover, which may or may not be the case, the clouds insulate the earth and the temperature doesn't drop so low.

These pages are not the place for a meteorology course, and I have only begun to touch on a few of the factors which can affect the weather forecast for a given region.

For the student forecaster, being suddenly confronted with a chart plotted with hundreds of data bits and being told to draw a map and make a forecast with insufficient time, the effort could be devastating. Nevertheless, I continued to plug away, confident that I would eventually pass. After all, I had been through four years of college and had mastered many a hard course in the past, even if this seemed particularly difficult.

I really appreciated being near my home in Muncie. It gave me the occasional opportunity to visit my folks, since Chanute was only about 150 miles from home. In those days, the fastest transportation available to servicemen was by hitchhiking. One weekend, I had gone back to Muncie and was being driven back to Chanute by the folks, stopping along the highway for a picnic. The food was great but our mood was subdued. Nobody knew when, if ever, we would meet again.

Throughout the war, servicemen were accorded an almost embarrassing respect and deference. Regardless of how they felt about the war itself, civilians were 100% back of the troops.

An event was about to happen which would change my life forever. In October, 1943, I attended the Ball State Homecoming parade, spotting an attractive, vivacious, and talkative brunette named Mozelle Smith, whom I seemed to have known for years, even though I had never met her before. I learned that she was an honor student, majoring in business education, and that her dad taught math in Marion. We began corresponding with each other, and visiting when we could.

Meanwhile, my grades in the vital map-drawing course fell below the critical cut-off point by less than ½ %, and I was informed that I would not be graduating. So near and yet so far ...I would continue as a weather observer, but not qualify for the higher classification of forecaster.

Earlier in the fall, I had a confrontation one night in our barracks. Most of us were worn out and ready to go to bed at the 9:00 p.m. curfew. As the ranking sergeant in the barracks, it was my job to enforce the few rules we had, including curfew. However, sometimes we'd bend them a little and allow a soldier who came in late to have the lights on long enough to get undressed and go to bed.

A loud-mouthed Texan came in drunk that night and turned on the lights. I gave him a few minutes and finally told him I would count to ten and then turn them off. "Well, you blankety-blank better not turn those blanking lights off!" We were on the upper story of a two-story barracks, and there was a stairway at each end.

I counted to ten, snapped off the switch, then moved a large trash can so as to block the stairway, before I went down it, pulled the master switch, came back upstairs using the stairway at the other end of the barracks and got under the covers. Just as I had anticipated, the guy lurched to the switch, stumbled over the trash can; fell downstairs, and came back up cursing. Lying under the covers, I could hear him vainly clicking the disconnected switch. Stumbling back to his bunk, he muttered, "Tomorrow when I get up, I'm going to beat up on you and *you* and YOU! And I'm going to **KILL** that damned little sergeant!" But in the morning he was gone.

INDIANAPOLIS

My next station was Stout Field. Indianapolis was quite a metropolitan area. Moreover, I could easily get away on weekends, hitchhiking as usual. Ordinarily, one could reach Muncie faster by hitchhiking than by taking a bus. But not always. One December night, I got a ride as usual, but halfway to Muncie the driver announced that he was turning at the next crossroads, leaving me in the middle of nowhere. I decided to walk back toward the intersection we had passed, only to hear a vicious-sounding dog who seemed unlikely to let me continue to the intersection. So I reversed direction, headed for the intersection toward Muncie. En route, I was stopped by another, equally mean-sounding dog. Finally, about 2:00 a.m., I was picked up.

Allan Robert Humbert

Most drivers were perfectly willing to give a soldier a ride, but at night they simply couldn't see us in time to stop. Later, I thought of a method to solve the problem. I would hold five ordinary kitchen matches in my left hand, ready to strike. As a car approached, I would successively strike each match and flip it over my head. At night the effect was startling, and it never failed to cause motorists to give me a ride.

Back at Stout Field, my weather observing job was routine. By training men to perform certain functions in the same manner everywhere, the army achieved the personnel equivalent of interchangeable parts in the military machine.

We were all subject to the Articles of War, a list of rules designed to apply to nearly every conceivable situation. If you understood them, you could operate freely regardless of your place in the hierarchy. According to rules governing weather observation, unless the visibility was a certain minimum distance, flight was forbidden unless the pilot had an instrument license. So a lowly sergeant weather observer could occasionally find himself in the position of keeping an army general from taking off.

Flying is never risk-free. Once, while I was on duty, a pilot put on the brakes too quickly while landing his light plane. It stood on its nose and broke the propeller. The pilot emerged unscathed but red-faced as he entered the operations room. A glance at the newspapers of the period reveal many other examples of worse events when students made some mistake while learning to fly fast, "hot" aircraft.

At the moment I was more interested in romance than in weather. I asked a woman at the service club for the name of a reliable jeweler. She recommended Rost Jewelers, where I bought a 1/4 carat engagement ring. My bunk was located where the rays of the rising sun would strike it. Sometimes before getting up, I would hold the diamond under the covers watching as a narrow shaft of sunlight was transformed into the colors of the rainbow.

On December 24, 1943, I drove to Marion and asked Mozelle if she would like to wear it. She accepted.

Our visits soon ended. By February, I had been ordered to Seymour Johnson Field at Goldsboro, North Carolina, a staging area for overseas duty.

WWII LETTERS TO MY GIRL BACK HOME
From Nigeria, Arabia and Turkey

Chapter 11

SEYMOUR JOHNSON FIELD
NORTH CAROLINA
FEBRUARY 1944

During our service at Dale Mabry Field in Florida, we had worked in an atmosphere of cordiality and mutual respect. There we were treated like professionals and responded accordingly. We had jobs to do and most of us tried to do them well. Seymour Johnson Field was different. As a large and busy training center supplying troops for overseas duty, its personnel didn't seem to care whether we liked the place or not.

Excerpts from a letter written to my fiancée describe the air base and give no hint of future problems:

February 16, 1944

Greetings from Seymour Johnson Field. It's 1400 in the afternoon, and we haven't done a thing so far except get located. Last night (about 0200) we arrived at the station and were soon picked up by trucks and taken out to the field. We went to bed about 0330, expecting to be awakened at 0530, but we weren't, and therefore slept till noon. At 1300 was chow formation, which we marched to.

Just as we were walking out to wash our trays, I heard a yell, and who should I see but Sgt "Red" Evans from Tallahassee. We were soon talking over old times. Most everyone but a couple of people I used to know have left. We had fun talking to each other.

He took the last forecasting exam, was 4th from the top, but 4th Weather didn't send any men, so now he won't be a forecaster either. He'd been up for staff sergeant for months, but left before making it.

This is definitely a big post—some people say 22,000. The climate is mild, and the barracks and buildings are dark green in color, and are located on sandy soil. They are heated by stoves—so far it's been rather cold inside. In many ways the field reminds me of Tallahassee, and it doesn't appear to be a bad place at all. There are lots of PXs, chapels and theaters.

Now for the rumors: These are strictly latrine rumors, mere idle conjecture, yet some of them will no doubt be true. (#1) We will be here 6-12 weeks; (#2) We will be here only a short while, being alerted for immediate shipment; (#3) We will sleep in tents; (#4) We spend 21 days on the rifle range; (#5) We go on an eight-day bivouac; (#6) We go on a ten-day bivouac; (#7) A big group of weathermen was marked off the shipping list right at the POE (Port of Embarkation); (#8) We can't go to the PX during duty hours; (#9) We have parade formation every night; (#10) We are going to England; (#11) We may go to South America. Confusing, isn't it? Well, don't put too much reliance on these; wait to see what happens.

On the 17th began our processing, a 4-5 day period through which we had to go before being eligible for pass or shipment. First was a lecture on the early part of the war in Europe, mostly a review of what I already knew. Then came a talk on allotments. We were told that it was wise to have a large part of our pay withheld in Class E allotments and sent home directly rather than having to send it home from overseas. With a base pay as a sergeant of $78.00 per month, plus $15.60 overseas pay, my total income would be $93.60. GI insurance would cost $6.60, leaving me $27.00 per month to spend after the automatic allotment had been sent. I told Mozelle that saving so much money would make us plutocrats by the end of the war.

WWII LETTERS TO MY GIRL BACK HOME
From Nigeria, Arabia and Turkey

From another letter:

February 18, 1944

Was it only six days ago that I saw you? It seems like weeks at least. So far I haven't received a bit of mail from anybody, which makes me miss you more than ever.

Effects of all those wonderful nights with you are beginning to show up, but the nights were worth it. I have a very bad cold and would go on sick call except it would delay me another day in getting out of this squadron. Let's make it a point <u>not</u> to visit North Carolina—I don't think it is worthwhile. Everybody has bad colds, and morale of course is low. Maybe the idea they have here is to make our stay in camp so unpleasant we'll be only too glad to go overseas.

As I read in the paper today about the troop transport that was sunk with a loss of 1,000 men, I couldn't help thinking that everybody at home would be worrying about that happening to me, when the actual chances of such an occurrence are surprisingly small. I hope you don't worry about me, darling; although on the other hand it's nice to know that somebody is thinking about me.

The transition from Stout Field to Seymour Johnson was a bit too abrupt for me to accept good-naturedly. To exchange the company of fellows at the station for these GI's wasn't much fun. Then, too, it's cold and damp here, and the usual permanent party scum to contend with, not to mention our heartily disliked General Francis Brady, who actually goes prowling all over the field to find people who are out of uniform, in the wrong areas, etc. Oh well, best I quit complaining—I won't be here long, and nobody enjoys reading another's woes.

This morning we had PT (physical training) and took physical fitness tests during the period. I did very poorly, scoring only 26 sit-ups (I did 52 at Chanute) and 5 pull-ups (11 at Chanute). Maybe some day I can better the score if it ever makes any difference.

Next we were each given a carbine to play with before the lecture. It is a very nice little gun (it's only 35" long and weighs but 5 lbs). All members of each outfit receive a carbine—it is to take the place of the .45 caliber pistol. It has several advantages over the pistol. First, it is much more accurate. Second, it shoots 15 shots as fast as one can pull the trigger, while the pistol shoots only seven shots. Third, it can be drawn and fired before the automatic pistol can. Statistics show that a man with a carbine can draw and fire 3 shots before a man can even draw the pistol. Altogether, it is a very nice gun and is receiving wide use.

This afternoon we saw and took apart another weapon, the M-3 submachine gun. It looks like something out of Buck Rogers, is fully automatic, all metal and shoots a magazine of 30 .45 caliber cartridges.

That concluded our training for today. Now to go to bed and forget the whole thing, and maybe recover somewhat from my cold, sore throat and fever blister.

February 19, 1944

—More greetings from your forlorn fiancé. Right now I feel as your grandmother might had she been kicked down a fire escape onto a coal pile and left lying in sub-zero weather for hours with two broken legs, two broken arms, a broken nose and double pneumonia. Yes, that is a bit exaggerated; actually, I don't even feel sick, but am merely bothered with a bad cold (which is getting better) a sore throat, usual PT stiffness and three more shots. So don't waste any sympathy on me, for in a few days I'll be in good shape again, probably by the time you get this letter. My arms are no sorer than they were the first night I received my earlier shots, but they are uncomfortable. At least we have obtained some heat in the barracks, and it is now almost warm.

The shots referred to were yellow fever, cholera and typhus. In addition, we had a POE (Port of Embarkation) physical, prepared power of attorney designation, a will (optional—I made none), and allotment.

Censorship was something to consider. How were we soldiers to write our sweethearts knowing that every torrid phrase would be seen by our commanding officer? Should we tone down our letters just because somebody else was reading them? No way! We'd just keep on writing as before and consider censorship as another necessary wartime invasion of privacy. Besides, looking at the matter from the censor's point of view, the novelty of reading the romantic sentences of homesick GIs may well have been pretty tedious.

February 21, 1944

I am writing this in your favorite letter-writing position, propped up in bed. The fire went out last night and it's cold in the barracks.
Yesterday we did almost nothing but see movies. We were given new gas masks and shown how to pitch a tent. While preparing to pitch the tent, a car drove up and who should get out but our confounded General Brady, who proceeded to bawl out the whole group. I huddled in the center of the group to keep from being "busted." This happens, you know, especially in a place like this.
There was no mail yet. If the mail situation gets any worse, I'll not even be here when mail comes. I hope letters are getting through to you more easily than they are to me. Sooner or later I will run out of things to write about. And when I go overseas, there will be a still longer gap when neither of us will get any mail.

We found many interesting fellows in the camp—a staff sergeant who returned from England to attend forecasting school only to wash out, a soldier who looks exactly like the current caricature of a Jap, but who is in reality an American citizen and a graduate of Dartmouth, as well as kids of 19 being sent overseas, and even one only 18 years old with three weeks in the army. We only hoped that Infantry troops were not being sent overseas with so little training.

As we drew closer to overseas duty, people at home became more fearful of what might happen to us. In my letter of the 24th, I tried to reassure Mozelle with our candid assessment of our genuine risks:

I'm not about to become a dead hero. As a matter of fact, I look upon the prospect of being overseas without the slightest fear. And I have greater confidence in my own ability to come through in one piece than in that of anybody else. Maybe you would feel reassured if I told you some of the reasons why, and attempted to give a few of my ideas on the subject of battle.

Modern warfare is as complicated as anything else in the machine age. There is nobody in the world utterly immune to destruction by the war. And even those who seem least likely to be hurt by war, may, in civilian life, lose their lives by such simple accidents as slipping in the bathtub.

So many people visualize battles as a constant stream of men "going over the top" armed with little or nothing, straight into a hail of machine-gun bullets and certain death. This simply isn't true. Before even the infantry goes in, there is a ceaseless bombardment by planes, as happened in the Marshall Islands. Men advance on the ground, carefully, and the percentage of loss is pretty low. This, my dear, is what happens in the worst of war, to people whose job is conceded to be far more dangerous than mine.

As a weather observer, I shall not be too close to the lines, and will probably never shoot a gun at anything. When the Germans got close to Corporal Sam Kurlandsky's outfit in Tunisia, one of the first things the commander did was to get a truck up to the weather station to move things out when action got too hot. Why? Because the cold military fact is that we are too valuable to lose. It just takes too long to make a good weatherman. We are not deemed as expendable as, say, a marine is.

Part of the frustration of being at Seymour Johnson was that of being constantly directed by the men who operated the post, and who would be there long after we had departed. So-called "permanent party," it was almost as if they took special pleasure in lording it over us. There was at least one orderly in charge of latrine details who literally couldn't write his name. So he would make the corporals and sergeants who were doing the dirty work write their names on his duty roster. He couldn't read them, either. Having stripes made no difference; about all it did was force those of who had them to be especially cooperative lest some angry officer or his minions take action which would reduce us to the grade of private.

No thought was made of economical use of manpower. For a job such as fire prevention detail, which needed barely two men, the "management" detailed six. On one occasion, I and some others were in charge of US prisoners. Not only were they no trouble at all; one of them assured me that he liked being in the guard house and as soon as he was released fully intended to go AWOL again so he could return to his favorite place. Besides KP which at least could be justified as necessary, there was always "policing the area." A group of us would go out with a sack and a pointed stick picking up trash, papers and cigarette butts. We called the sticks, "dive bombers."

We finally received word that a missing barracks bag of mine had turned up in Louisville. Rather than bothering to return regulation clothing items available on our post, they kept them, sending me just the personal possessions. So long as the barracks bag was in limbo, I could not join the others in the overseas contingent, a matter of two weeks.

From another letter:

March 3, 1944

Today has been a very busy one. At least a hundred bullets have whizzed over my head, but don't be alarmed, for I was working at the rifle range "pulling targets" safely out their way. We ate out of mess kits, and had wieners, boiled potatoes, slaw, ice cream and coffee. Tonight I missed chow due to getting off work late and having a GI party. While on the range I fired the M-3 submachine gun at a couple of targets. It was pretty easy.

For the next several days, our routine continued—KP, the restriction of the barracks because an inspecting lieutenant found one pair of unshined shoes under the bed, efforts to get off the post for recreation, and the usual burdensome details to which we were assigned. Some of us had civilian items which we were not supposed to take overseas, such as a radio I had brought. I managed to sell it for $10.00, even though its cost a few years earlier was only $9.45. A bald-headed captain with a Purple Heart and service in World War I casually told us that we could be charged with desertion if we missed only one roll call!

Allan Robert Humbert

However, there had been good news earlier. The weather outfit had all been transferred to the 712th squadron, our last stop at the base before going to the as-yet-unknown port of embarkation for shipment overseas.

In a letter of March 8 I wrote:

Today I got my very first really GI haircut. My hair is so short that it doesn't matter whether it's combed, because it stands up on end. But it's just one more part of getting along at Seymour Johnson, and I'm willing to comply if it keeps me out of the doghouse. Two fellows in the barracks had their names taken today for failing to salute a major. Just to play safe, I salute everything that has wheels, whether driven by a civilian, enlisted man, or officer. The habit simplifies things even if it does waste a few salutes now and then. Anything to escape from Seymour Johnson as a sergeant!

And from a letter of March 9th:

This has been a busy day but an interesting one. In the morning we heard a lecture on censorship which was quite revealing, and reminded me again of the danger incurred by letting the wrong people in on seemingly harmless knowledge.
The lieutenant told this true story. There was an American landing field on one of the Pacific islands, cleverly camouflaged and separated by some distance from a dummy airfield. The Japs, being fooled, bombed the dummy field, while the Americans watched in high spirits. One of the guys was so proud that he wrote his mother about it, telling how they'd outsmarted the Japanese. She, too, was proud and called up the local radio station, telling them about it, and they in turn reported it on the air, mentioning no names or places. But enemy agents got hold of the story, searched their files, checked their records and discovered which field it was. The next raid was a complete success, because they killed most of the men on the airfield and wounded the rest, including the fellow who wrote the letter. Moral: Don't tell nuttin' to nobody.

We had a gas drill in earnest. We started by lectures on proper use of the mask, then put it on and entered a room filled with tear gas. Aside from a slight burning around the unprotected part of one's face, there wasn't the slightest inconvenience due to the gas. Next, however, they made us take it off, walk to the door and exit. The stuff felt like concentrated acid, and simply blinded us instantly. We groped our way to the outside door out into the wind and in ten minutes were OK.

Now for the real business. We put our masks on and entered the other room, which contained a lethal concentration of chlorine. A few minutes in such a place without a mask would cause death, but with mask on, we couldn't even smell the stuff.

Last of all, we put away our masks, first having left the room, of course, then took a breath, walked into the room and put our masks on while in the lethal concentration. Once again, I didn't even smell it. However, after we got outdoors the odor of chlorine clung to our clothes for a long time. No jewelry could be worn in the chlorine because it would have been corroded.

A letter of March 11:

This has been a rather dull, though easy, day. About a third of our barracks, including myself, were put on clothes-marking detail for the remainder of our stay at Seymour Johnson. The job isn't hard, but I have to work on Sunday again, which will be the third week in a row without a day off. Yet to request relief from the job would be to invite KP or guard duty, so about all there is to do is stick with what I have.

There is a feeling of restlessness permeating all the fellows in this camp—a desire to get going, to be on the move, to be overseas. Rumor has it that we meet our officers tomorrow. This constant strain of doing jobs that require no special aptitude would get on one's nerves in a little while. We have trouble sleeping at night, and there are even a few nightmares. Not the idea of going over, or the possibilities that exist once we are there, but the insidious pressure that this field keeps on everybody. Just this week, for instance, some major "busted" a staff sergeant for having a dirty tie. Obviously, no

Allan Robert Humbert

one in this outfit is so perfect that similar shortcomings cannot be found, including myself. All this pressure does no good whatsoever.

The censor in his lecture the other day mentioned that we must always be cheerful, tell the folks the chow is good, etc. But should my letters, especially overseas, ever become too complimentary regarding things, remember that there may be more to it than meets the eye.

March 13, 1944

Today on the bus I talked to a WAC (Women's Army Corps) who has charge of educating a group of illiterates. They were all unable, at first, to read or write, and their IQs haven't been measured. These people are very happy when they learn to write a little. She told me of a fellow who actually wept when he wrote his first letter to folks at home.

March 14, 1944

You asked when I am leaving for the POE. Right now our shipment seems to have cooled off and it appears that we may be here for weeks yet. But again, we may go out in only a couple of days—not even our squadron officers know when it will be. All information comes from Washington. However, the organization that will prevail on ship has been decided, and fellows appointed to various temporary jobs, such as payroll clerk, acting first sergeant, etc.

March 15, 1945

At 1345 we again fell out (took our places in a military formation); this time for swimming instruction. We were told how to use clothes, packs, barracks bags and even helmets as a means of flotation in water. The pool was that of the local Y in nearby Goldsboro.

Upon returning from chow, I lay down and re-read a bunch of your letters. Near the barracks is a skating rink which plays Strauss *waltzes very beautifully. Also near the barracks are dozens of little frogs. The combination of croaks and notes is quite pleasant. It certainly would be nice if you were here now—who knows how long our shipment will be delayed?*

March 18, 1944

We have just spent 24 hours on guard duty, and I am very sleepy. It's a silly arrangement—we're on post (guard) two hours and in the barracks the next four hours, following the routine for 24 hours. The only sleep we get is between shifts, and never more than three hours at a time. However, we are then off duty for 24 hours, and can sleep, etc. as we please, except for the daily ceremony of "Guard Mount"—more Boy Scout stuff. And it's all very boring.

The first three shifts (6:00 to 8:00 p.m., 12:00 p.m. to 2:00 a.m, and 6:00 a.m. to 8:00 a.m.) I rode a jeep and didn't so much as see the Officer of the Day, or challenge one soldier. The next shift 12:00 a.m. to 2:00 p.m. we just sat around for a while, and had to take prisoners out for half an hour. I had three on one truck. They loaded smashed-up tin cans for salvage. None of the prisoners caused any trouble; in fact they have life easier than we, except for being unable to get passes.

March 19, 1944

Once again weathermen outwit the GIs. In spite of our clothing check, I remain in possession of all the stuff I wanted to keep: binoculars, tools, fur-lined gloves, and scarf.

We were told that there was to be a search of the barracks and therefore we must take every single bit of personal equipment and send it home, or it would be confiscated, so it was necessary to hide things.

In the barracks is a ceiling, of course, but there are several large and small holes in it. Standing up on one of the beds, I put the valuable stuff back up in the hole, behind one of the beams, far out of reach and sight. This was the real prize. Near the opening though, I put a few bottles of ink, etc. which any searcher could find easily, leading him to suspect that that material was all there was. Next, I scattered razor blades between the two sets of stuff, and finished by sticking an old jar of apple butter (origin unknown) very close to the hole, where any searcher would probably knock it off on the floor, scattering the "terrain" with apple butter and broken glass. This, I figured, would make the hiding pretty safe. It did, too. In fact, nobody looked at the hole at all. There's nothing like being prepared. Of course, they may take the stuff away from me at the POE, but if I don't bring it along, it's certain I can't have it until it's sent overseas from home.

On March 21st we received word that the 22nd would be the last day we could send in laundry. Some of the officers had gotten disgusted with our shipping delay and wired Washington. They were informed by headquarters that we would be gone by March 31.

From my final Seymour Johnson letter:

March 23, 1944

Tonight is the last night we are allowed off the field, and we'll be gone in a week for sure. Our officers talked to us today; at least one of them is a weatherman himself. Remarking on the fact that a two-star general is visiting the field, he said, "And when you see a car with two stars, for Pete's sake, salute! Those stars don't stand for two boys in the service." Nice guy!

On March 25th came the final word. We were leaving on the 26th.

WWII LETTERS TO MY GIRL BACK HOME
From Nigeria, Arabia and Turkey

Chapter 12

CAMP PATRICK HENRY, VIRGINIA
MARCH, 1944

The lower left hand corner of the envelope of my letter dated March 27 is signed by the army censor. Private correspondence would now be a thing of the past, another casualty of the war. Our location was indicated as "Atlantic Coast," and the army post office was 12934-A. We were to avoid using any numbers in our letters which might be a secret code, to divulge no military information. Even the use of X's to represent kisses was forbidden.

Except for a lecture on censorship, we had nothing to do. It was fun sleeping late and being free from the everlasting harassment by some of the permanent party people of Seymour Johnson Field. We were advised to write that the food was delicious. In truth, it was some of the best we ever ate.

On Sunday night I went to church and enjoyed the music. Outside our quarters the next day we could hear dreamy Strauss waltzes, as if the army were trying to calm any lingering fears we had. The privilege of sleeping late continued, and we had time to think and write long letters about our post-war future.

On April 2nd, I wrote:

...This was a pleasant day. We were orderlies at Mess Hall— which amounts to being waiters on the officers. However, I didn't mind because we only worked a couple of hours or so at each meal. In general, the duty is a very distasteful one to many guys because they didn't enter the army to be servants. Being a little more practical, I considered the matter from the standpoint of the amount

and difficulty of the work involved. Since the work is easy, it suits me.

Camp Patrick Henry had a music room. We could listen to Beethoven's Pastoral Symphony, Schubert's Unfinished Symphony and many others almost as we did in college Rec. rooms. Moreover, church services were held every night. I attended often.

Part of my letter of April 4, 1944, follows. I started it on a new blank page so the censor could remove the censorship story without destroying the rest of the letter if necessary:

There was a prisoner of war in an American prison camp, a German woman. She received mail from Switzerland, all of it censored by US censors before she got it. One day she got a letter saying that one of her friends or relatives had been going across the street daily to the beer hall, after not having done so for weeks. That city was Essen, Germany. The letter was taken to an expert who knew Essen as well as you know your home town, and the expert realized that there never was a tavern at that specific place. But there was a chemical plant that had supposedly been bombed out of operation. That one letter gave the clue that the factory was again operating, and within a day a special mission left to hit that very plant. Moral: Even the walls have ears.

Another censor, one H. Sigmon, Captain, Infantry, did delete part of my second letter of April 7. I had been on a pass, but the details had been cut out. Missing from page one was a section 3/4" x 4 1/2," and from page 2, 2" x 6."

In a second letter of the 7th, that had nothing cut out, I wrote:

...This being Good Friday, I went to church. Communion followed, and with it an unfamiliar ceremony. Instead of our receiving the cup and bread seated, as we ordinarily do, we knelt around a prayer rail, while the chaplain quietly dipped a thin wafer in wine and inserted it into our mouths. Then it would be the next group's turn and we'd retire to the pews. The service seems more impressive and personal given in this manner.

Some day this place will be commended for its excellent handling of a potentially difficult adjustment. Instead of the mad rush that was typical of Seymour Johnson, there is an air of quiet peacefulness about this camp the like of which I've never seen in the army. There is music wherever we go—not GI stuff but the old well-liked classics—the kind you and I like. For the first time I find myself looking forward to church services during the week. This camp is one of the very few projects I couldn't run better myself.

Our pleasant stay at Camp Patrick Henry was drawing to a close.

Allan Robert Humbert

Time out for Milkshakes

Cleaning the Barracks Floor

WWII LETTERS TO MY GIRL BACK HOME
From Nigeria, Arabia and Turkey

Cairo: Red Cross Tour Group

Feluccas on Nile

Allan Robert Humbert

Cairo: Citadel Mosque

Pyramid and Sphinx

WWII LETTERS TO MY GIRL BACK HOME
From Nigeria, Arabia and Turkey

Scene near Cairo

Egypt: Camels

Allan Robert Humbert

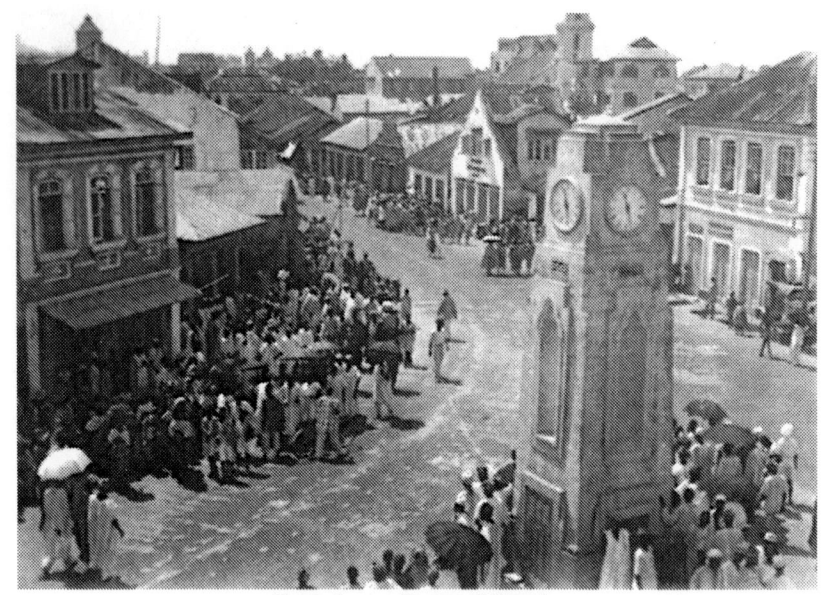

Downtown Lagos, Nigeria

Lagos, Nigeria: Native Market

WWII LETTERS TO MY GIRL BACK HOME
From Nigeria, Arabia and Turkey

Swimmers: "Bathing Suits" added by Author

Nigeria: Native Canoes    **Author and Friends near Lagos**

Allan Robert Humbert

Natives along Beach in Nigeria

"Pop," Favorite Arab Waiter

Author on Seacoast

WWII LETTERS TO MY GIRL BACK HOME
From Nigeria, Arabia and Turkey

Masirah Weathermen Barracks

Howard Swan at Monument

Allan Robert Humbert

Masirah Ceremony After Death of President Roosevelt

Palestine Tour Group 1945

WWII LETTERS TO MY GIRL BACK HOME
From Nigeria, Arabia and Turkey

Tel-Aviv along Mediterranean

Jerusalem: General View

Allan Robert Humbert

Jerusalem: Mount of Olives

Tiberias by Sea of Galilee

WWII LETTERS TO MY GIRL BACK HOME
From Nigeria, Arabia and Turkey

Jerusalem: Citadel

Wailing Wall

Author: Jerusalem

Via Dolorosa

Allan Robert Humbert

Sea of Galilee

Russian Church **Holy Rock**

WWII LETTERS TO MY GIRL BACK HOME
From Nigeria, Arabia and Turkey

India: Camel Hauling Grain

Karachi Shopping District

Allan Robert Humbert

Boarding SS Margarita for US

Entering New York Harbor

Chapter 13

LAGOS, NIGERIA
MAY TO JULY 1944

Having covered the US part of my army service, the following chapters resume with the plane having landed in Nigeria following the trip over French Equatorial Africa. My letter of May 23, 1944, read:

...So far, I'm uncertain as to how much we can tell about our location. You can perhaps guess that it's on the west coast of Africa though that isn't too specific. The natives here are a rather high type and can do many things as well as any white person. Unlike those in Egypt, they seem to have plenty of food and are much happier. Whether the job is driving a car, directing traffic, waiting tables or what have you, these people do it eagerly and well.

Strange how one must get to equatorial Africa before he finds civilization. From the time we visited Khartoum till reaching here, civilization has increased. We have tablecloths, china, waiters, and even two spoons. No more mess kits. No more being room orderly. No more carrying our own bags—these people do it all, and are glad to do it. They certainly have my consent.

We soon learned that Lagos in the '40's was a city of some 80,000 situated on an island also named Lagos, separated from the ocean by a lagoon. At one time as many as 100,000 slaves were shipped through it each year. Malarial mosquitoes thrived in its hot, humid climate. It was a British protectorate. Trade was carried on in palm oil, palm kernels, cotton lint, cacao, mahogany, tin ore, and in sheep and goat skins. One could buy beautiful gold bracelets and exquisite figures of

Allan Robert Humbert

natives carved in ebony. Mahogany was plentiful—even latrine towel racks were made of it.

The weather officers lost no time in putting me to work. Observation methods and instruments were the same everywhere. Weather stations operated 24 hours daily. Observers on the midnight shift had to become accustomed to the problem of sleeping and eating at irregular hours.

Regarding the natives, I wrote:

I find it difficult to pass one of these chocolate-colored citizens without bursting into a smile. They practically worship us, and I, for one, hate to do anything that would lower their opinion of me. Such whole-hearted admiration as theirs is to be found elsewhere only in a hero-worshiping pup, and is a very subtle form of flattery.

A long time ago, these people were in possession of a rather high civilization—at least one that was well organized. And many of them can do lots of things we can, and some things that I can't. Here in the library I saw one of them reading and I glanced at the book as I passed by. He was studying shorthand!

One never sees them on the street carrying loads in their hands or arms. Invariably the object is balanced on their head, whether it is a five-gallon oil can, a basket of fruit or a stack of laundry. When they smile they sparkle like a light bulb. In short, I'm getting a big kick out of them, and many of us could take lessons from them.

June 1, 1944

...This has been a typical June day. Bright sunshiny hours, warm but not hot, made this an ideal day. Actually, it isn't over yet, because I go to work at midnight and work till breakfast. But so far, I've had a very good time.

We get laundry twice a week here, and it is very well done, costing only $1.50 a month. Hogendobler and I had to wait on it before starting out on a little excursion this afternoon. We took a canoe to town, enjoying the conversation of the native kids who paddled and poled the boat. They like America and aren't forever *begging as are the Arabs. They speak English quite well and seem pretty intelligent. On the return, the kids asked us to write down the name we thought their boat should be called. Its former name was "Liberty." We decided that the name "Brooklyn" would be more likely to attract customers, and wrote it down for them. Their boats are not so much canoes as long, narrow rowboats without oars. The kids were pretty dexterous, but hardly exceptional. They charged us one shilling each way, which is about 20 cents.*

British money is simple. There are 20 shillings to a pound, and a pound is worth in our money $4.055. Thus, a shilling is worth about 20 cents; the British 3-penny piece corresponds in value and size to our nickel, and four of them make a shilling. So a penny equals about 5/3 cents, roughly 2 cents. Prices are listed in pounds, shillings and pence. Thus a price of 2/6 means two shillings and 6 pence, a total of 50 cents.

Upon arriving in downtown Lagos, we walked down a street paralleling the water and lined with native tradesmen. They were friendly, lacking the mean and beggarly attitude of some Egyptians. I think I was addressed as "Sergeant" at least 25 times. Walking on down the street, we were accosted by a pair of kids each riding one bike and pulling another. So, finding they charged only 1/6 an hour we rode out into the country to the beach. The temptation was too great, so we got rid of most of our clothes and got in the water, allowing some of the big breakers to come rolling in upon us. Upon seeing a wave coming, one takes a big breath and holds it while the wave passes. There are various ways of meeting waves. One is to face them and jump as high as possible before they strike. Another is to do the same but with your back toward them. Or you can dive through them. Any of these is fun—the feeling of being hurled back by the waves is a grand sensation, one you'd like. We withstood one wave 15 feet high, a real thrill! Finally we returned to camp via bicycle and canoe, resolved to do it all again in the early future...

Sometimes when the waves were too high for swimming, we would visit the wreck of a British freighter which lay half on its side, parallel to the shore. Abandoned, it still contained wooden chairs aboard, long since too weathered to be of value. When we would toss a chair overboard on the side of the ship toward the Atlantic, the waves would quickly smash it to bits against the steel hull. It was easy to understand the fear which sailors have of shipwreck.

June 2, 1944

Today a half dozen of us went swimming where several people have drowned in the past year. It was near the place where we swam yesterday. The surf was high and we had to be quite careful. The undertow almost carried one guy under. Actually, playing in the waves is safe enough, provided you keep your head and watch your business. There are two main rushes of water, first the wave, which may simply bowl you over and cast you up toward shore. Second is the undertow, or the wave sliding back down into the ocean. So long as you aren't in water that is too deep, everything is easy, provided a wave and the undertow from a previous wave do not hit you simultaneously. In that case, it's comparable to the old grade school trick in which one person kneels behind you while another gives you a shove from in front. Maybe you and I can practice wave playing some day in the States.

The sand is clean but rather coarse. There are dozens of little sand crabs about the size of a big thumbnail. However, they are even more anxious to stay out of your way than you are to stay out of theirs, and they don't trouble you.

When we were about ready to leave, we noticed a few native kids selling oranges and bananas. For an English penny, I got three good-sized bananas, and for another penny, two oranges. You see, darling, not all the advantages are with you civilians. We get bananas!

These natives are surprisingly clean and prosperous, and have excellent posture and physique. Moreover they make a living themselves, instead of begging from us. Rationing seems unknown. In fact, I think I'll prepare a list for you of all the products hard to find in the States but readily available here.

June 3, 1944

This afternoon I drank some English tea. It was quite delicious. On our table are three kinds of pills: salt tablets, vitamin tablets and Atabrine tablets. I take them all. Thus far they have had no ill effects on me, but since I already feel fine, they could hardly improve my health.

June 4, 1944

Today I saw a large chameleon found by the natives. It was about ten inches long, green in color and nasty in disposition. We brought it into the barracks and placed it on the cement floor. In a few minutes the color was a much darker green. When I attempted to handle the chameleon it puffed its throat away out as if the lizard were being strangled, made a gasping sound and snapped at me. There are tiny claws and its feet can grip almost anything. Another odd feature is its eyes. They stick out as if the lizard were being strangled, and the eyeball itself is a bright leaf-green in color. Instead of being round, its eyeball is egg-shaped so that the "egg" points out. But the oddest thing of all is the fact that the eyes work independently. One eye can look straight ahead while the other looks back over his shoulder, so the critter almost has eyes in the back of his head.
When we had finished looking at him, we put him in a low nearby palm tree. Later, I returned, and it took five minutes to find him, so well did he blend in with the foliage.

June 5, 1944

…Have you ever noticed how a rather small incident can spoil many subsequent hours? Last night I came to the library early to get a seat for the movie being shown. During the arranging of the chairs, I was asked by a guy who seemed to be in charge, to move to the other side of the room. Meanwhile, the remaining seats in the room rapidly filled up. Just when the movie was to start, the commanding officer of the post came and requested my seat.

Allan Robert Humbert

Naturally I gave it up, went to the back of the room, waited a minute and left.

Situations such as that infuriate me out of all proportion to their importance. Probably it is just the unfairness that makes me mad, though every enlisted man has a certain animosity toward the line that separates officers and himself. In such cases, the line of demaracation seems more appropriate for the Nazis than for a supposedly democratic America.

Changing the subject, I get a big kick out of observing the English. The ones I've seen hardly exemplify the quiet, self-controlled efficiency one hears about. Sometimes they get mad, yell over the telephone and use profanity that we wouldn't think of using. But by the time I've been in the army as long some of these fellows, though, perhaps I'll do that, too.

June 13, 1944

This is a small world. Today, while taking inventory, I picked up a battery-powered lantern. I saw it was "Delta" brand, made right in your home town of Marion, Indiana. I believe you yourself worked there one summer. If that is true, you might possibly have helped construct that very lantern, little dreaming that I, in Africa (you didn't even know me then) would later use the same lantern.

I like the English. There is one couple at the station in whom I detect the same traits we might ourselves have some day, Mr. and Mrs. Gulliver. Both are short; in fact, you and I are taller, respectively than they. They must be around 40 or older, but they remain very much in love, and are constantly showing little favors to one another like a couple of newlyweds.

He is a typical English gentleman, quiet, rather reserved, with a calm air of efficiency. He usually wears shorts to work, yet he suffers no loss of dignity from doing so. We refer to them as "Gully"—Mr. or Mrs., though not in their presence.

Mrs. Gully is small, which, because she reminds me of you, may be why I admire her. She uses perfect English and it is a pleasure to hear her speak. Women definitely make more of language than men. She is interested in everything, especially the war, and could well have played the part of Mrs. Minniver. Hmm—best I quit telling you how nice she is, lest you think I have fallen for her. But they are such an interesting couple, and so obviously in love that I can't help noticing them. People who are in love belong to a society all their own. Once, back in third grade, I got a Valentine with the following sentiment on it:

> "The whole world loves a lover,
> They say, I hope it's true
> 'Cause then the whole world's in love with me
> 'Cause I'm in love with you."

June 14, 1944

...There is a satisfaction that comes from planning, not so much for the material benefits that come from it, as the mental satisfaction of anticipating a situation, preparing for it, and seeing one's plans click. On the folks' place outside Muncie there is an electric tower across the railroad that borders their property. Dad and I used to use it as a rifle target. It was so far distant that we seldom hit it, but now and then would come floating back a 'ping' telling us we had registered a hit. It's the same way when your plans succeed.

I get frustrated by people who wander through life like an aimless cow, never imagining anything, never accomplishing anything and laughing at people who try.

I remember the attitude that prevailed at our Florida weather station. We had a class "A" station, lots of work, and crack station personnel. There were schedules to meet, standards to be maintained and rewards for accomplishment. We took pride in operating, in every sense of the word, a class "A" station. Every shift cleaned the place before leaving. The observer going on duty studiously checked the entries of the previous man, and woe to him if an error could be found! When the end of the month came, we didn't expect the records to be good. We expected them to be <u>perfect</u>. And they usually were. There was a spirit of keen professional competition and everyone was better off for having it.

Allan Robert Humbert

One observer (Hal Stanton) had charge of the records, and he literally rechecked the calculations for any questionable entry.

On the 18th I went to church services in a British chapel. They were rather unsatisfactory to us, the only two Americans present. Just a dozen were in the congregation—not even the English knew the songs being sung, all of which had at least six verses. The priest was all right—he wore conventional priest's robes, but the service as a whole was weak, insipid, and ineffectual. I decided not to return.

June 21, 1944

Lately my day has fallen into a very nice routine. I wake up at 6:45, shave, shower, eat breakfast and arrive at the station about 7:30. There I work till 11:30, finishing the required four hours. Then I return about 12:00, put in a couple more hours and am free to do as I like.

Nice big desk, large electric fan, tea, books, stationery and a comfortable chair complete the picture. I stay there until six, return to chow, go to the library, get located in a good seat, and read till 8:00 when the show starts. There are about three or four a week. By ten the show is over; I go to bed, getting about 8 ½ hours sleep.

June 27, 1944

Our barracks is now the home of a bit of machinery that I hate. One of the fellows got a clock—not a silent clock, or one that chimes the hours away, but an (unprintable) cuckoo clock. Twice each hour that wee wooden birdie pops out, gives his cheery little whistle, and retires. But does he cease at night? No; the confounded little insomniac whistles blithely his twelve times at midnight the same as noon. And last night I heard every whistle from 11:00 p.m. to 1:30 a.m. How I wish I had my 20 mm machine gun again! I'd send a blast of red-hot tracers through him. Sherman was right.

WWII LETTERS TO MY GIRL BACK HOME
From Nigeria, Arabia and Turkey

June 30, 1944

I like to talk with the British weather observers, and discuss things with them. Both are quite intelligent and reasonable, and they often win me to their way of thinking.

Once when we were talking over the post-war future of Europe, I mentioned that some country such as Russia should simply dominate the whole continent, and thereby keep wars from taking place. But LAC (leading aircraftsman—equivalent to US Pfc) Hollands pointed out that England could never allow this because she must have trade in order to live, there not being sufficient land to grow enough food for the people. And, he reasoned, Britain simply cannot afford to risk the domination of any European power.

We talked about Winston Churchill, whom he admires just as much as I do. According to him, that speech of his defying the Germans during the darkest hour of the British Empire, acted as a shot of adrenalin in the veins of the people. I remember the speech, and recall getting excited, too. If I were given my choice of hearing Churchill make that speech, or Lincoln, the Gettysburg address, I'd take Churchill.

It was a treat to hear him. First, the utter crisis of the hour, with people trembling in their boots at what might come. And then his magnificent defiance of the whole German nation, as though he were Horatius of old holding the Tuscans at bay on the Tiber River. His phraseology was wonderful, and every syllable was given just the correct inflection. Perhaps never in history has there been a situation of like significance, nor a man better fitted to meet it. Here's wishing that grand old warrior a long life and a successful one!

D-Day had been a sobering event. There had been a short prayer in our outfit for the men. The Gullivers had a big war map showing both the eastern and western fronts, indicated by long strips of rubber band held in place by pins. Each day, as the war news came in, the English would carefully adjust the rubber strips to indicate exactly the location of the fronts.

Allan Robert Humbert

July 2, 1944

Last night there was a GI movie called "The White Cliffs of Dover." For some reason, the picture appealed greatly to me. It was rather tragic because it showed the terrible price of war in suffering of the people back home, yet it carried a message of triumph and accomplishment.

This morning I awoke about 6:30 and arrived at the station to do a bit of work that must be kept up daily. Then I went down to the spots where the canoes for crossing the lagoon are. As soon as I got near, a score of natives began jabbering for me to take their boat. So I chose one named the "Zorenda." I had no sooner seated myself than a repulsive native girl sat beside me. As she munched her piece of bread, the ugly creature announced that I was going to pay her fare. I told her I was only going to pay my own fare. So she said, "Thank you." At any rate, I paid only for myself—one shilling, making a mental note to avoid that boat hereafter. People do very silly things here. One is to ornament their skin by inserting small pebbles beneath it. The result is an appearance something like that of tooled leather. At least, it looks better than tattooing. Still, I dislike anything but skin, without such applications.

By 8:30 I was in town, where I immediately began looking for a church. I found a very nice one, known as The Cathedral Church of Christ, and arrived just ten minutes before the service began. Unfortunately, the usher seated me very near the front of the church, and I strained my eyes getting cues from men to my right. And they were mostly old, with such slow reactions that there was an appreciable delay. One moment, we would stand up. The next, we would kneel. A minute later, we'd sit down—very confusing.

Yet I found the service very satisfying. First of all, there was an organ, a fine and powerful one. That alone would have been enough for me. I thought of all the other times I'd heard organs—Moon River, with your head on my shoulder, the one at Chanute during the forlorn days of a year ago; the one at the Rivoli Theater in Muncie that very first night I met you; the organ at the port of embarkation where hymns were sung by people suddenly brought face to face with a real need for religion—But the organ I heard in *my imagination was the one that will perhaps play when we get married. That is the one I long to hear.*

These Negroes have a wonderful sense of harmony, and the choir was the equal of many an American one. I almost chuckled at those rows of sober little cue-ball heads, with white eyes and ivory teeth. Of course the kids cut up a bit, like all choir members of any spirit. The girls' and women's section was clad in white, while the men and boys had black choir robes with stiff white collars.

Fifty years ago, some Nigerian natives were still practicing cannibalism. Today, because of Christianity, they have a considerable amount of culture and civilization. I take my hat off to those first courageous missionaries, who, with the British government undertook to convert this place.

The sermon was far better than the average American one. The minister kept it simple. First, he read the story of the ten lepers whom Christ healed, and told how many people are ungrateful. Then, after an example or two, he proceeded to a discussion of ingratitude, pointing out how many people are ungrateful. He cited three causes of it; envy, pride and covetousness, and gave a very clear explanation of each, even using English poetry. Very well done.

I was a little embarrassed at the close, when the collection was taken. Being on the front row, I received the collection plate first, and had only enough time to grab a coin out of my pocket without looking. I intended to give a florin, which is worth two shillings. Instead, I accidentally got a penny, worth only 1 ½ cents. There that big shining penny was, lying bright and conspicuous on the plate. But the worst part of it was when the entire church collection was combined on one plate. I saw the collection that came from the children's section and it was composed entirely of the same shining pennies as the one I so generously gave! Still, the service was very good, and definitely better than any I've seen since leaving the States.

Walking back to the business section of town, I was greeted with cries of "Hi, Sergeant!," "Yankee!," "Yankee-Doo-Doo," "You're ———right!" (I hadn't said a thing.) Espying a fellow with a bike for rent, I agreed to pay him a shilling for half an hour, and proceeded to ride around town, past native quarters, and nice sections under long arches formed by very old trees, beside the lagoon—a very nice ride. After paying for the ride, I walked to the boat landing, and got aboard the "God Bless You" and rode back to camp. Then came chow.

After chow, I organized a swimming party, got transportation and finally arrived at the beach. We swam a couple of hours, came ashore to eat coconuts and bananas costing only a dime for all that six people could eat, and waited for the truck.

On the way back, we amused ourselves counting "culluhd chillen" in their birthday suits, and admiring cute little baby goats no larger than medium-sized pups, and laughing at dozens of little naked babies each supported by a broad cloth belt attached to their mother's waist. The arrangement was somewhat like that of an Indian's papoose carrier, except for the support being made of cloth, and the kid riding at hip level. From a scientific point of view, they have good support, and the baby doesn't object. I saw at least a couple of them comfortably snoozing their little lives away.

Home, chow (shower first) and next a concert on our phonograph, strictly high-brow, and arranged by your proud fiancé.

And that, my lovely, brings us up to now. My. My! All that fun for only 64 cents. But I'm a little tired now ...

July 5, 1944

Many of the GI movies, that is, the ones actually made by the government, are really excellent. They make great use of animation. The one last night showed the tremendous amount of gas required for a single thousand-plane raid over Europe. It showed a car taking off today and running 24 hours a day for year after year as it burned an amount of gas equal to the amount used in that one raid. The years moved past in an endless stream, and the poor old car was faithfully rolling off the miles until the driver had a long, white beard. Seventy-five years later, the venerable jalopy shuddered to a stop, out of gas, stood for a moment and collapsed like the "One Horse Shay." Such animation makes gas consumption figures real.

WWII LETTERS TO MY GIRL BACK HOME
From Nigeria, Arabia and Turkey

July 7, 1944

We had a chance to ask for a transfer to some other African station today. Of course I didn't. By the middle of October, I will be eligible for a furlough, which I hope to spend in Palestine. Hollands left today. It seems strangely quiet without him. Funny thing about the army, when you tell somebody goodbye, you never see them again, though you may. Today was a British "bank holiday." Nobody seemed to know why the holiday exists, not even the British.

The army is making every effort to see that we vote, even to the extent of making us come up and sign for an absentee ballot. What we do with the ballot is another matter, but they intend to see that everyone gets a chance. The army sometimes does all right. Just recently, the Air Transport Command completed an entire year of operation without a single fatality—an outstanding record.

Military services seemed determined to provide their soldiers with as many comforts of home as they could. A British custom that we came to appreciate was tea; as noted in a letter written earlier:

Promptly at 4:00 p.m., Holly and Smithy come in, and a messenger brings tea and sandwiches. Since the RAF furnishes it, they always order a bottle of tea for me, too, and now and then I bring them oranges, etc...They are good kids and I get more satisfaction out of talking to them than anyone else in camp ...

We Americans grew so fond of their custom that we would remind the English when it was time for tea.

The army does an excellent job of caring for soldiers. Nevertheless, no amount of organizational effort by leaders who are highly social, sports minded and aggressive could make up for the intellectual void which characterizes most armies. One can visit museums and find intricately carved scrimshaw or ship models made by sailors, who, had they been home, would have found other creative outlets. In particular, those of us who as civilians had fun making things with our hands were frustrated by this situation. I even went so far as to acquire a portable tool kit with which I could make various small inventions; I would work on them zealously until discussions with men who, before the war, had been in product development convinced me that commercial success was highly unlikely. However, I would reach this conclusion only after months of effort.

Sometimes our quiet post was enlivened by unusual events, as I wrote:

July 17, 1944

Another day, but rather exciting in spots, due to a fight. It happened this way. About a third of the post was restricted for a week due to their failure to sign out when going to town. Those restricted were mostly of the wilder element, so some friction was to be expected due to their confinement.

A couple of guys, one a weatherman and the other a communications fellow, were quite tight and even at 0200 were very high. To amuse themselves, they got a horse belonging to two other soldiers and went galloping through a nearby swamp. This got the horse quite muddy, and was very dangerous, because of holes into which the horse might have fallen and broken a leg. Around that time, I heard laughing outside the window, and sounds of the horse. By and by, the owners of the horse woke up, mad as hornets, and were threatening to do everything to the riders, including killing them. (All were more or less intoxicated.) The communications man tried to keep one of the owners, the camp butcher, from fighting the weatherman, since the idea of taking the horse was originally his and he felt responsible. They fought, and in the process he got several severe blows, according to report, and after they separated, I could hear him in the latrine saying, "Look at my face! Look what they did to me!" Upon returning to bed, he swore to battle the guy in the morning.

The fellow is one of those loud, argumentative individuals who instantly takes sides against any opinion and argues far into the night. His philosophy is quite nihilistic; he doesn't believe in anything and has nothing but contempt for religion. Having lots to do, I avoid contact with him, but evidently plenty of the guys dislike him.

Just as I was returning from chow, I looked outside the barracks, and sure enough, there was the battle. The butcher is built like a bear, and must have landed a square blow, because the practical joker's face was rather a mess. Five times the communications man was knocked down; as soon as he would get up, the butcher would knock him down again. By and by it broke up. I personally had neither interest nor sympathy for either side, but I prefer they squabble where it doesn't bother me.

July 20, 1944

Today came the sensational news of the resignation of Tojo and the entire Japanese cabinet. This seems like bigger news to me than does the second front itself. I got considerable pleasure in hearing that the emperor told the people that seldom in history had Japan faced such a crisis. Things must be pretty bad for the entire cabinet to resign. May they all soon sleep with their honorable ancestors in Hades!

Comments made to my fiancée regarding excerpts from a letter written to me by Mrs. De Motte, a favorite journalism professor:

Compliment on my letter to her…She's glad we're getting something out of the war, at least… "We feel the war is progressing in our favor—that you will be home some of these days." Our engagement…she feels it's best to wait till after the war to marry.

Casualties: Ed Williams, a former member of our Navajo fraternity, one of the twins, who was handsome, intelligent and popular, was killed on "D-Day" in Normandy. Ernest Wallace was killed in Italy. He was practically the best friend of a very good friend of mine. We worked side by side at Ball Brothers factory. I imagine he was a pretty good fighter.

I suppose that I should really feel rather badly about the guys who were killed, but having been out of touch with them so long makes their deaths seem like those of people I don't know. There is a curious finality about death that is much like a dead-end street, and of course it always seems that the people are still living. The waste of war seems particularly impressive when someone useful and educated is killed.

There are many less morbid things I wanted to tell you, about going to the beach, eating bananas (5 cents a dozen)—having steak for supper—how my mother wrote that you looked cute in a green dress and a pretty apron ...

July 21, 1944

The Armed Forces Institute course arrived today. It is on advertising and the material I received consists of a 404-page paperbacked text and a 135-page workbook. These courses should be all right. By taking an examination at the end of the course, it is possible to get a certificate of proficiency which can be used much as high school or college credit. Moreover, the initial two dollar fee pays for as many courses as I choose to study, provided I finish one before starting another. So it seems like a good idea all the way around.

July 22, 1944

This was a good day brightened by various events...Some humor came this way. A couple of the boys were doing their hour of drill, occasioned by the little incident I told you about a few days ago. Nobody takes punishment too seriously here, since it is seldom given and is usually moderate. The boys receiving it looked very GI—pistol belts on, hats, and carrying rifles. Naturally all of us were laughing at them giving them commands as though they were rookies, and in general enjoying their discomfiture. Then somebody said that our doing so might result in our getting the same medicine.

This gave some guy an idea, and he promptly walked over and told me I was wanted in the office by the lieutenant. It seemed strange that I alone should be discriminated against, but nevertheless I buttoned my pockets, put in my shirt tail, marched promptly into the office, saluted smartly in my best GI manner, received an equally snappy salute and a grin from the CO, and reported to him, "Sgt Allan R. Humbert reporting, Sir." He asked what I wanted and I realized it was all a joke. He then asked who the fellow was that sent me, but I didn't remember, having left so quickly. I understand that he would have received five hours drill, so maybe it's good for him that I did not remember. Just an incident, nothing to get excited about.

The rest of the morning I worked on filing, noting that the whole system needs to be reorganized, then to chow at noon, back to the weather station in the afternoon and finally stopped in the communications department.

The communications department has fixed up a neat little radio broadcasting station there, consisting of a mike, a couple of turntables, and a powerful transmitter reaching out the tremendous distance of not quite two miles. Receivers are located in another barracks and in the mess hall; it's really nice having music with chow.

The advertising course (US Armed Forces Institute) that I began recently is very interesting. I'll probably finish it in three months or so. There are 23 assignments, one for each chapter in the book.

July 26, 1944

We are now receiving an Atabrine pill every day, which is four times the dosage given on the ship. The stuff colors one's skin slightly yellow, but is better than having malaria. The few people who are allergic to it take quinine. One tastes as bad as the other, though of course it isn't necessary to taste them at all. Both quinine and Atabrine are known as "suppressants." Virtually everyone contracts some malaria, but the pills eliminate the effects of it, so one doesn't show malarial symptoms. Formerly it was common for people to develop malaria as soon as they left the infested area, due to a stoppage of Atabrine. Now, however, those leaving are given several weeks supply of the pills, and by taking these, prevent malaria. Once they are away from the mosquitoes, the malaria dies out and vanishes.

Those of us who had done some reading on tropical diseases came to realize that mosquito-borne diseases could not only be unpleasant, but deadly. Nor did the army consider the mosquito menace trivial. We slept under mosquito netting; some of us went so far as to put newspapers inside the net lest we get bitten by allowing our arms to get against the net. And in our first contact with bug bombs, we saw natives spraying with DDT several times each day, not only in the barracks, but in the screened double doors through which we entered.

As a further precaution, we were required to wear long-sleeved shirts even though we were in the heat of the tropics, and also thin, leather, knee-high boots. Plotting weather maps in such conditions could be a real problem. One literally perspired so much that sweat would run off the end of our nose and spoil the map, while more sweat poured from our forearms as we leaned on the plotted map. So we learned to work using three pieces of paper, one under each arm, and one on the map to catch the sweat which dripped off our nose. With a little practice, we managed to keep the map dry.

During the dry season, the climate was milder, but it was oppressive during the two rainy seasons. Each afternoon rain would occur with hardly a breath of air stirring, almost as if one were under a bathroom shower. Sometimes we would literally walk back to the barracks without raincoats, just to cool off.

July 27, 1944

Today an incident occurred that would make Hitler happy. Among the natives who work here is a little colored kid named Peter, who works as the officers' mess boy. He is a likeable kid, bright, smiling, alert, and clean as can be. Everyone on the post admires the little African for his courageous spirit and for the degree of independence which he has, despite the fact that he is just twelve years old. At an age when American kids are only in the sixth grade, this small guy is earning his living.

WWII LETTERS TO MY GIRL BACK HOME
From Nigeria, Arabia and Turkey

While the station wagon was waiting in front of the mess hall, he came over and said that Lt Wasson wanted to see him. So I told him to hop in, since there were only two of us at the time. Along came a red-faced corporal who ordered him to get out, in a loud, insulting tone of voice. So as soon as he left, I told the kid to come along anyway, which he did. However, there were too many soldiers so he didn't get to ride all the way after all.

Of course it didn't hurt the Negro to walk a couple of miles. But what infuriated us was that this corporal should so flagrantly demonstrate his inferior ancestry and lack of education by picking on someone too small and weak to strike back.

It is all very well to be arrogant toward superiors, for they can reply in kind. And even toward equals it is hardly unforgiveable. But when a person mistreats those who are helpless and unable to defend themselves, he places himself below the very pigs in the gutter.

In short, this guy's attitude is precisely like that of the Nazi "Master Race," that the mere possession of a white skin entitles one to trample on the rights of those who happen to be colored. So long as people have ideas like this, there will always be more wars, even though we win this one.

July 28, 1944

Regarding Mrs. Gulliver—Women are so scarce as to be practically non-existent, and she does have a tendency to mother the whole camp. She and Gully are as much in love as we are, and I think their affection extends to the whole world. They have a good time in the British Met office where I work. Often in the evening they walk away holding hands like a couple of seventeen-year-olds. Yes, I like them both because they are such fine people and partly because they exemplify our own romance.

July 29, 1944

Joe Gracyzkowski and I were lamenting the fact that we are in Africa rather than the States. We agreed that the worst in America

Allan Robert Humbert

is better than the best in Africa and that Africa surpasses us only in coconuts.

Of course the first item on the list is women, which means you, primarily. But I miss other girls, too, Barbara and Rosemary, and my other sisters. I think that one reason Mrs. Gulliver is so popular even though she is years older than us is that very fact.

And we miss music. Here, again, there is music of a sort, but nothing really fine—no Prudential Hour, Moon River, no Longines Symphonette. Instead, we get a steady stream of "wailing corn," typified by those great ballads, "Mr. "Five-by-Five," "Salt Lake City Blues" and such.

Moreover, we miss having a place of our own, a garden, surroundings which we feel belong to us, and on which we can bestow our work and care. Of course nothing can be done about that.

And we miss people from our own culture (In Nigeria, we were the vastly outnumbered minority, lost in a sea of natives.) *I get tired of seeing wogs*, and one always has the feeling of being foreign and of a "master race." The natives themselves foster this by their humble, subservient manner.*

*According to Webster, "wog," perhaps short for "golliwog" (circa 1929, chiefly British), was a term used for dark-skinned foreigners, especially one from the Middle East or Far East, usually used disparagingly. One meaning of "golliwog" was "grotesque black doll." For us, "wog" simply meant "native," though doubtless with an implication of perceived inferiority.

Still another thing we miss is group activity. People are so made that they enjoy doing some things with a large group of people like themselves. A small detachment having only a few dozen men can never have the feeling of mass morale, of belonging to a great organization, of esprit de corps. Remember our college functions, such as ball games? Then, all the students were united with one idea; bands were playing; there was a team to root for; excitement was keen, alert and active. In times like those Ball State seemed like a very real organization, something to be proud of and enjoy.

To a large extent, a sizeable congregation in church gives a similar feeling of participation and unity; here, church is insignificant, and in native churches one has that left-out feeling. I used to get a thrill out of church youth groups such as Wesley Foundation and our own Youth Forum, in leading discussions, planning meetings, and organizing parties. All that seems infinitely far away now.

We miss peace, too. In peacetime, there are many times when one goes to bed with a serene, placid feeling that perhaps the world is getting better, and that one's own effort is helping. At times such as Christmas and Thanksgiving, there is a certain harmony among people of thankfulness and appreciation.

But the war makes everything different. At the very time that you yourself are reasonably comfortable, there is a constant realization that men just like you who were a bit less fortunate, are being blown up and torn apart every minute of the day. And every now and then crops up the name of some casualty, some person whom you knew, away back when the war was as far away as America is today. Still, life must go on, regardless, and the only thing to do is avoid thinking too much about the war.

Despite our sincere efforts to be tolerant of others, we were reminded more than once that the ways of Africa were not necessarily those of our home town. Once in Egypt, I saw a boy about six years old happily swimming in the Nile River. A few feet away from him floated the rotten carcass of a dead pig.

Or the woman in Cairo holding what appeared to be a fly-covered doll. Suddenly it moved, and I realized that it was her baby.

Then there were the thieves and pickpockets, kids of maybe nine or ten, who would ask if you wanted to buy postcards, holding them up to your face. Only later would the victim realize that the thief's real goal was to steal the pen of the soldier by hooking it from his shirt pocket with the card and running.

At the market in Lagos were merchant stalls where food was sold in bulk, not merely beans and peanuts, but such delicacies as roasted grasshoppers. One day I saw a native woman, naked from the waist up, jogging down the street with breasts the size of loaves of bread, one tucked under each arm to keep them from bouncing. I saw another woman carrying a huge platter on her head. As she overtook

Allan Robert Humbert

me on the street, I saw on the platter the freshly-severed head of a cow. Blood from the head was overflowing the tray and running down her back. She seemed not to mind.

I noticed a smallish, tired-looking man in Lagos preceded by five huge women who were all dressed in brilliant purple and green. I was told that they were his wives. On a bulletin board for native troops, I read that one soldier had been reduced in grade. It seemed that he had wet his pants while standing in a military formation.

On the nearby ferry, as natives returned from work, instead of waiting to get off the boat via the gangplank, they simply jumped off the upper deck of the two-story ferry, landed lightly and dashed toward home, more like agitated insects than people.

Army cooks and bakers were held to high standards of sanitation; nevertheless, a native baker must have gotten a bit careless, because I received a slice of bread that contained a neatly sliced dark object. It was the remains of a large cockroach.

July 30, 1944

This Sunday was rather different because I actually did two of the things one is traditionally supposed to do. First, I went to church, attending a service at 10:30 given by a Jewish chaplain, a captain. He preached on sacrifice, using the willingness of Abraham to sacrifice his only son as a chief example. The second deed was visiting the sick. One of the weathermen is in the hospital for a minor operation, and three of us took an ambulance to visit him. There were only two seats in front, so I rode reclining where the victim is supposed to go. We found our colleague as healthy as ourselves.

There we met a British nurse, a first lieutenant, and had quite a long chat with her. Of course British and Americans never meet but what they begin talking of the great superiority of their own country. This nurse, (Miss Dunn), appeared to be about 30, had a nice complexion, and was rather pretty. She was completely imperturbable. We told her the traditional news story "Now that the Americans have conquered England, they have invaded France." And we told her the presence of the Yanks would raise the standard of love-making in England benefiting the girls immensely. She didn't agree and continued making a rayon negligee as cooly as ever. We left to see the patient shortly thereafter, and Miss Dunn told us to come again. The British are very nice people.

Here are a couple of items: a sailor had a pet chimpanzee here last night, trying to give it away. Later the little critter got loose and escaped into the bush. No doubt it will be happier there. Wogs...the other day we saw one with a stick he wanted to break. Did he break it over his knee? No; instead he put it over his head and pulled down on it with both hands. He certainly knew which was the hardest part of his body.

Allan Robert Humbert

Chapter 14

LAGOS, NIGERIA
AUGUST TO OCTOBER 1944

August 1, 1944

More notes on native customs in West Africa. We are told that human sacrifices I mentioned aren't all over yet—travelers who go into the wrong places still disappear into the bush and don't come back.

One of the fellows here said that in Liberia strange things also go on. He told of standing guard on dismal nights, guarding the runway, which ended right in the jungle itself, and hearing tomtoms of the natives. There is also supposedly a Leopard Society; men who dress in the skin (and head) of a leopard, and carry on savage rituals at certain times of the year. One of the natives from the field mentioned returned from the village in terror. It seems that he had been informed that he was being made a human sacrifice! Of course these natives still carry on wars, and when a warrior kills an enemy, he eats the man's feet so he will be a good runner. Even in Nigeria, various odd customs prevail, and a man can legally marry all the wives he can support. Some wogs can afford 30! We have a fellow in camp who stabbed to death a native in another camp. He showed me the knife. All that happened to him was that he was "busted." It seems the native was a policeman and slugged a companion of his for no good reason.

However, my dear, you must realize that all this happens away from here. (They always keep weathermen in a safe place.) So far, *no trouble of any kind has ever occurred here, because this is the oldest civilized place.*

August 1944

Tonight I'll talk about money. We were paid today, and I therefore sent home $20, in addition to my regular $60 monthly allotment. That makes my total cash at home $505, just over half the $1,000 goal. That amount, incidentally, is $30 ahead of schedule. While working ten hours per day, there is no reason for expense, and saving is just natural.

It is nice to think about that amount of cash, of what it means in terms of purchasing power. A long time ago, whenever I had contact with money, I didn't consider the gold or silver equivalent. Instead, I used the "ice cream cone" equivalent. A dollar and a half represented 30 ice cream cones, etc. Thus I had a very tangible idea of the value of any amount of cash, because it was measured in terms of appetite.

Well suppose I <u>did</u> buy nothing but ice cream with the money. At $1.00 per gallon, I could buy 500 gallons of the stuff—ten fifty-gallon oil drums of it. That amount will buy 10 fine watches; it should also buy five fur coats. It equals my salary over nearly six months time. It would pay your next year's teaching salary for ten weeks, and it would pay Johnson, our Negro typist, for 20 months, longer than I've been in the army. $500 will buy a pretty nice used car; in fact, that's what Dad paid for the new, wrecked 1941 Dodge. That much money is twice what we figured would be needed a few months ago to get married. In normal times, it should go quite a distance on the purchase of a home. It could be used to pay for a couple years' college tuition. It should be plenty for a long trip over the US. In short, $500 is a very nice thing to have. Guess I'll have to get busy and save another $500, just so I can write and tell you all about it. Add to the amount mentioned what you're saving, and also the $300 I am certain to get when discharged and the result is a very comfortable sum. Still, we'll need it, because there are lots of things to be done, and they all take money.

Allan Robert Humbert

Half the pleasure in setting goals is in surpassing them, in staying ahead of schedule. The proper attitude toward goals is not one of stern sacrifice, but rather just of a cheerful game. Goals make time pass faster, give a measure of daily accomplishment, and achievement that otherwise would not likely be made.

...Furloughs: we are apparently eligible for furloughs in Africa after six months foreign service. The date of service begins from the time we left the states, and we are allowed 10 days, plus whatever time is needed to travel to our furlough destination and return to our station. We can go to one of three places: Alexandria, Egypt, Palestine, or Eritrea, which is on the east coast of Africa. I'd prefer to be home with you; still, I might as well see what I can in Africa, because I never intend to come back.

August 6, 1944

This was a quiet, nice day. The sun shone nearly all day, but the weather wasn't hot. I spent the morning working on an advertising assignment, and we went swimming again after dinner. The water seemed quite cold at first, but we soon got used to it. As usual, I took a walk, swam, and bought a penny's worth of bananas.

I enjoy lying on a blanket under the sun and listening to the booming of the surf. The seashore is a wonderful place to think, though it is better when fewer people are around. The soft breezes, the lazy waves and the warm sunshine are all just like a travel advertisement. There is an atmosphere of mañana. Nothing seems very important; one could almost lie down and sleep the war away.

The weeks fairly race by, and it seems I get virtually nothing at all done. A bit of conversation here, a letter written there, and a few other interruptions, and lo! The day is gone.

August 9, 1944

...Once again the camp is restricted, allegedly for window-peeping on the part of someone. Rather droll coincidence, but simultaneously posted with the restriction notice was a letter congratulating our base, the Air Transport Command, for its

excellent work. However, restriction is the most convenient punishment in camp for me, because I seldom go anywhere.

Needless to say, these stupid occurrences hardly add to one's pleasure overseas, and make me wish I were home. Sometimes I get very lonely for a bit of the civilizing influence of Indiana. I don't believe in living in an ivory tower; yet it would be nice again to associate with people of culture and refinement.

After a rather unkind reference to some of the less desirable guys as pigs, I continued ...

Certainly some of these soldiers eat like pigs, sleep even more than pigs, and have standards of value approximately equal to those of pigs. And further, when the least little thing goes wrong, how they squeal! Pardon my undemocratic criticism, sweetheart, but every now and then the realization of the enormous void between their attitude and ours expresses itself in protest.

August 10, 1944

Greetings from your virtually British fiancé. This evening I drank no less than six cups of tea, compliments of the RAF (Royal Air Force). By the way, they never say the letters "R" "A" "F" individually but call the organization "RAF," rhyming with "laugh."

Today I thought about you even more than usual. The incident was my sending home the letters you wrote. There were no less than 125 of them, over three pounds altogether. Being written materials, it was necessary to send them first class and the postage was $1.68. I couldn't help thinking what that little box represented, and it seemed as if I were sending home part of you rather than mere letters. A great many of them I can recall as if they were part of a novel. The one you wrote realizing I had left Seymour Johnson Field, and the one when you knew I must have left the country—even some from Stout Field. The letters you wrote while I was on the voyage—the terribly anxious one you wrote when you thought our ship had been sunk, and the happy, relieved letter you wrote *when you knew I was safe. Yes, darling, those three pounds were more potent than a hundred USO shows, and they contained the very essence of morale building. Nothing could take the place of your letters, except you in person.*

Last night I entered the barracks after writing you, and noticed a small group of people in the corner of the room very quiet and sober, except for one fellow who was sobbing quietly. He had just received word that his father had died. The fellow was Sam Katz, a cheerful, considerate fellow from Brooklyn, one of the really fine people in the camp. We all felt very sorry for him. There was very little conversation about death—we tried to cheer him up by talking among ourselves about various subjects, in order to keep his mind off the telegram. Sometimes the best sympathy for such occasions is just companionship. Death is inevitable and nearly everyone must sooner or later lose their parents, but this is no reassurance to the bereaved.

Yet I believe that death is far less terrible to those who are Christians than to people who believe in nothing, and that single fact should be strong persuasion for church attendance. I never fully realized the enormous influence of the church till being compelled to do without it. Right now, I would cheerfully pay five dollars for one good Indiana service, for church fulfills needs that simply can't be satisfied elsewhere.

August 11, 1944

Natives ... today a native weather observer came to me and said, "Come here. I see something complicated in the sky. It looks like the sun and the moon!" So we went out, and the phenomenon consisted only of the moon in the sky. The poor dope had never noticed that sometimes the moon can be seen in daylight!

It is pitiful to hear these people sing our songs. They never get the words right. For instance, this same guy gave the lyric, "The night was young and you were so beautiful" the following complimentary twist, "The night was young and we were so beautiful." And they have a way of pronouncing numbers that is all their own. One="wan," Four="foah," Five ="fife," Six="seex," Eight ="et" and Zero="Oooooh."

And they use "please" with utter superfluity. A native will answer the phone and say, "Mr. Obogo here, please. Whom do you wish to speak to, please? Yes, please. I'll call him, please."

They glide to and fro like silent, smoky ghosts, and many a time I have thought I was all alone when working, only to look up with a start and see a messenger standing beside me. Stories are told of the Senegalese troops from the Belgian Congo. In France, some of these colored troops were working at the front, side by side with Australia's best. There was an Australian sentry on duty, and he nearly jumped out of his skin when a Senegalese soldier suddenly appeared and spoke to him. But that wasn't the climax. Before the native had even spoken, he had glided silently up behind the Aussie, and identified him as not being an enemy by feeling his shoulder insignia, without the slightest knowledge of the soldier. I'm glad they're on our side.

August 12, 1944

Last night there was a bit of a farewell party for Sgt Art Kammer, a fellow who is being sent to another station because he has had malaria three times. It wasn't so much a party as a farewell conversation. Because this is the army, there was naturally a bottle of Scotch involved. I sometimes like to watch people get a little tight—the way they sometimes become friendlier, happier—the way their statements take in more and more territory till they think things are either wonderful or terrible. I am not in favor of drinking; yet there seems to be very little harm in indulging as they did. So few people can do this, however.

Curiously enough, we had an Englishman there as company. He claimed to have been a pilot during Dunkirk days, to have been shot down on the Norwegian coast and to now have an important position with the British Overseas Airways Corporation. He told many funny stories about the animals he has supposedly caused to get drunk.

Allan Robert Humbert

His father kept a hotel in Scotland, I believe, to which was attached a bar. Below the beer spigots, there was a small tray which inevitably became full from the overflow which was not drunk for sanitary reasons. So his sons would take the stuff and get the animals drunk with it. He told how they would soak bread in liquor, and feed it to the parrot and watch him stagger around in his cage. They even got their dog drunk. But the climax occurred every Sunday morning when they would give beer to their pet donkey, and put him in the yard where people going to church would pass by. The donkey would roll over, stagger, wiggle his ears, hee-haw, and in general perform antics which horrified the strait-laced parishioners.

August 13, 1944

Another Sunday passes, and for once I did very little at all, except listen to our newly-acquired radio, relax and take it easy.

We planned to go swimming in the afternoon, but the truck wasn't in running condition. I did invite Smithy over to eat supper with us. He liked the meal, which consisted of steak, potatoes, green beans and ice cream with pineapple topping. After the meal we attended the RAF theater and visited their billets. Their beds are smaller; they have almost no light, and the building is hotter than ours.

August 14, 1944

Believe it or not, dear, I was quite busy this morning. The occasion of my labor was the monthly inventory which I must always take. I had some work to do this afternoon, but not much.

This as usual was a very routine day, enlivened only by our afternoon tea. Smithy was there, and both Gullivers, and there were lots of wisecracks—I told them that it seemed we hardly needed a weather station here, but Mrs. Gulliver replied that at least we were very pleasant company, and I remarked that they are pleasant company, too, that it was good to see a couple of civilians left. Whereupon, she accused me of saying they were both relics, and called on her husband to take her part. All in fun, of course—I like them both.

They have an enviable set-up. As head of the Met office, he never has a lot of work to do, and for all practical purposes, is his own boss. Theoretically, he is her boss, but since she is his wife, that makes little difference. So they work together, play together, sleep together—a very enviable set-up indeed. And here you and I are wanting nothing so much as just that—but we are separated by thousands of miles of water. Still, it's nice to know that some people still live normally even if we can't, and seeing them reminds me how happy we shall be some day.

August 21, 1944

A few weeks ago, one of the fellows in our barracks was laughing at my habit of putting my billfold under my pillow at night. He said that nobody ever took anything here, that all the natives were honest, etc. I listened carefully, and continued sleeping on my wallet as usual.

That was good policy, because last night between midnight and dawn, someone robbed most of the fellows in our barracks. The fellow who sleeps next to me (named, oddly enough, "Cash,") lost the most—over $120. About all they got from me was a few coins. The thief must have known about the room arrangement, because he woke no one. Moreover, he was quite bold, because he stood in the doorway and searched at least two wallets. Other wallets were found outside the barracks—empty, of course. The police are working on the case, fingerprinting, etc.

So much for the robbery. Now to my nightmare. I began the dream in a small town which might have been Marion. Somehow I had been told that various people had disappeared under mysterious circumstances never to return. For some reason, I felt the urge to go into a part of town only a block away. However, there was no road or alley leading to that part of town, and the only route seemed to be across people's lawns. I was just starting to cut across them when a pleasant fellow said he knew of a shortcut through a tunnel. So I took that route. It was very dark inside and the ceiling was low.

Allan Robert Humbert

About a half block into the tunnel, it ended, and the only exit was a ladder leading into a pit below, so I went down the ladder, came to the bottom, walked a bit more, and came to another ladder which slanted up over a great hole and seemed to lead to the upper level of the tunnel again. The ladder led through a maze of beams that made climbing confusing. It was a bit lighter there, and I was startled to hear a heavy, muffled sound caused by some big animal. Just then, a whole section of the ladder to which I clung, folded, throwing me deep into the hole. Looking below as I clung to the ladder I saw a monster hog, bigger than the biggest bull you ever saw, reaching up to make a meal of me. I managed to scramble out of reach, and finally made my way to daylight. Then it dawned on me that the ingenious and pleasant man had been securing food for his hog by the clever trap I had almost fallen into.

I awoke very glad to find it was all a dream. The question is, where did the dream originate? I should have had difficulty working out such a plot even while awake.

Maybe the dream was due to a subconscious realization that we who are in Africa by the merest chance, have been spared some very terrible things by missing actual combat. Still, the subject hadn't been on my mind before. Or maybe I was just vaguely conscious enough when the native searched my clothes to put the event into a crazy dream.

...Being used to dealing with words, I am a bit too adept at expressing uncomplimentary opinions about those who cross my path. Benjamin Franklin said, "He who makes a jest makes an enemy." So while an apt remark may get results, it does so at a loss to the person making it. For instance, Bob Hale and I were going to a movie, and because he was about a minute behind me, he asked that I reserve a seat for him by putting his hat on it. This is quite customary, and is done by everyone. But a big guy plopped himself down on the seat, even though it was reserved. I reminded him that it was, and received the reply, "I see you ain't been in the army long!" to which I replied, "I see you come from Brooklyn!" He got up, but my remark was a little too strong, and I had to be extra friendly to get him in a good mood again.

WWII LETTERS TO MY GIRL BACK HOME
From Nigeria, Arabia and Turkey

August 21, 1944

Before I so much as finish this page, the date will no longer be the 21st, but will be the 22nd. I feel surprisingly chipper just now, quite prepared to put in the seven hours between now and the time I can start going to bed...Why do I feel chipper? To begin with, I lay down for about 45 minutes, though I could not sleep. Then I got up, washed my face, brushed my teeth, and came to work on the "hoot-owl" shift, as it is called, and I was pleasantly surprised to find a delicious piece of apple pie, plus sandwiches, bananas and oranges. The sandwich was cheese, but such lousy cheese that I threw it away. But the other items were quite good, and I took along an orange to eat a little later.

What to do on the midnight shift? To tell the truth, not very much. I take weather observations, write up an occasional balloon run, keep the weather written up to date, and fix little messages to be sent out on the radio. Which means there is quite a bit of spare time, especially early in the evening. Glancing at the clock, best I correct that statement to read, "early in the morning," because it is now morning of the 22nd, 0007, to be precise.

And just in case I happen to want a bit of variety, I brought my advertising course and a book by Robert Frost, having such poems as "Mending Wall, Stopping by the Woods on a Snowy Evening, Death of a Hired Man," etc. So all there is to do is to keep busy for the next six and one half hours, and Lo! The night will be gone and I can go to bed.

September 2, 1944

The GI show last night was called "Section VIII" after the title given to the statute which lets insane personnel be discharged. It was an all-male burlesque show, although there were several good songs, including "Back Home Again in Indiana." Most of the jokes were pretty raw, but as Mrs. Gulliver said, "The show was well suited to the audience."

There were a couple of fights. One occurred between a weatherman and a mess sergeant. Both of these people have been annoying one another and their associates, and by a strange coincidence they had a fight, but were later separated. Also, two of the fellows got drunk and beat up a native. That barracks had not less than 1 1/2 gallons of whiskey in it last night. So a new regulation was made—no more liquor in the barracks area.

The only other event of note was another robbery, this time in the officers' barracks. (At least the thief is democratic—he steals from them as well as us!) The natives who work for us have all been told that all will be fired unless the culprit is caught.

September 3, 1944

The war news gets better every hour—one report said people of our army are within 14 miles of the German border. They say the Germans realize the war is lost, and are allowing the British and Americans to enter so they can avoid Russian occupation.

September 5, 1944
Somewhere in Nigeria

I hope you aren't startled by my mention of Nigeria. It's perfectly all right to tell people now, because an order from headquarters authorizing it came through today. I'd be interested in knowing where you thought I was. Of course I have been here since May.

Last night I dropped in at Gullys', at Mrs. Gulliver's request to show them some of the things I bought for you; she liked them. As it happened, Smithy and Grant were there, and of course Gullys offered everybody something to drink. I chose ginger ale, which she spiked lightly with some mild wine. British ginger ale is not so good as ours, because it tastes as if there were pepper in it.

American soldiers sending home presents are far luckier than are British subjects. All we have to do is sign a slip stating that the article is a gift, and it enters the US duty free. But they must pay a 40% export tax and 100% import tax, making the final cost of the article 140% greater than the original price.

September 6, 1944

The natives like to bargain. I bought four photographs today, and our conversation went something like this:

"How much for these four?"
"One and six" (30 cents)
"No. One shilling for four."
"No."
"No. One and three" (25 cents)
"No."
"Okay. I don't want them."
"Wait. You pay me one shilling."
"Okay."

September 10, 1944

Another Sunday is gone. I worked this afternoon, and spent a good bit of time talking to AC Raymond Grant, PhD; I didn't know till today that he has a doctor's degree. He is thirty years old. I'd really like you to see his picture. Maybe when I get the film from you, I can take it ...

September 11, 1944

Britain is our standby for news; most of our American music and programs come from recordings supplied by our tiny local radio station. We get the broadcasts of Jack Benny, Gildersleeve, Fibber McGee & Molly, Henry Aldrich, etc. Occasionally we pick up a shortwave wave broadcast from the states; now and then some nice German propaganda, and occasionally a station in the Congo. An odd combination of ultimates presented itself one day as I turned on the radio, "You are listening to Station—from Leopoldville, in the heart of the Belgian Congo. We bring you the Mountaineers singing, "My Old Kentucky Home."

Allan Robert Humbert

September 12, 1944

This post owns a motor boat, fitted with an old 4-cylinder marine engine. Lately the fellows have been fixing the boat up, and one of them, Young, invited me to go boating; I accepted. We donned bathing suits, took along a gallon of water, one life ring, and a bilge pump (which looks like a tire pump but is used to get rid of water in the boat) and set off to go by boat. We were driven out to it by the RAF launch and were soon aboard. It is pretty big, there being room across the middle of it for me to stretch out at full length. There are two sections in which people can sit—the cockpit, seating two, and the bow, seating four. We took along one other fellow.

The first thing we noticed was the sound of the motor. It sounded just like a Model T Ford, and smoked like a V-8. It chugged along, though, and we jokingly told the RAF to come after us if we weren't back by 4:00 p.m. Pretty soon the motor started missing. Presently it stopped. We started it. It stopped again. So we decided to head for shore. But the engine kept stopping oftener and running less until it finally stopped dead. We drifted about a mile before it occurred to me to throw out the anchor! So we hailed a passing canoe and sent one guy ashore to send for the RAF. We managed to start the engine again, but it soon stopped. We whiled away the time for three quarters of an hour just relaxing while the boat rose and fell with the swells. At last the RAF launch came along, tied on, and began pulling us. I was at the wheel, and we were really having fun, breezing along at 25 mph, kicking up a spray, etc. Of course the faster a boat goes, the more strain it puts on the steering apparatus. All at once, the tiller cable broke. So I jumped on the stern and handled the tiller much as the rowers in the ancient galleys used to. Finally we arrived at the pier, where I debarked and dashed for work.

On September 16, 1944, I moved to a different barracks in which there were only two persons to a room. My roommate was Joseph Graczkowski.

September 16, 1944

My good turn for today is done. While moving over here, I began piling my books into a box, while one of our dusky assistants watched. He pointed to a book and said, "That's a good one!" I looked, and saw that it was the Bible. I asked whether he had one and he said, "No." So I told him to take mine, which he did with a broad smile and great gratitude. Originally, the Bible was given to me, but somehow I seldom get around to reading it. Although I am not a missionary, I do believe that anyone who wants a Bible should have one, and he certainly did.

September 23, 1944

I'm sitting in the library listening while our very un-GI first sergeant plays our new piano. He's pretty good. This camp keeps improving all the time—the other day they shipped out one of the dissipated windbags I told you about—now if a couple more would leave, I should be very satisfied.

By September 26, 1944, I had evidently received word of an impending transfer, because I mentioned a new A.P.O. address.

September 27, 1944

Dad has been suggesting for a long time that I should keep some kind of account of my overseas experience. I believe I shall, even going so far as to write a long story about it. Of course to be complete I should have to include material that could be censored, which could mean not writing the story till after the war. If things keep up, I could even write a book! The experiences you and I get writing to each other should make a little item like writing a book very simple. But that can come later. (Author's note 2002 A.D. 58 YEARS LATER?)

Allan Robert Humbert

October 4, 1944

This being Raymond's day off, we made arrangements to go swimming in spite of a very foreboding sky. The weather still looked bad when we got down to the landing, but we climbed into the canoe, one of the smallest ones there, while a wog put my bicycle in beside us. It usually takes about 20 minutes to make the trip, but before we got halfway across, we saw a thunderstorm approaching, with low black clouds and a curtain of driving rain. It hit us just as we were in the middle of the bay. Some natives paddled up in a very large canoe, and asked whether we wanted to climb under the hatch of their boat till the storm was over. We looked inside—the canoe was filled with sand, there was at least four inches of water in the bottom, and the shelter was already occupied by dripping, odoriferous wogs. We preferred the rain, and told the natives to continue toward the other side, meanwhile wisecracking with such statements as "The congregation will now sing 'Let the Lower Lights Be Burning'." It's a wonder we didn't upset. My sole worry was about property—mine and the government's, namely my wallet and the bicycle. All arrived safely, however; we paid the natives double the usual charge, and stood under one of the tin huts you saw in the picture of the native markets.

The shower ended just as quickly as it had begun, so we proceeded to the YMCA where our clothes were thoughtfully dried and pressed by the natives. Instead of swimming, we sat and talked, whiling away the time till 4:30 by eating chocolate and drinking tea. We returned via the ferry, which brings us right up to now.

...Several hours have passed since I wrote the above lines. Bob Hale and I went for a bicycle ride, visiting Raymond. After a long conversation we left. Hale wanted to go to bed, but I wanted to look at the moon through the theodolite. It always seems a bit wonderful when you set the crosshairs of the telescope squarely on the center of the moon and watch it glide steadily out from the field of view, as only a heavenly body can do.

I was glad to be alone on the two-mile ride back to camp, and I would have given anything to have you beside me. Say whatever you wish about the tropics, the nights are the most breathtaking on earth. The water of the lagoon was so still it looked like a silver mirror, reflecting the moonlight. There is always a deep satisfaction in looking at the stars. It gives one a feeling of perspective, of understanding and harmony that lasts for days. I always feel reassured after such experiences, seeing the stars and realizing that you see the same sky, and feel as I do about it, and that one of these days we'll be looking at the same stars together through the nights of spring, summer, fall and winter for many long years to come.

On October 6, 1944, I was still in West Africa, waiting on transport to my next station.

Allan Robert Humbert

Chapter 15

MASIRAH ISLAND, ARABIA
OCTOBER 1944 TO MARCH 1945

Whenever we were assigned to a different station in the 19th Weather Squadron, we went through Cairo headquarters, traveling always by air. For me, the distance would eventually total 25,000 miles. Usually the move would take a week or so, giving us a welcome break.

Cairo, Egypt
October 7, 1944

Another day passes in comfortable ease, with nothing to do but do as I please. I am having a vacation—nothing whatever to do but look at the bulletin board three times a day.

Tonight we had some extremely delicious ham for supper—the very first I've had while in Africa. It's nice being where activities are a bit more organized—there are movies every night, a big PX (serving chocolate ice cream, too), good bus transportation, a newspaper, a radio station, a beach—in short, most all the comforts of home. I keep seeing people I know.

One of the people in our barracks is a corporal who is an authority on camp broadcasting stations. Before the war, he was a drummer. He says there are four most important factors in the morale of any camp. These, in order of importance are: chow, mail, PX and movies. Personally, I would rate mail at the top of the list.

Postage in this area is calculated curiously. It is figured as though we were in Miami, and any place in Africa is "local." The result is that we can send 15 pounds 3,000 miles for 15 cents. Not bad—one cent for 200 miles.

October 16, 1944

It's mid-afternoon, and my vacation has come to an abrupt end, which probably means a few days will elapse before you hear from me again. This has been the equivalent of a 10-day furlough, with no work required whatsoever.

**(Masirah Island, Arabia)
October 18, 1944**

Greetings from the desert island above of your sleepy and plane-weary fiancé. Before long I'll examine a few censorship rules in order to see just what I'm allowed to tell you and what I'm not.

We found that Masirah was an island about 30-40 miles long some 10-15 miles off the east coast of Arabia. Strategically, it was part of the system of air bases for shipping war materials to the China-Burma-India theater.

Climate here makes me very happy—an ideal location for sleeping, loafing, or working. Today it was warm, but already there's a cool evening breeze blowing, about like a lovely fall day at home.
One pleasant result of my visit to the weather station was the discovery of six nice letters from you. I'm writing this in the dayroom.

Our barracks were plain but adequate. We lived in Quonset huts, prefabricated buildings made of galvanized steel, with semicircular roof, wooden floors and screen doors. We slept comfortably on folding metal beds, with mattresses supported by strands of steel wire. Our folded flight jacket served as a pillow. The beds were in two rows, one along each side of the barracks and perpendicular to the wall with a center aisle between the rows.

Allan Robert Humbert

Arabs cheerfully performed all the housekeeping, working for ridiculously low wages. We could get a haircut for ten cents. The workers were trucked in each morning from a native village; most went home in the evening, standing in the rear of army trucks in their flowing white robes, wearing either fezzes or turbans. One could see and hear them in the distance, as they rode toward home, singing. One of them, "Pop," grew to be quite a favorite with the fellows.

Our Rec Room chairs were of ingenious native construction. Instead of a wooden frame, they were built using flimsy reeds to form a vertical cylinder sewed together so the reeds extended entirely around the chair with a cut-out front for the seat. Goatskin leather was used for the seat and strips of leather bound all the reed edges. Result: a sturdy, comfortable chair made of the materials locally available, yet so light in weight that it could be lifted between thumb and forefinger.

October 20, 1944

...Speaking of budgets, I should do pretty well in this place, because even the guys who want to spend money can find nothing to spend it on here. We're using rupees for money now—16 annas=one rupee, and one rupee about 30 cents. I made a rupee yesterday by selling a little whistle.

An interesting coin with which we became acquainted in the Middle East was the Maria Theresa Dollar. It contained about 28 grams of silver and was originally minted in 1789 by Maria Theresa, the Empress of Austria-Hungary. To finance the war effort in Middle Eastern countries, the US made legitimate copies of the coin, dated 1789 even though made in the 1940's.

Since the coins had the same intrinsic value as the originals, they were readily accepted as legal tender.

October 22, 1944

Sunday evening again. There was a brief, but sincere church service in the evening and a relatively large attendance. The

WWII LETTERS TO MY GIRL BACK HOME
From Nigeria, Arabia and Turkey

chaplain, Captain Kermit Jones, has an easy-going, friendly attitude that automatically puts everyone at ease. He's coming back the 3rd Sunday in November.

I worked at the station all morning, but had the afternoon free. In your recent letter you mentioned flies. This little haven is the most thickly populated with flies of any station I've seen. And there's never any fly spray... regarding religion of the Nigerians, many of them are Christians. All three of our house boys were: Christian, Andrew and Johnson. Incidentally, the brown skin of the natives here is a change from the black we had there.

One pleasant bit of news last week was the death of General Rommel. I get the keenest pleasure about the end of people such as he. Thinking about all the destruction he has caused, and the casualties, it seems very fair that he should be killed! Here's hoping that when the German war does end, every possible Nazi leader is executed. And I do not favor restoring Germany to her previous position. They believe in a Master Race; very well, let them live beneath a master race for a hundred years or so, till their pig-headed leaders finally realize their place and keep it...So much for the war.

October 20, 1944

I just returned from an ENSA show, the British equivalent of our USO show, (Entertainers National Service Association). It was very good—an all-girl cast, with entertainment which varied from classical piano numbers to semi-burlesque.

The war news is good today—a big naval victory. I'm not positive, but I believe the commentator said 1/4 to ½ of the Japanese fleet has been knocked out. Also, I read an article in <u>Liberty</u> magazine that this war is the will of the Japanese people, and is being conducted with their consent; once the situation becomes dark enough for them, they will make an armistice rather than wait for a land army to invade. The Japanese, according to the writer, are not subject to the same measures as the German people, and once they know their country is licked, they'll quit. I hope so.

October 27, 1944

Allan Robert Humbert

...The army certainly does vary in the demands it makes on different individuals, and the rewards it gives them. By the way, Warren Blackman is a sniper in the infantry. It's unfortunate that all the sons in one family should have dangerous jobs. The guys who leave Africa, incidentally, don't always return here—many go to the South Pacific.

November 3, 1944

...Not having seen a movie for several nights, I attended "Navy Way," despite grim admonitions. Seldom have I seen a show with more faults, propaganda, clumsiness and drooling sentimentality. However, there were several interesting shots showing the AAF shooting up German and Jap transportation. Frankly, I'm glad to be in the American army, because I have a hunch we're going to win. The enemy should have known better than to have fought with us.

Last night was the first night I'd spent in this barracks. It has several features, mostly bad. The good features: a radio, better insulation against outside heat, company. The bad ones: lights on all hours of the night, people that get drunk and lie in bed babbling to themselves, long walks to chow and work, and lack of any table on which to write. However, I'll get used to the arrangements.

I like having a radio for a change. Music is one form of entertainment that brings back the times when we were together. Next to mail from you, it is the biggest morale factor for me.

November 4, 1944

Do you mind if I tell you my troubles? I have just gotten up feeling sleepier and more miserable than when I went to bed. This weathermen barracks contains only ten people but it's the worst I've stayed in yet, including the ones in basic training.

Friday night the lights were out and the place fairly quiet by some time after midnight, except for a drunk who lay singing himself to sleep. But last night the "party" didn't break up till after

WWII LETTERS TO MY GIRL BACK HOME
From Nigeria, Arabia and Turkey

2:00 a.m., and it was nearly 3:00 o'clock before the last lights were out. At 4:00 a.m. I was just beginning to drop off to sleep when the 4:00 o'clock man was awakened. I finally fell asleep a little later, getting less than three hours rest out of a possible eight.

Believe it or not, I find myself wishing for the discipline of such places as Seymour Johnson Field. True, there were inconveniences, but at least the lights went out and people were quiet at a certain hour every night, whether the men liked it or not. Moreover, no liquor was tolerated in the barracks. Here, nobody cares about anything, drunkenness least of all. The whole camp is filled with the lazy, shiftless don't-care attitude of typical GI's, who believe that the mere fact that they're overseas is justification for all that their officers will let them get away with.

The rights of a soldier are exceedingly few, but even the Germans and the Japanese recognize one, namely the right to get a decent night's sleep.

November 8, 1944

...It's 8:35 a.m. here, even though election day isn't yet over in America. According to the latest reports, our old, familiar friend is leading in 23 states to 15, which probably assures his victory.

As a Republican, I felt that the US was moving toward socialism, but that we were outnumbered in our views. At any rate, perhaps it would have been unwise to change presidents in the middle of a war which was being won.

At about this time a nagging worry vanished. While I was in Nigeria, we were all required to take a test on weather, with implications that we might be demoted if we failed to make certain scores on the exam. However, my score was in the "Very satisfactory" group, and it turned out that demotion was only a scare tactic used to encourage people to study.

Allan Robert Humbert

Armistice Day, 1944

In this letter I am introducing you to a little yellow pill with which you should be acquainted. Some day you will read the story of this famous little product. It is none other than an Atabrine tablet. I had a few extra beyond the month's supply needed here. You should taste it, in order to know why people aren't very fond of it. One other objectionable feature is the yellow color it imparts to the skin of those who take it. After a few months' steady use of the tablets, you become as yellow as a Jap. But when you quit taking it, your color returns to normal. So examine this pill because some day it will be famous.

Chow is over, and I'm eating peanuts again. We had roast beef, tougher than the sole of a barefoot wog. I think the cattle we eat must walk all the way here from Johannesburg. Thus only the toughest old bulls can get through, because the others die en route. Maybe that's why the meat is so formidable. Actually, dear, the food here is usually quite all right.

November 14, 1944

I went swimming at 3:00 p.m. This particular beach is one of the finest I have seen; the waves are the merest ripples; sometimes the water is so clear you can see your own feet through it, and the sand is clean and white, and hard enough to drive on. The sun is mild and pleasant—not at all like the blazing rays that reach Accra and Lagos near the equator.

I swam until tired of it and then set out on a long walk along the beach. The place was almost deserted, and by and by I was out of sight of the trucks and even the fishing boats. Standing there on the shore, I could look out on a perfectly straight horizon of blue water. I could almost recapture the feelings of some long-ago shipwrecked mariner on a desert island like this.

The seashore is one of the finest places of all for dreaming. I thought of you every minute, walking there completely alone, of all the things we'll some day be doing and of the good times we've had together.

The long walk back to the spot where the truck left us, followed by another two-mile hike back to camp left me with a drowsy, relaxed feeling.

November 16, 1944

...just returned from the picture, "Follow the Boys." This was the second time I'd seen it, and I liked it as well as the first. A really fine movie affects me more than the majority of church services, particularly when there is a very real point to it. Whenever you hear that Hollywood is doing a magnificent job for men overseas, you may bet your bottom dollar that they are.

American movies and songs dominate the entire world—no other country seems able to produce so many as the USA. But that is to be expected, because the United States is simply the best country on earth—and the only comparison is the degree to which other countries are worse.

The people here are Arabs, of course, and are no darker than someone with a very heavy sun tan. There aren't any towns, except maybe a native village somewhere, which is off limits to soldiers.

November 19, 1944, Sunday

Life here seems very dull just now, and studies even duller. Last night, as usual, was brawl night, with drunks staggering in and out of the barracks till long after midnight.

Our barracks has lately acquired a contingent of lowly but active bedbugs, and I am forced each night to "fight the good fight." Darling, when we build our house, let's not have bedbugs. Really, I am not at all accustomed to them. The captain in charge of the dispensary believes they were brought in by the RAF. He advised control measures which we'll soon put into effect.

Just to make this discussion of pests complete, I should mention that we caught a mouse in the barracks a few nights ago. And as for flies, I had to kill, by actual count, a total of 76 before beginning this letter. They're pretty scarce now, though.

Allan Robert Humbert

Last week I read a very entertaining book, <u>Animal Reveille</u> by Dempewolf. It told the varied but vital parts played by animals in the war. Written with the sympathetic outlook of an animal lover, the book pictured each creature as an individual with a distinct personality. All sorts of curious facts came to light—the superiority complex of the camel—all kinds of war dogs: messenger, Red Cross, sentinel, attack, wire stringer—how the humble slug has an uncanny sensitivity to poison gas—the homing pigeon that was on a hundred mile race, had his wings clipped by someone, and <u>walked</u> the full hundred miles, of dogs trained by Japanese to pull a little cart with bombs in it into Allied camps, allowing them to blow dog and all to kingdom come—plus dozens of other stories.

Thanksgiving, 1944

Thanksgiving Day is nearly over, and an excellent day it was. I imagine that you've read the menu already—I enjoyed the chocolates and mixed nuts particularly. To supply the feminine touch, twenty girls and women were brought in from India, mostly from upper-class British, but some of native descent. Each of the natives wore a sort of sash over her shoulder. The average age of the people was greater than ours; still, the fellows all considered their visit as a very generous gesture, and everyone had a good time. True, there was the usual subdued and cautious speech due to the presence of women, but we enjoyed ourselves nevertheless. I believe there is some kind of party or dance later—I may go.

This, my lovely, is my third Thanksgiving in the army. The first, you remember, was spent on a troop train, the second at Chanute, and this one in Arabia.

It is appropriate that we should consider not only the holiday atmosphere, but also the reason for celebrating the day. I am thankful that the war is progressing so well, that my fate in it has thus far been a lucky one, that I have the United States to return to, and that some day I will be returning to you.

WWII LETTERS TO MY GIRL BACK HOME
From Nigeria, Arabia and Turkey

Occasionally we could get a three-day pass to Karachi, 600 miles eastward, a welcome change from our desert existence.

December 7, 1944

The first day of my three-day pass is over, and a very nice one it was. There is always a certain thrill in any flight, however routine. The giant planes look as solid and formidable as locomotives, and there is room inside to show a movie. I enjoy looking outside at the motors at night—seeing the red-hot engine parts and the fiery four-foot trail of escaping exhaust. Flying in such a plane gives one a feeling of complete safety and isolation. Just to make the ride more pleasant, I stretched out on one of the seats and imagined that you were along, what a good time you would be having, and how much fun I would be having with you.

Soldiers here have much less comfortable quarters than we do. We're in a tent right now sleeping on cots. The mosquito net covering the cot had ten holes in it last night. Guess how I patched them? Chewing gum. The owner of the net may not be especially happy, but better he should be unhappy than I should have malaria.

This morning we spent sleeping and getting ready to go to town. After a mad scramble virtually resulting in a riot, we got seats on the GI truck jammed like sardines, while a bemedaled captain bewailed the disorganization which made it necessary for him to sit on someone's lap.

Karachi, India, (Now in Pakistan) was a city of tree-lined streets along which were the homes of British officials. We toured the residential part of town in a horse-drawn cab called a gharry, then walked in an area of small shops. While separate from my companion, I stopped at a jewelry store which bore the imposing name, "Cheap John." The proprietor brought out a battered shoe box which contained a handful of diamonds, rubies and other precious stones, some mounted into finished pieces of jewelry, others lying loose, carelessly as if they had been a schoolboy's marbles. I bought Mozelle a pair of sapphire earrings.

Allan Robert Humbert

Strolling on, I came to a less attractive part of town, where a native boy asked if I wanted a shoe shine. I told him I didn't. So he picked up a rock and demanded, *"Now do you want a shoe shine?"* With a few choice, unprintable comments, I convinced him that assaulting me would definitely be counter-productive to his welfare. He dropped the rock and took off running.

To top off the day, we went to a very modern Chinese restaurant, the ABC, for a wonderful meal. I ordered filet mignon, a delectable steak buried under a savory heap of mushrooms, peas and thick gravy. For dessert we had apple pie a la mode.

As the returning plane circled Masirah in the moonlight, a thrill came over me as I thought, "Gee, it's great to be home again!"

December 12, 1944

We returned to find the camp suddenly very GI, with saluting again in effect, etc. Frankly, it's all the same to me; following regulations is simpler and takes less thought. Before, we didn't know whether to salute or not—the unwritten law seems to be "salute only visiting officers above the rank of captain." Anyway, it was an aggravating situation and I'll like the new procedure better.

You probably realize that weathermen are not usually GI. Most of us regard the army with tongue in cheek, and we haven't any fond illusions about making the world safe for any long period of time. The army is merely a game, one that's illogical, expensive, tragic, but sometimes funny. It's not a game to be taken too seriously. So if people want me to conform in these tiny particulars, they'll find me as docile as a little dog being led by a string.

Really, dear, it's downright funny hearing the furor being caused—comments are being made such as "Now if we're going to have discipline, that wog who makes up the beds in the morning will have to knock before entering. And that one who sweeps up will have to knock, too, but even when he <u>does</u> knock, we won't let him in." I'll continue to report all developments of this amusing

situation, meanwhile continuing to be as GI as General Marshall himself.

December 13, 1944

A sort of sullen lethargy has settled over the camp—showing a definite decline in morale. It's too bad that had to happen.

December 16, 1944

...After working the midnight shift, I was rudely awakened by a thunderous explosion. It turned out to be merely routine blasting, so I got up, shaved, and took a bath.

This is Saturday. How do I know? Simple—today I changed razor blades. One blade lasts about a week, so long ago I began using a brand new blade each Saturday. But for that one tiny act, I might never know the correct day.

You should see the ultra-convenient writing arrangement I have. My bed rests with the head against the wall. Next to it is that of Cpl Andy Knapton, our popular and practically Americanized RAF observer. Between the beds, against the wall, is his foot locker, a box about two feet square. It is so placed that I can recline comfortably on my stomach, using his locker for a desk.

A few minutes ago, we were again shaken by a terrific explosion that blew stuff off my shelf and frightened our little dog. We considered running up a white undershirt on a pole as a surrender gag, but thought better of it, realizing that some wog would probably steal it.

December 30, 1944

...Believe it or not, sweetheart, I can hardly remember what civilian life is like. Everything is planned for us here—such items as food, recreation, and clothing never need be considered, and we live without thinking.

They say that discharged veterans feel lost at first, and a bit frightened at the prospect of being forced to live on their own. In

Allan Robert Humbert

the army, everyone is your brother. You may not have the remotest thing in common; yet the uniform does bind you together, whether you like it or not.

Some ex-soldiers try to live on their laurels, feeling that their service automatically entitles them to extra-special consideration. Before I left Muncie, I was stopped by a veteran of the first world war who moaned about how little the government was doing for him. Yet he seemed quite capable of helping himself, and probably never amounted to anything before the war. All that the world owes any ex-soldier is a chance to get back on his own feet, unless, of course, he has some disability incurred in the service.

Getting back to the subject of demobilization, I rather expect to feel lost also, at first. I imagine that, close as we are, you and I will still have plenty of getting acquainted to do. We may feel a lack of things to talk about which will last quite a while. Frankly, I don't feel like a veteran at all—I could drive straight to your house without hesitating. And believe it or not, I can remember easily every street on the way to your house. All of which means, that, essentially, we still are what we were and are unlikely to change during the coming year or so we're apart.

On this pleasant December afternoon, as I lie reposed on my bunk while warm sunshine flows in the back door on my stocking feet, I feel inclined to be a bit philosophical. Surely I must have gotten something out of the army during the past two years—but what?

Maybe "experience" would be the biggest item. Nothing surprises me any more—well, nothing <u>much</u>...I have talked to people whose IQs ranged from 160 to far lower—to hillbillies from Appalachia, lawyers from Brooklyn, natives all the way across Africa—liars, preachers, generals, privates, roues, religious fanatics—and the list could go on and on.

Perhaps "poise" is another item. (Maybe I should have used the word "detachment" here.) *I can feel at ease wherever I am. There is a large part of me which sits by and makes fun of what the rest of me is doing. Many things which once seemed personal now seem impersonal; I can accept minor disappointments often without letting associates know I am disappointed. Then there's insight.*

WWII LETTERS TO MY GIRL BACK HOME
From Nigeria, Arabia and Turkey

Come to think of it, maybe time in the army isn't as wasted as we sometimes think.

January 4, 1945

Last night a movie played here that I saw three months ago at Lagos. Evidently films are shown there first, and shown here later...
Sophie Tucker certainly does a fine job, capitalizing on her age, weight and reputation. She seems to have taken upon herself the task of improving romance among this generation of sweethearts. Of course she says little that people don't already know, but she simply makes a point of the art. A very practical old girl.

January 5, 1945

...Chow is over, and the less said about it, the better. Sometimes I marvel that army cooks can go on producing the same inedible grub for months on end with monotonous regularity. The food they are given to cook is quite decent, but these ingenious individuals can do strange and ghastly things to the finest stock, rendering it unfit to eat. The present mess sergeant likes onions—but <u>likes</u> is such a tame word. I might better say he loves them, delights in, and worships them. We are given beets—certainly a thoroughly respectable dish, but nothing satisfies him but that he must add sliced onions. We are given hamburger, another nice dish, but once again that onion-loving sergeant impregnates the meat with onions. We are served "C" rations; these could be good, except—onions again.
If only I were permitted to teach him a lesson! All I would need would be a cell, a jug of water, and a 100 pound sack of onions. I would simply lock him up with nothing to eat but onions until he groveled on the floor, swearing never to eat, touch, or serve another one. Happy dreams ...

Allan Robert Humbert

January 6, 1945

Having been out of bed less than half an hour, I have already started the day off wrong by slicing a large area from my lower lip while shaving. As you can imagine, it bled quite a bit, so I finally went to the dispensary in disgust, where they gave me a gauze pad to hold over it. In a few minutes the bleeding had stopped—now all I have to do is avoid disturbing the cut. That means keeping my mouth shut (a very difficult task), so I'm writing you. There is another reason, too, however—I work at 3:00 and a brief quiz is being held at 1:00 concerning the weather observers' examination.

...Cold weather you mentioned—that is the least of my worries—I don't believe the temperature has fallen below 60 since I arrived here. Are you jealous?

I heartily agree with you that the things purchased for our house should be of high quality. In the long run, the cheapest stuff wears out sooner, gives poor service and creates a bad impression.

Somewhere in the Humbert family is a pack-rat trait of trying to save everything and to economize through using junk. My grandpa was the worst offender. He wouldn't throw away anything—not even a rusty nail. I believe I told you that he raised apples, and always ate the bad ones first, so that by the time the first bad ones were eaten, the others had become rotten, meaning he never had any apples to eat except rotten ones. Life is worth too much to fritter it away nursing broken-down pieces of junk.

The observers' examination came in. Having seen so many GI examinations, I am inclined to be a little cynical about this one. Officers are a bit too trustful—no one likes to feel that his own men would cheat, which makes conniving easier still. If such material is locked up, its safety is usually trusted to a two-bit lock that can be opened with a hairpin.

There are ways and ways—I've heard stories how people prepared an envelope exactly like the new exam's, copied the new one and resealed it in the old envelope, destroying the old exam— and no one was ever the wiser.

Mail came today—a letter from you and a package from home. It contained candy, nuts, cards and underwear and was very welcome.

You can certainly get ready for school in a hurry—I always need to shave so I can't very well match your record. Your facilities are probably a good deal better than ours. By the way, I've heard rumors we are to get hot water soon. If we do, I shall enjoy my first hot-water shower in ten months...(Nothing speeds up bathing on a chilly morning like a shower in cold salt water.)

January 7, 1945

Insurance is the chief topic tonight. As you know, I am now paying $6.60 per month, which gives my folks $10,000 life insurance in case I am liquidated. But when the war is over, that insurance ends and I lose all that I've paid in.

A government insurance agent had met with us and explained to me that by making a lump sum payment of $418.88 and paying $20.10 per month back to the date of enlistment; and for 20 years thereafter that I could keep the $10,000 insurance for life. It seemed like a good deal so I accepted.

January 10, 1945

Today arrived two more letters from you, written on that cute blue stationery. I have come to the conclusion that something has happened to mail which left the states on the 27th of December. Most everyone I know has three or four letters missing. And those from the east are missing letters later than I. If this is true, we may never get them.

So maybe you should repeat whatever news of interest occurred on the 24th, 25th, and 26th of December. Ordinarily, I wouldn't mention missing mail, but I am particularly interested in how you spent Christmas Eve, what you thought, what happened, and how you liked the presents.

Allan Robert Humbert

Ration points are all Greek to us here, and I didn't know any ration trouble existed till you told me. Before I went overseas we usually had plenty of all kinds, because the kids ate less than the adults but still received the same number of ration points. Most civilian difficulties are pretty well glossed over for us. Bad news is presented, of course, but is played down somewhat.

Tonight the chow was delicious—steak, mashed potatoes, gravy, lemonade, hot biscuits, coffee and a fruit cocktail. Now in a few minutes I'll go to the movie, "Gildersleeve's Ghost," mail this letter and go to bed for the few hours sleep remaining before 4:00 a.m. And at that time begins a new day, or rather a work day.

January 15, 1945

Tonight, instead of a movie, we were entertained by an ENSA show. There was a variety of simple acts which went over well. Some of the audience criticized the actors and actresses, but I thought they were good. In both ENSA shows I've seen, the people seemed to be putting forth every ounce of effort. Such spirit makes any performance enjoyable and causes me to overlook any minor shortcomings.

Howard Swan and I sat on the very first row, getting plenty of opportunity to size up the characters. There were various combinations of single and double acts. First came a strictly leg number by a couple of nice-looking blondes, followed by some concertina and violin music, plus assorted roles of different description. The old man who played the piano was good, banging away like an old-time pianist in some western saloon in the gay nineties. A funny little Scotchman had a cute act, too, playing the part of a Scotchman celebrating his 94th birthday. So I repeat, I liked the show.

January 20, 1945

If I've learned anything during the 24 years I've been around, it is this: People are the same, not only the world over, but over all stretches of time. If Plato were alive today, he might make very good company. And if old Ben Franklin were with us, you might feel surprised and a little shocked to discover just how up-to-date he was. Ben, you know, was quite a wolf in his day. He wrote, said, and did things which just weren't, and for that matter, aren't done.

As soon as I noticed that the book of quotations you sent me was originally edited in 1891, I became curious to see what people had to say about sex. Only <u>four</u> quotations in 734 pages! <u>This</u> can't be, thought I, people are people, and there have to be more than that. So I looked under "love," and there, spread out on eight pages, I discovered 182 quotations. People are still people.

Paraphrased from my letter of January 21, 1945:

1. *Went to beach—blue water, balmy breezes, smooth white sand.*
2. *Returning, walked to within a few hundred feet of camp, picked up by British Wing Commander Young. Very nice of him. I believe he ranks equally with an American lieutenant colonel. He's rather famous—shot down 4 planes, etc.*
3. *I'd like to be home, if times were normal; still, life is easier here than in the USA. I'm glad I'm in weather. A signal corps fellow at chow told me of a friend who went back to the states for rotation. Since there were plenty of men doing his type work, he was listed as surplus, reduced in grade from master sergeant to corporal, and placed in the infantry. Fortunately, there is no surplus of weathermen. Such deals as that, however, make me quite satisfied to stay here till the war is over and I can go home to stay.*

January 25, 1944

Some mail drifted in this afternoon, most of it rather old. I received two letters from you, one from Dad and one from Lee.

This place is pretty hot today—about 80 degrees, and there isn't a breath of air, so I am sitting beside the screen door wishing it would cool off. This will soon happen, though because the sun will be down in a couple of hours.

Allan Robert Humbert

Lee wrote about getting set up in the Philippines, and enclosed Japanese invasion money which you will find in this letter and may keep. The largest one has a value of a nickel in Japanese occupied territory. Just to make life complicated in one more way for the Japanese, the US has been dropping large quantities of counterfeit Jap invasion money behind their lines.

If plans go all right, I am to receive a furlough to Palestine in March. That will be fun, and educational to boot. Before long, I'll need to read up on the place, so I know what there is to see.

Now it's cool again. The desert is nice—when the sun goes down, it gets cool very quickly.

January 26, 1945

For once, the end of the day finds me tired—I feel that I've earned my $3.10 pay. Tomorrow, though, is my day off, since I don't go to work till 9:00 p.m.

Furlough plans continue to percolate nicely. Today the letter requesting it was written. So in a few weeks, I'll be off to Palestine for ten days leave.

February 2, 1945

Do you remember my mentioning Sgt Punch who slept in the same tent with us at Cairo? He's stationed here now. He's an easygoing, solid, dependable fellow, as reliable and conscientious on the job as if he owned the business. I'm glad he's here.

The turnover in our outfits is amazing. People are forever moving about, and I no sooner get to know one group before it is broken up and separated. However, the process results in knowing more guys, and makes it more likely that we'll meet people we've known at the next station.

For reasons unknown to me, virtually every person I've met in weather has been a distinct personality, a character difficult to forget. True, close contact with anyone makes the person distinct in your mind; still, I believe weathermen invariably have more fully developed personalities. Very few groups are so clannish.

WWII LETTERS TO MY GIRL BACK HOME
From Nigeria, Arabia and Turkey

The Russians are 45 miles from Berlin, or closer. Translate that into distances in Indiana, and the result is surprising; it's as though you were in Marion and the enemy were in LaFayette. It would be great now to be back with our old crowd in Nigeria.—Mrs. Gully, Hollands, and Smithy. They would be dancing with glee, betting on when Berlin would fall, etc.

Last night I heard a motor running, which sounded exactly like an old tractor. Suddenly I remembered being in grade school again, in the spring. At that time of year, the distinct roar of tractors could be heard nearly every day as the neighboring farmers were ploughing. School was an absolute waste of time during those days, because we never paid attention to dull classroom subjects when more alluring sounds competed for our attention ...

War, in those days, was something we never dreamed of ...

Paraphrased from a letter of February 4, 1945:

I constructed a bedside cabinet for storage of personal items. It consisted of an orange-crate, fitted with a door having a shelf on the inside. Inside the cabinet is a shelf for a toilet kit and candy. On top the cabinet is room for handkerchiefs and stationery. Hanging on the outside of the cabinet next to the wall are a canteen, knife and flashlight. I also made two bookends for the top of the cabinet by splitting a tomato can vertically.

February 5, 1945

My chief activity this afternoon was talking over old times with Sgt Punch. I found out several interesting bits of information. "Red" Evans, due to an unfortunate incident, was "busted." That seems odd, because he did good work when I knew him. I hope he takes the reduction in grade more gracefully than I could. Demotion is a very bitter pill to swallow. Red has had more bad breaks than he deserved. From the very first, he worked as hard as I did, missing forecasting school acceptance by almost as narrow a margin as the one by which I washed out.

Allan Robert Humbert

Such events can virtually be considered as casualties because they would never have happened but for the length of the war and the feeling of gloom that long lack of progress causes. Still, what will be the difference a hundred years from now?

Even though you know I am at Masirah Island, Arabia, remember to address your letters as before, without writing "Masirah" on the outside of the envelope. Incidentally, spellings of this place vary. I've seen it written also as Moserah and Mosera.

February 6, 1945

Greetings from your faithful but sleepy fiancé, who remains up only because there is interesting conversation. After rising at 4:00 a.m., I worked at the same old place doing the same old things in the same old way. Getting up at 4:00 a.m. is a grim business. You go to work without washing, shaving, or brushing your teeth and feel as frowsy as a drunken sot stumbling into a flophouse. However, by 10:00, all the work is over and the remainder of the day is free to be spent at leisure.

This morning the wogs cleaned the barracks, moving all the beds outside and making the place temporarily uninhabitable. By evening it was normal once more. Feeling so sleepy, I decided to read, reading <u>Science and War,</u> Bob Hope's <u>I Never Left Home,</u> and Lin Yutang's <u>Moment in Peking</u>.

The philosophy of Chinese Taoists may be comforting, but it is a bit too passive for me. The Chinese could hardly be expected to get anywhere with such ideas. Still, their passive attitude would make easier the life which many must live.

February 7, 1945

Every time this post has the misfortune to acquire a new commanding officer, the result is a series of uncalled-for and bewildering changes. The latest move happens to affect me personally, and it messes up my plans to a considerable degree.

The Enlisted Men's Club, which was built and partly paid for by the men of the post, is to be stripped of its furnishings and converted into a barracks, leaving the whole post bereft of one quiet place to read, study, think, or write. I am uncertain where religious services are to be held, quite possibly in the latrine. It is my expectation and sincere hope that Chaplain Jones will make the biggest possible issue of this matter.

Frankly, I feel hopeless about the situation. It's the same old "Bread and Circuses" philosophy—entertain the masses, and let minorities take care of themselves—the same philosophy that has ruined so much already. Still, there is no use passing my anger on to you.

Last night between 7:30 and 11:00 p.m., a Jewish student from Palestine was attending a concert given in the Rec Hall, and later talking to a couple of us in the barracks. Formerly, he lived in Austria, but escaped in time.

The fellow is named Deutsch and is now in the RAF. Before enlisting, he was studying social science. Evidently he is quite intelligent—his quick thinking and remarkable command of English both suggest it.

He outlined the places I should visit in Palestine, and told me a little about what to expect there in the way of expenses, weather, etc. Since the places are just names to me, you probably wouldn't be interested in them, either. Later, of course, I'll tell you everything possible, and I'll keep notes for future reference about such matters as may be censored.

February 12, 1945

It's now 3:30 in the middle of a long, drowsy, desert-island afternoon. Of the seven guys now in the barracks, five are asleep, and one is up only because has to go to work soon. I myself am active to the extent of writing you, but I nevertheless feel the desire to relax and let life go by, as though it were a lazy, slow-moving river ...

Allan Robert Humbert

February 18, 1945

The chapel situation is going to be taken care of. In a few days, there is to be another barracks erected, which will serve as a temporary chapel and reading room until the arrival of a large prefabricated building, which is to be the permanent one. The chaplain is on the post now, and there is church this evening. Services are to be held in an unused transient barracks, the first ones in several weeks.

February 21, 1945

I turned in some clothing for salvage. Due to salvage, I am now the proud possessor of four pairs of socks <u>without</u> holes, and a suit of underwear. You should have seen that undershirt! I bought it in Tallahassee, and it contained more holes than a fish net. True, the one I received in exchange was too big, but my two years in the army have taught me not to expect all clothing items to be the correct size.
In your letter, you mention Karachi. Quite a bit of it is off limits; the white people are mostly British, who live in fine, modern houses. The main section of town, where we were, has paved streets, streetcars and street lights.

February 25, 1945

Last night Andy and I walked down to the beach to see the phosphorescence in the water. The moonlight was so bright that the sea could be seen quite clearly, even had there been no phosphorescence. However, we experimented by dipping up handfuls of water, meanwhile looking at it using our flight jackets to keep out the moonlight. Sure enough, in every handful would be luminous little globules, shining brightly. In a few days we'll go down when the moon isn't shining; then the effect should be very bright.
As usual with typhoid shots, I have a slight fever—you know the symptoms—the room seems too warm all the time, but only to you.

If a person didn't expect that reaction, he'd probably disregard the slight effects altogether.

...We just returned from a good ENSA show, another sincere and enthusiastic performance making up in pep whatever it may have lacked in talent.

Today being Sunday, I deliberately did very little. The result was that I began thinking of you and missing you more than I have yet, taking out all your pictures, remembering the conditions under which each was taken, and wishing I were back with you again.

February 26, 1945

The pendulum of military discipline swings to and fro, and the field is now beginning another cycle of being GI. So far, the changes have been minor and reasonable, being for the most part rules which should be followed regardless of enforcement. Many things are proposed, but the practical thing to do is wait and see just what develops, rather than anticipate in detail that which may never happen.

You may or may not know that a great many trivial details of post arrangement are left up to the commanding officer of the post. Whenever a new CO arrives, he institutes changes, quite without regard to the ideas of the previous officer.

Lately we have witnessed the amusing little variations dictated by the whims of three successive CO's. The first, famed for anything but sobriety, liked to have a post free of natural hazards to those slightly intoxicated. Because of his work, it was possible to walk with one's eyes closed, and never bump into a single object. I appreciated this, since it became easier to go by bee-line routes when working after dark.

The next fellow, a personable young captain with background in weather, had a passion for making big Army Air Forces stars on the ground, using the rocks we have here. However, he placed them without regard to common routes of travel, and soldiers frequently stumbled over them.

Now we have still another CO who has returned to the policy of the original captain, and therefore removed some of the ornamental stonepiles. That's the way it goes. Still, the inconvenience had been slight and several useful innovations have arrived, including a fast and efficient chow line.

March 3, 1945

It's a good thing furloughs don't begin till we reach Cairo, or mine would be over before I ever saw Palestine. In short, I'm still stuck here on this island.

By this time, my furlough to Palestine had been granted; actually getting there was another matter. Naturally, war-related transportation was more important than the recreational travel of soldiers. Sometimes more time would be spent waiting on planes than on the furlough itself. Because we had to be ready to depart at a moment's notice, our regular work routine was out of the question.

You would think there would be nothing to do under this set-up, since I'm off shift. Actually, I spend more time running back and forth between the station and the barracks than I would spend working. The billeting hillbillies whose duty it is to call passengers can't be trusted to call us in time.

Receiving a furlough should be good for my morale. All my life until I entered the army was spent in an environment of perpetual advancement, from the day I entered first grade in primary school, until the day I made sergeant. True, there were exams, disappointments and setbacks but life was a going, advancing concern. Each year saw us further ahead than the preceding one. But now, the only values to be gained are formless, intangible ones. A great effort yields a small return.

Still, to return to a philosophical point of view, it isn't hard to see why we feel this way. By all the laws of nature, you and I should be married and living together this very minute, engaged in raising a family instead of living so far apart. So the only thing to do is get this__*__&__war finished. Then we can get married and live normally.

WWII LETTERS TO MY GIRL BACK HOME
From Nigeria, Arabia and Turkey

March 4, 1945

Sunday rolls around again, and I'll bet you can't guess where I am—that's right: Masirah Island, Arabia. At present I am held here by a combination of flat airplane tires and sandstorms. So passes this day.

Welcome supplies arrived at the PX today: cigars, chocolate bars, Baby Ruths and a wealth of other items. So far today, I have that "stuffed" feeling, due to eating breakfast and dinner plus a large Hershey bar and a box of pretzels. Soon, for no earthly reason, I'll eat supper. In this climate which requires few calories, I get along fine on two meals per day, so long as the stuff is fit to eat.

A letter posted on the bulletin board announces that this CAFD (Central African Flight Division) receives the best mail service of any army post office in the world, that all first class mail goes by air, and that it is never delayed over 24 hours but for weather. Other outfits receive much mail by boat. Good mail service is just about the most important morale item to us.

Allan Robert Humbert

Chapter 16

PALESTINE FURLOUGH

To reach our Palestine destination, we first flew northwest to Khartoum, then north to Cairo before boarding the plane to what is now Israel. Travel took nearly a week because our transportation priority was low.

Anglo-Egyptian Sudan
March 5, 1945

Censorship: now what can I discuss or write about without sending you a letter which will arrive full of holes where the censor has cut out words?
I'm writing you while sitting in a particularly nice spot in the large, airy library of the post Rec Hall. A quiet-running electric fan wafts rather warm breezes near me, and in the distance a radio is playing, "Amour." In short, this place is a perfect one in which to work and write.
Various features of this post are desirable. One is the presence of a patch of fragrant green grass surrounded by a few shade trees. Do you know what my first reaction to that grass was? Now is this grass really necessary? At first, a desert seems desolate and bare, but once you get used to it, trees and grass seem like unnecessary luxuries.
I enjoyed a fresh-water shower this morning, too, not to mention a coke and a fresh-vegetable salad. It just goes to prove, honey, that there isn't much of anything we can't appreciate if it's been denied awhile.

WWII LETTERS TO MY GIRL BACK HOME
From Nigeria, Arabia and Turkey

March 6, 1945

Now that I am away from the island and am no longer subject to censorship from our weather officers, I shall take advantage of the opportunity to write candidly about them and the station.

In general, the only topics which I avoid in my letters to you are the personnel and management of the weather station. True, I feel a little awkward having every affectionate thing said about you read by people I know, but in the army it can't be helped. Our officers, First Lieutenants Haider and Vaughn, and 2nd Lt Youngman are very tactful about their work, never mentioning censorship.

I get along fine with everyone at the station, particularly the officers. Most of the guys are extroverted and not quite my type. The only fellow I pal around with much is Cpl Howard Swan, who has a high IQ, a thorough background in science, and a somewhat pessimistic outlook.

All three officers seem downright eager to comply with my wishes. Haider and Youngman are easily the best men in the station, introverted but tremendously conscientious. These traits are responsible for their lack of popularity among the men. Most of the guys resent the fact that the officers aren't back-slappers, but I admire them for it.

You have probably guessed that my letters are often written as much to educate the censors as to inform you. Usually, when I complain about the camp, it's pure propaganda, although honest, mostly intended to influence them.

Sometimes I feel it would be better to complain less in letters to you, but I think it preeminently important that our letters be sincere and earnest. Otherwise, we'd hardly know what to believe. Besides, moods when writing vary, and we aren't always thinking along gloomy lines.

Rather hot here these days—max temperature yesterday: 105 degrees.

Allan Robert Humbert

Egypt
March 8, 1945

 This has been a very busy day. We were awakened at 4:30 a.m., and by noon were thinking about eating dinner in this place. On the way I read State Fair, *an entertaining, if ordinary, novel. The countryside looked the same as ever—forlorn and miserable.*
 I've been meeting fellows from all over; believe it or not, dear, Africa seems a great deal like home, and I find a faint feeling of nostalgia at being away from my familiar surroundings.
 To a transient, the field appears rather GI. We no sooner got out of the plane than an MP told us we must wear ties. Then our identification, orders and shot records were checked, and we were given two hours to have our money converted to Egyptian currency. Next came a visit to the orderly room. En route, I was bawled out for walking on the "grass"—there was literally not one blade of it on that dust-covered surface! But I soon recovered a good mood and went to the orderly room. We were assigned a barracks, given a list of winter clothing to draw out and went to Supply for that purpose. By the time we got back to our barracks, the afternoon was over. So I got a shine and shave, returned here, ate, and spent the remainder of the time talking over old times. As soon as I finish this letter, I'll sew insignia on my uniform and go to bed, since we must get up early.

Tel-Aviv, Palestine
March 9, 1945

 It's 6:45 p.m., the grass is green, the sky is blue; Tel-Aviv is a wonderful city and I'm as happy as a kitten in a dairy. All afternoon, fellow tourist Calvin Copper and I have wandered around town soaking up the civilized atmosphere, and taking more delight in meeting people than Ebeneezer Scrooge did on Christmas when the Three Spirits finished visiting him.
 The shops are splendid. Prices are quite high but there is a wide variety of articles available—cameras, binoculars, electrical appliances, silks, jewelry, pictures—nearly every small article you

could find in Indianapolis. The clerks are cultured and courteous, making no effort at all to force you into buying anything.

Most of the people look just as we do, and it is particularly delightful to see them. Children are appreciated just as much here as they are at home. I saw dozens of immaculate little kids, well clothed, well fed, the very picture of health and happiness.

There are the usual elements of civilization, automobiles, taxis, buses, theaters, modernistic architecture, etc. Copper and I walked along the street which parallels the Mediterranean. It is a smooth, modern boulevard about 15 feet above the water, separated from it by a broad sidewalk. We didn't travel much, but our impression was that the streets are rather confused, not being laid out symetrically.

We are staying in tents at the rest camp located about seven or eight miles from Tel-Aviv. Conditions are quite nice—the place isn't GI; everybody is friendly; the Army and Red Cross have splendidly organized services; food is as good as or better than Khartoum's in the Sudan where we stayed en route to Cairo; in short, this spot is as ideal as can be, and I am honestly enthusiastic about it.

Tomorrow evening we are to be guests of Mr. and Mrs. Greenburg at a party. That should be fun. On Sunday occurs a tour (There are at least a half dozen of these available) and many other things remain to be done.

A few minutes ago, we heard an excellent lecture accompanied by Kodacolor pictures shown on a screen. Virtually every spot of historical significance in Palestine was discussed.

Tel Aviv, Palestine
March 10, 1945

Not being able to get on any scheduled tours at this time, we slept quite late. However, at 4:00 p.m., a few minutes from now, we meet at the Red Cross for a party at the home of Mr. and Mrs. Greenburg. He is the General Electric Company's representative in Tel-Aviv. It should be very interesting.

Allan Robert Humbert

Tel-Aviv
March 11, 1945

The only way we could have done any more in the past 24 hours would have been by being ourselves and a couple other people at the same time.

First, the party at the home of Mr. and Mrs. Greenburg. It was held from 4:30 to 7:30 last night. Ordinarily, an equal number of fellows and girls are invited, but last night several fellows failed to show up, causing a shortage. The fellows are, of course, all soldiers, and the girls, local people. They were very nice, well-educated, English-speaking and typical sorority kids. For entertainment, we sat around and talked awhile, then ate doughnuts and drank coffee, rolled up the rugs and danced to phonograph records. Such delectables as chocolate cake, nuts, oranges, bananas, etc. were available at all times.

Frankly, dear, I hardly knew how to act, and the party was almost over before I felt at ease. Such social niceties as dancing and small talk are easy to forget on a desert island. However, I had a wonderful time, soaking up the warm happiness of the occasion with as much appreciation as I had soaked up the warmth of my first hot water shower after leaving the ship. I left the party, one big lump of gratitude, loving them, and Palestine, and best of all, you, more than ever before.

Since Greenburg's son is stationed with me at Masirah, I had an "in" from the very first. I told them all I knew, playing the guy up considerably. They are so eager to hear news of him that the tiniest bit of information was accepted with open ears. They have already promised to send me away laden with salami, chocolate, and an electric hot plate for the barracks.

As for the tour, we left Camp Tele-winsky at 8:15 a.m., arriving in Jerusalem to the southeast after 9:30. Jerusalem, you know, is built on hills something like those of southern Indiana. We were on the Old Testament tour, and by noon had seen and walked on the site of Solomon's Temple, the Wailing Wall, the Mosque of the Rock, located on the very rock on which Abraham nearly offered Isaac as a sacrifice, Solomon's stables, and a museum there.

WWII LETTERS TO MY GIRL BACK HOME
From Nigeria, Arabia and Turkey

The site of Solomon's temple overlooks the surrounding hills on which can be seen many of the places where Biblical events took place. We saw the area of the crucifixion, the shadows on the wall from which the word Golgotha ((place of the skull) comes, the place where Stephen was stoned, in short, everything possible to see in that area. Then we walked through David Street, a narrow lane thronged with people and lined with shops something like those in Nigeria, but having much cleaner inhabitants.

After dinner, we visited the quarry from which the stone for Solomon's temple was taken— the original home of freemasonry, then the Garden of Gethsemane and the Tomb of the Kings.

In a few minutes, I must eat, when John Calvin Copper and I are going to hear the Palestine Symphony Orchestra.

We did attend the orchestra and enjoyed it to the utmost. Nevertheless, there was a poignant note when the entire audience stood for a moment of silence in respect for the millions of their fellow Jews who had been killed in the Nazi death camps.

Tomorrow, we set out for Damascus, by ourselves. There is a chance of getting a plane ride to Beyrouth, or Beirut, as it is called, a distance of 150 miles. We already had some money changed— Syrian money is worth only 1/10 the value of Palestinian money.

Beirut, Syria
March 12, 1945

I wish you were here! This YMCA lounge is deserted, ideally suited to a quiet get-together (Hmm—I no sooner got that written than I see an RAF chap arrive and begin writing. He's a nice bloke, though).

Hearing that there was some chance of getting a ride to Beirut by air, Calvin and I arranged to be awakened at 6:00 a.m. in order to catch the 6:45 bus to the airport. Just as we were ready to set out for the bus stop, it began raining. Against my better judgment, I deferred to his wish to postpone leaving till the shower ended. That delay was just enough to make us miss the bus, though we didn't realize it at the time. By 7:30, it seemed that the bus wasn't going to arrive, so Calvin decided to eat; I wanted to hang around to catch any ride going to the airport, so we separated.

Talking to some lieutenant, I was informed that our plane went <u>away</u> from Beirut rather than toward it. Therefore, I walked back to camp, looking for Calvin. Meanwhile, he caught the 8:00 a.m. bus for the airport. I supposed he would ride out there, discover that no plane was present, and return. After an hour's wait, however, I had seen no sign of him. Becoming frustrated, I stored nearly all my luggage and set off for the airport, determined to go to Beirut if I had to crawl. Stopping at the weather station, I was told that he'd been there, that the plane had indeed been going our way, but that there were no seats available. Also, he had seemed inclined to hitchhike there. After a brief wait, I bought a couple of chocolate bars, ate one for breakfast, and was driven to the road by a German Jew. I decided that Calvin must have gone on ahead or given up the whole idea. Anyway, I wanted to make the trip despite rain and the advice of some people not to do so. The bus driver tried to dissuade me, saying that little traffic went along the road.

Luck was good, though, and I caught a ride within a couple of minutes, and then another one following the end of the first. The second ride was with an RAF fellow, who believed in batting along at a merry clip. We had a swell time all the way, driving with the mountains to our right and the Mediterranean to our left.

At 11:15 we stopped for tea. I ordered the same things as the others who were there—an egg sandwich and tea. Since one of them paid for the whole order, I returned the favor by buying some small cakes for us. The cafe was quite modern, containing a nice radio, good food, and a pin-ball machine!

By 1:00 p.m. we were in Haifa, and there I learned that I could catch a free train to Beirut... Some British sergeant informed me (woe to my informers this weary day!)—that the train never left till after 2:00. My watch was two minutes slow. Result: I had the unhappy experience of seeing the train pulling away, a good 500 feet beyond me. So I ran like everything, gradually overtaking the darned thing and grabbed hold of the hand rail of the brake car, hanging on for dear life. A bit of gingerly climbing brought me to

WWII LETTERS TO MY GIRL BACK HOME
From Nigeria, Arabia and Turkey

the floor level, and I rode hanging onto the side of the car for a while. But upon looking forward, I noticed looming ahead a post located uncomfortably close to the track. Not wishing to be swept off the car by the post, I walked or climbed between the brake car and the one in front of it. As soon as the coast was clear, I asked them to let me in, which they did, through the window. Soon the trainman and I were having a pleasant conversation, and at the first stop he let me get off into the regular coaches. Then after 4½ hours of chilly riding, we arrived here. I noticed a truck leaving the station, and clambered aboard just as it pulled out. It happened to contain a couple of naval officers. Result: a trip right to the YMCA. where I registered and am now staying.

Tomorrow I'm going to Baalbeck (wherever that is). Supposedly, one of the Seven Wonders of the World was there. If plans continue OK, I shall later visit Damascus, and the cedars of Lebanon. Then I come back here. Now you know why I'm sleepy.

Beirut, Syria
March 13, 1945

...Somewhere in Syria, a weary soldier huddles under a 40-watt light bulb, striving vainly to keep from shivering. Curiously enough, that hapless wastrel is your loving fiancé. Last night we had only one blanket, so I piled everything on my bed except my shoes, and, after filching another blanket from an unoccupied bed, managed to sleep quite snugly. But tonight, all the beds are to be occupied, and unless I can promote a blanket or think of something, "I've 'ad it."

Actually, this place is not a hotel, it is a hostel. The food is decent, the prices are OK, and the people are pleasant. I don't remember what I'm paying, but it isn't much.

We didn't get a ride to Baalbeck at all. The road was blocked because of ice up in the mountains. Not having seen snow for ages, I decided to hitch-hike up to the road block. First I caught a street car crammed with people, getting off at a road intersection where a large sign announced that riders would be given lifts if they waited. A ride with a British captain took me a couple of miles into the

Allan Robert Humbert

country to a spot where I could see mountains above me, a valley to the right, and the town of Beirut between the road and the sea. I ate at a little place for warrant officers and sergeants only. It was a "ducky" little spot, called "Moon Garden." From the window of the curtained, pink-walled booth where I ate was a beautiful view down into the valley below. The other item of interest was a brightly-painted 3-foot high figure of Mickey Mouse, and an intriguing little bar featuring a man and woman on a desert island. (Author's note: next three inches of handwritten line cut out of the letter by censor.)

Interruption...I've just been loaned a blanket by a British army chap. Now I won't have to set the building on fire, after all.

After eating, I got a lift to Aley, a nice little village, then another to Sofar (sic) 18 miles from Beirut, and beyond, where the road was blocked. I walked beyond the block a half mile or so, then climbed up a gently sloping peak, looked around, and started back, after throwing a few snowballs. I had to walk a good way back from Sofar before getting a ride, and the ride I did get was in the mud-and-snow covered bed of an open truck. But it got us there, so we didn't mind. Altogether, I must have walked ten miles in those mountains. The temperature up there was about 30. Tomorrow, we go to Damascus, I hope ...

Beirut, Syria
March 14, 1945

It's night again, and I'm thinking of you. This time tomorrow, I should be back "home" in Tele-winsky.

Our trip to Damascus was interesting. The proprietor of the tourist agency kept piling men into the bus until there wasn't an extra inch of space. We started off half an hour late, some 20 people, ranging from a British major to a little Palestinian private enlisted in the equivalent of our WAC.

Our driver is wasting his time. Nerve like his belongs in either the combat tank forces or in a fighter squadron. All morning long we caromed madly over the Syrian hills, boldly defying the laws of physics and everything on the road. We passed donkeys, horses, camels, Arabs, street cars, dogs, chickens and cats, miraculously hitting none. The practice here is to rely on your horn. We drove alongside another native vehicle for a good two minutes before the blasting of our horn broke the driver's morale and caused him to let us pass. Ice and snow lay along the road, and in places where the road had been blocked were big chunks of the stuff four to five feet on each side. After a time we passed below the snow line and had a clear track from there on.

Some day I'd like to return to the shops of Damascus with a few hundred dollars and buy out the whole bazaar section. As it was, I bought only a couple of souvenirs, jewel boxes for my sisters and a nut-cracker for the folks. I was offered $20 for the pen with which I am now writing, but patriotically refused to sell it.

As for sights, we saw the wall down which Paul, the apostle, was let down at night, the street called "Strait," and the church over the house of the woman who restored his sight. Also, we visited a famous mosque there, but not so impressive as the Mohammed Ali one. Nevertheless, much of the inlay in the mosque was beautiful. I gave a roll of film to a British lieutenant, with the understanding that she is to send me prints of the pictures taken. She was quite nice, as most of the British officers are. The consensus of opinion of the forces I've met seems to be that American officers are the most "stuck-up" of the lot.

Coming back, we ran out of gas, though very near a station. This caused a delay of about half an hour, so that we had to do part of the driving at night. The scenery all the way there and back was a treat, especially sunset over the snow-covered peaks and the distant twinkle of the lights of Beirut as we came down the mountain.

Tel-Aviv
March 15, 1945

Our return ride was in two big jumps, namely a train to Haifa and an RAF car to Tel-Aviv. The train was very slow, but the auto made up for lost time, buzzing along at a fine clip reminiscent of speeds in the States. Speaking of reminiscences, I saw a 1941

Allan Robert Humbert

Dodge sedan in Beirut exactly like Dad's. That's the way with these foreign countries—you see the very new right beside the very old.

Recently, I read an article in a British magazine about actresses. This author believed that men's preferences in types of women varies with the local and world-wide conditions, and that an actress' popularity is largely influenced by the kind of women men happen to prefer at the time. At present, Greer Garson is supposed to be the most typically suited, being the sort of girl about whom guys sing, "You'd Be So Nice to Come Home To."

Yesterday there was a fine couple, an American soldier and a British WAF who were on the tour with us. She was quite nice, reminding me of you, and with her extremely feminine way of standing close beside him, modestly but lovingly.

Tel-Aviv
March 16, 1945

I can virtually see the last minutes of my furlough ticking away. A couple more days, and the whole trip will be over.

Every day seems like Sunday here, partly because there is no work to be done, and partly because there are always so many well dressed people on the streets.

Last night I wrote from the room of a fellow in the Canada House, a sort of USO for Canadians. This fellow, a tall, slender airman, invited me to dinner, and I eventually stayed all night and had breakfast with him in the morning. He refused to accept any payment, saying I was his guest and that he had been treated with similar hospitality by Air Corps men during his stay in the States. His name is Clyde Evans, and his home, Stratford, Ontario.

I endeavored to repay his hospitality by taking him to see "For Whom the Bell Tolls." My opinion of that show is the same as that of everyone else—namely that it was a great picture, and that Ingrid Bergman was wonderful.

It must be grand to have helped produce an epic Technicolor picture, to realize that millions of people the world over will sit spellbound as the story that you have worked on unfolds before them.

WWII LETTERS TO MY GIRL BACK HOME
From Nigeria, Arabia and Turkey

As for Tel-Aviv, I couldn't feel more at home here if I were Jewish. I like everything and everybody in town, down to the very cats and dogs. I only wish there were some way of expressing my gratitude to the whole country.

Tel-Aviv, Palestine
St. Patrick's Day, 1945

Last night I posted a notice on the bulletin board offering to pay one pound for a ticket for the New Testament tour of today. Until 7:45, there was no sign of success, though I had eaten and got dressed just as if I had one. Shortly after 7:45, a fellow appeared with the desired ticket, so I paid him a pound and got into the bus. The regular price is a little over 1/3 of a pound, but I didn't want any slip-up to occur, since this was the last time that tour would be made while my furlough lasts.

It took about an hour and a half to reach Jerusalem, via a flying GI truck which only touched earth occasionally. We parked at the million-dollar American YMCA, went in and ate a bite of breakfast. Soon we were back on the road again, and shortly thereafter, in Bethlehem. The guide, a fine man with a deep, resonant voice, told us the Christmas story again, each time pointing out the particular location of that part of the story.

You know the Christmas story, of course. There is now a church known as the Church of the Nativity built over the presumed birthplace of Christ. It is the oldest Christian church in the world, all earlier ones in Palestine having been destroyed by the Persians. The only reason it was spared was that the king noticed Persian garments on some of the people depicted in the building, concluding that it was an old Persian structure. Later, the Bethlehemites ransomed the place over 100 times from the Arabs, who threatened to destroy it every time they needed money, as we were told. Certainly the place has changed hands many times, and for a good while the Muslims turned the church into a stable, causing Christians, upon recapturing it, to block the main entrance so there wouldn't be room for livestock to enter. People, even those small in stature, must stoop to enter. Before the Muslims had it, but after the

Christians, the Romans worshipped Adonis there. After wild parties and drinking, men and women retired to the grottoes below the church.

We didn't get to the actual manger site since work was being done on it, but we saw most of the rest of the town, including tombs of various church personages. I remember especially the little room where Jerome made the first Latin translation of the Bible. It is impossible to see these places without a feeling of awe and reverence. The church is the one from which carols are annually broadcast to the world. On the way back to dinner we stopped outside Bethlehem while the guide told us the story of Ruth, and saw the well of Rachel.

After dinner, we visited the church supposedly located on the spot of Calvary, the Church of the Holy Sepulchre. Also, we saw and walked along the Via Dolorosa, where I had my picture taken, and saw the pool of Bethsaida, about which there is absolutely no question. There I bought an actual "widow's mite," one of the very coins used in the days of Rome.

Tel-Aviv
March 18, 1945

We were on the road shortly after 7:30, bound for the Sea of Galilee, some 70 miles northeast of Tel-Aviv. The country between here and there is hilly and considerably above sea level. A short distance from the sea, the country drops suddenly to a point 613 feet below sea level, I believe. We ate dinner in Tiberias—camel steak, of all things! The last stop of importance was Nazareth, where we saw the church built over the spot where Joseph lived.

Galilee is really only a lake about six miles wide and 14 miles long. It seems that the translators came across a word meaning either a sea or a lake, and wrongly wrote "sea" when translating the Bible. Regardless of the nomenclature, though, Galilee is a beautiful body of water, and the scene we witnessed was one to remember. After a leisurely look at the sea, from the cool shade of surrounding groves, we walked up to a small porch overlooking the water. There Dr. Hart, a benign and saintly old man, told us all the

WWII LETTERS TO MY GIRL BACK HOME
From Nigeria, Arabia and Turkey

Bible stories of Galilee, pointing to each spot in turn, while the warm spring air barely rustled the leaves, leaving the sea quiet, except for the frequent splashing of many fish. As he spoke, softly, of course, because he is old and feeble, he preached a lot, but in a manner so kindly no one could take offense. He was a chaplain in the War of 1898—a good while ago. After the talk, he showed us some relics and said goodbye.

I suppose I'll always remember the old man's talk, for it took place in a setting of inimitable poetic artistry. The locale, the day, the contrast between our youth and his age, and the shining saintliness of this fine old minister combined to produce an almost heavenly peace.

Cairo, Egypt
March 19, 1945

Good evening again. And it really is a good evening, for I can soon go to bed without the prospect of being disturbed or awakened till 6:30 at least. That, you might think, is a little early, but I intend to be in bed tonight by 7:00 p.m. which should supply ample time for recuperation.

Our trip was uneventful, and our reception here, OK. The takeoff was so smooth we couldn't tell when the plane left the ground. We flew in the clouds part of the way—I like the sensation of being completely surrounded by them.

In an effort to save the government a bit of time and money, I arranged to have my teeth and eyes checked here before returning to Masirah. Some fillings really were in need of replacement; as for glasses, mine hadn't been changed in two years, and I want to begin wearing civilian ones again, so the prescription needs to be correct.

...Now the radio is on, a variety of old but tuneful records. Already, I'm looking forward to mail from you, wondering how you're doing, and what you're thinking. I can see the stack of mail this minute, fragrant, feminine letters, each one different but each closing with the same sentiment and feeling.

(From Cairo, Egypt, but name of city cut out by censor)

Allan Robert Humbert

March 20, 1945

Another day, another dollar, and another visit to (cut out by censor). Frankly, dear, I don't care if I never enter this town again. That statement, incidentally, applies to the vast majority of places in Africa. Once the novelty wears off, each metropolis is just another wog town.

Efforts to sell those binoculars I brought from the States were fruitless—they're just a $45 white elephant, good only as a lesson not to spend money on needless things. Nevertheless, at the time I bought them before going overseas, there was no proof I wouldn't need them.

One of the boys here loaned me his ration of Toddy for the month, so I'll be able to bring back some to Masirah. Toddy, you remember, is canned chocolate malted milk, a delicious drink which has not yet reached home.

Also, I bought a little item for you, a small inlaid jewel box made in India. You'll get it one of these days. And did I mention seashell beads? They're nothing but colored sea shells that happen to have been picked up on the shores of the Sea of Galilee.

Now Bob Hope is on—rather distracting, especially when combined with a ping pong game, miscellaneous card games, and several conversations.

The fur-lined gloves you sent have certainly been nice to have lately. I wore them most of the time in Palestine. In weather observing, one's hands aren't toughened at all. Callouses become thin, and by and by hands don't have much protection against the cold. Warm hands help a person stay warm all over.

I'm a creature of routine. I like a little variety now and then, but not the variety of wondering where I'll sleep tonight, who's going to wake me up, how I'm going to comply with all the regulations, etc. And after a certain amount of traveling, I get bored. A line of sleek C-46 airplanes would excite me no more this evening than a line of rusty box cars setting along some siding. If a phosphorescent green elephant were to walk in the door, sit down beside me, and begin speaking Hebrew, I wouldn't even give it a second glance ...

WWII LETTERS TO MY GIRL BACK HOME
From Nigeria, Arabia and Turkey

Egypt
March 22, 1945

The thought occurred to me, why do people write "somewhere in Egypt"? After all, how can one be in Egypt at all without being somewhere there? Perhaps the "somewhere" is to designate to the censor that the writer is complying with censorship regulations.

Lately I've spent quite a bit. Soon I must get back to my budget. Today, though, I've bought paper, envelopes, a razor, sun glasses, coke, Toddy, tooth paste, toothbrush holder, and a subscription to <u>Time</u> magazine. The <u>Time</u> subscription is the cute "pony" edition, which is much smaller than the one you receive.

Strict budgeting is perhaps a good idea, but I prefer having a surplus to spend any way I please. As Angus McPherson said, "Damn the expense. Give the canary another seed!"

Egypt
March 23, 1945

I am convinced that American soldiers have no respect at all for the safeguarding of military information. Time and time again, I've been told stuff which few people should be permitted to know, merely because I, too, was a soldier. Only today I overheard one guy in conversation with a civilian, blithely telling him information the Germans and Japanese would like to know. True, the fellow being spoken to had probably been investigated by the FBI, but even the most loyal people cannot always be trusted to be careful regarding those to whom they speak.

One interesting feature of a large army post is the ceremony of retreat. If I were running a post, there would be a huge formal retreat about once each month, but no oftener. When observed now and then, retreat is morale-building and inspiring.

Not having stood retreat for a long time, I found today's ceremony refreshing. Although I saw the ordered ranks of soldiers, I had forgotten how near the hour was for the ceremony of lowering the flag. On the way to the retreat, I was half-way across a large open area when I realized I was sure to be caught in the open.

Allan Robert Humbert

Suddenly over the loudspeakers came the final strains of band music, followed immediately by the explosion of a cannon. So I halted instantly, saluted and held the salute rigidly until the Star Spangled Banner had been played. Frankly, dear, you can't resist feeling very proud of your army when retreat's going on.

Just before being caught out during retreat, I heard a dog barking, and looked around to see where it was. There, a few feet from me was a kennel labeled "Muggsy" and to it was tied an adorable little dog, no larger than a half-grown kitten. He made a show of being very ferocious, but a few minutes of woofing changed his mind, and we became well acquainted.

Egypt
March 24, 1945

I'm getting more anxious every day to get out of Egypt and back "home" again. This constant waiting around becomes tiresome, and if I don't get back by the 1st of April will cause all sorts of aggravating complications—delayed pay, lack of any chance to work on the weather records next month, and possible discontent among the officers and the guys back at the station because I spent so much time en route. However, there's nothing I can do about the matter.

Anglo-Egyptian Sudan
March 25, 1945

This letter will probably reach you before the one I wrote last night, proving that I finally got on my way after all.

You know the army—"hurry up and wait." We did lots of rushing, for during a single hour, I told the boys goodbye, signed out at the desk in Headquarters, checked in my bedding, carried my bags to the terminal building, after packing them, had my money changed from piasters back into rupees, and had finally taken out of check a case of Toddy. A few minutes later, we weighed in, answering routine questions, "Are you carrying any undeveloped film or any uncensored mail?" and began waiting.

WWII LETTERS TO MY GIRL BACK HOME
From Nigeria, Arabia and Turkey

It was nearly two hours later that we finally boarded the plane—majors—captains—USO girls—and even a small dog, the pilot's mascot. There wasn't any heat in the plane, and our originality was sorely taxed to keep warm under the single blanket each of us were given.

We got to bed at 0415—a very poor time to get there. I slept through breakfast, and deliberately missed dinner in order to get cleaned up. Now the time on this Sunday afternoon is 2:30 p.m., and I'm lying on my feather-soft bed, relaxed, comfortable, and indifferent, while a warm afternoon breeze blows luxuriously on my back, legs and shoulders. What a pleasant change from chilly Cairo! With almost imperceptible effort, I could nestle into this downy mattress and go back to sleep, dreaming you were beside me. Or, with a little more effort, I could finish dressing and go to the library. You see, dear, I'm a lord of leisure... Those dots represent a four-hour lapse in time, during which I've talked to people and eaten a delicious supper. In 25 minutes, I'm going to the movie.

Honey, I feel as glad to get back in the tropics as if I were coming into a warm house after being out in the cold all day. I like the mood of this post—a "southern gentleman" grace and dignity, quite unlike the army.

I suppose that I've received more than a fair share of beautiful days and lovely nights. Much as I want to be back in the States, I will miss certain features of this place. If you were here, dear, you'd know what I mean. Still, Indiana nights are nice, also, and I'll be delighted to get back to them.

A few more days, and I'll be back on my island again. There I hope to find 20 or more letters, which I'll read lying down, putting the unread letters on my right and the read ones on my left...

Aden Protectorate
March 26, 1945

Another day, another dollar, another plane ride, another country, and still I'm not "home." I would like to tell you about the exciting plane ride we had, but alas, the description might never reach you.

Allan Robert Humbert

I had been relaxed into a fitful slumber when some corporal awakened me, saying, "Be ready to go in 10 minutes." Frankly, at 0230 in the morning, I'm not too keen about going anywhere; the normal place to be at that ungodly hour is in bed, and all my being shouts to be there.

The fellows here have a neat method for keeping the Quonset huts barracks cool, by planting ivy all around them. Each building is so heavily festooned with vines that the structure itself can hardly be seen.

Had a nice long visit with Joe Graczkowski and Al Cohen this afternoon.

I wonder what's new on the island. Any news short of death itself would never reach me, and all kinds of good or bad news could be waiting unknown to me, having been gone for three weeks.

Aden Protectorate
March 27, 1945

...Now I'm on my way again, after a day's delay. This aircraft is a far cry from the type I'm used to riding. We're sitting on upholstered seats, modern, adjustable—the twin of those found on new trains. I'm on the left side of the plane, where there is a double row of seven, sitting beside a window trimmed with light blue curtains on chromium plated curtain rods. Outside, I can see a few stars, a shadowy void which is the earth below us, and a flashing red light out on the wing. Over five hours will have elapsed before I'm back, and by then it will be past 1:00 a.m.

Five more seats are in a row on the right side of the ship, with another near the tail, just in front of the rest room. The cabin is lined on either side with a smooth, streamlined luggage carrier, which, like the walls, is painted ivory. A couple feet from the floor and downward is painted buff, and the carpet is brown. There are four lights in the center of the ship, set into the ceiling, making the place bright and cheerful. But if we wish to read or write while the main lights are off, each seat is provided with a small but powerful reading light built into the luggage rack above us. The final accent on comfort is an adjustable ventilator between each pair of individual lights made to direct cold air onto us, and adjustable to point in any direction while simultaneously being adjusted to maintain any volume of air desired. And for those who smoke, ash trays are provided, one for each seat.

As for company, it consists primarily (for the present) of a USO troupe, three girls and a man. Since there is lots of room, we're spread out, one person occupying a pair of seats. If any service is lacking, I don't know what it is.

Ordinarily, fountain pens tend to leak at flying altitudes, the ink being forced out by expansion of the air contained in the pen. As yet, this hasn't happened. The ride is just a little bumpy; every now and then I can feel the plane suddenly falling, or pushing upward beneath me. Moreover, it is wobbling from side to side somewhat. However, I enjoy a bit of rough weather, and so long as our little buggy stays in the air, I don't care what she does. I have a curious, almost fatalistic faith in all forms of transportation, flying not excepted, looking on this thousand-mile jaunt with considerably less apprehension that I used to have in the drive from Marion to Muncie, after a date with you.

Allan Robert Humbert

Chapter 17

MASIRAH ISLAND, ARABIA
MARCH TO MAY 1945

Masirah Island
March 28, 1945

Last night after writing you, I mounted a few pictures and dozed till we reached here. The island seen from the plane looked very enchanting in the moonlight, and our landing was as smooth as a bird's. An "ancient, fish-like smell" greeted us, conveyed by a soft offshore breeze. I went to bed, after reading one of your letters and checking to see that my bed wasn't in use. While answering her questions, I added points of my own.

Before me lie a stack of 24 letters from you, plus several from the folks. Surprisingly enough, there were no casualty reports—the only death was Queen's, our old Newfoundland dog—So the little dog you once had is dead. Funny thing how we'll cry over the death of a dog, while men remain dry-eyed at the death of a comrade. As for my trip, I passed through both Tyre and Sidon by train, but didn't get to the Dead Sea.

"Yappety, yappety, yappety." This barracks is filled with confusion, and I can't hear myself think, much less understand what I'm writing.

As for the weather observer exam we took, I made "excellent," which is the second best classification, a grade higher than last time. The chief satisfaction from this is knowing that RCO has no kick-back, and that there is no shadow on my stripes. I have a hunch that these exams will mean something, in a negative sense.

WWII LETTERS TO MY GIRL BACK HOME
From Nigeria, Arabia and Turkey

March 29, 1945

Your letters came today...Exercise? If pinned right down to it, I'd favor moderate exercise, too. We get a reasonable amount just walking. If I object to exercising, it is for the time used rather than the effort. Temperatures such as today's 96 hardly increase one's desire for exercise, either.

March 31, 1945

Should this letter reach you with a strange, unsavory odor, it is the direct result of a party we had last night. Our menu included soda crackers, pretzels, sardines, raisins, Limburger cheese spread, and beer. I partook of everything except the beer, making sandwiches consisting of Limburger cheese on pretzels, with raisins for that little extra touch. Maybe that's why I dreamed last night— but the dreams were about you and very pleasant.

Statistical sidelight: There are 181 pin-up girls posted in our barracks, although only three fellows go in for the sport in a wholehearted manner. I have one very small one—a calendar about the size of an envelope. The calendar is an Esquire folder decorated with the famous Vargas girls.

My new job is interesting, in a way. After the weather records have been made for a day, I go over them and correct all the errors. Besides this, I do various odd jobs, putting in approximately the same number of hours as people on shift, but during the day only. This leaves the evening free.

April 2, 1945

This has been a busy day. Besides doing a lot of routine work, I managed to go swimming. The water was cool and pleasant, and clean as could be. The sea was as beautiful as ever—a cool, green shade which you wouldn't believe without seeing.

Really, dear, I don't mind at all if you occasionally let off steam. Dealing with people can be frustrating. Dad used to complain about

Allan Robert Humbert

the PWA, the WPA, etc., never to the papers, but always to us or someone he knew. That's why I never complain. (!)

Your grandparents seem to be "good to the last drop," but why shouldn't they be? You know the poem, "Father William"—not the humorous version. As you say, FDR looks a bit emaciated lately. However, he'll probably last for years. The good die young.

An argument is developing here in the barracks, over the topic "is adventure—dangerous adventure, good or bad?" I say, for the sake of argument, that it is good.

April 3, 1945

This is a beautiful morning—calm, cool and very quiet. Naturally I feel great, having got up early, taken a bath, shaved and put on my "camping" shorts. That swim yesterday did enliven me. You know how muscles feel the day after using them vigorously—not tired, but just stiff enough to remind you that you were busy.

Isn't it strange that people are blind to the value of peace and quiet? In two or three hours, the radio will be blaring; at least two arguments will have begun, and all silence will be shattered.

Ordinary people very seldom produce anything remarkable in the way of creative work. I shouldn't wonder if the noise and confusion in which they live may not be the reason they don't. I find it nearly impossible to concentrate in the midst of such noise as we live in here.

…I just now took time to get a chocolate bar. Come to think of it, chocolate Toddy would also taste good. Guess I'll have a can of it, too. It's part of the case of 24 cans that I brought back from Cairo. So far, I've drunk about 1/3 of the total amount consumed, since it is the custom here to share anything edible, not to mention all forms of drink.

April 4, 1945

Yesterday was a very long and exhausting day. After writing you, I worked on the advertising course awhile, and then went to the station. Since this is the beginning of a new month, there is lots to do, and lots for me in particular, since I am taking over a new job with all the organizing it means, and must also handle a long report. After working till supper last night, I went to see "None But the Lonely Heart," returning to the station again to work past midnight.

April 5, 1945

This being laundry day, we have ours ready to be picked up early in the morning, and as usual prepared it last night. I happened to be thinking about you at the time, and I asked Howard whether he thought my unsuspecting fiancée realized that the job would some day fall on her. He went so far as to say she not only did, but even looked forward to the task. After considering the matter, I realized that it's fun doing little things for people we love, even things we'd do for no one else.

Aside from the many other advantages it affords, love brings fun to shopping. A man is not expected to wear such items as silks and jewels, but once engaged, he can purchase those things he can afford, since they're for his girl. In short, he becomes an Indian giver, having both the pleasure of ownership and of giving at the same time.

You mentioned someone being 37. Thirty-seven seems pretty old to me. In fact, 25 seems old, no more than I have accomplished in three years. I can remember my dad, at least as a person, when he was 25. He was 37 only nine years ago. However, age depends on conditions other than years alone. I know one old man who at the age of 87 is still full of pep, not at all tired of living. The old guy gets rather profane at times, a characteristic I secretly admire in him, not because profanity is good, but because it indicates his vitality and courage.

One of the venerable ancestors on my mother's side (she could tell you who) lived a long, full life, and a conscientious one, though not as a church member. When he was on the verge of kicking the bucket, some over-eager minister called wanting him to confess his sins so he could get to heaven without any delay en route. Apparently the old boy had some self-control left, for he refrained from telling the simple cleric where to go.

Allan Robert Humbert

April 6, 1945

Parents can be quite discouraging at times. Why must people (civilians) always think in terms of safety and convenience? Believe it or not, dear, much of the pleasure of being on furlough was simply the ability to do as I pleased. My trip to Beirut, for example, was a minor triumph over bad weather, poor connections and the inertia of my companion.

It is quite easy to do as you please away from home, but once back in the family circle, it is very hard to be different. Plenty of kids are flying bombers now who weren't trusted out with the family car back home.

My plans for the summer are rather scanty. I intend to go where the army sends me and do what the army tells me. Simple, isn't it?

April 8, 1945

By the way, do you people at home ever see any action shots of actual combat? The ones we see are restricted, not necessarily available to civilians, and are usually limited to scenes showing shooting, either heavy artillery, or strafing. However, there is considerable variety in the films, and most of them are quite interesting. Confidentially, I don't miss the excitement of combat at all.

People accuse me of being bloodthirsty, merely because I get a kick out of any kind of excitement, whether it is dangerous or not. If it's exciting to be on a ship when depth charges are dropping around you, why not say so?

We kids used to take considerable risks climbing up in the hay mow of our barn, playing tag with the rule that you could chase each other anywhere except on the floor—by clinging to rafters, walking on elevated beams, etc.—but keeping our nerve made these feats comparatively safe. A person ought to know the possibilities of success in any dangerous endeavor, in order to deal with emergencies that arise.

April 9, 1945

Today I purchased a money order for $12.16, which I shall send to Cpl Cohen, repayment for the funds which he gave me for purchase of the desk set, even though I also was swindled by the person who was to buy the sets for us. However, giving him back his money will prove that I'm honest, though I part with each of those dollars as if it were a tooth.

Two lessons are clear: Never trust strangers, and NEVER, NEVER, NEVER Trust Strangers with Money Belonging to Another Person!

April 10, 1945

Your fiancé has invented, designed and built a Toddy cooler, all in the same morning. This canned chocolate-flavored milk, which I've mentioned before, is great, but it really needs to be cooled, and we have no refrigerator in the barracks.

The cooler consists of only a few parts, namely, an old sock, a can of water, a small plate suspended from the ceiling by three strings, and the can of Toddy. The can of Toddy is inside the sock. The sock extends into the water in the can below, with the Toddy can on top the water can, both cans supported by the plate. Capillary action causes water from the bottom can to flow into the sock, and up around the can of Toddy, the sock functioning as a wick. Result: the Toddy becomes 10 degrees cooler than the air temperature. The drier the air, the cooler the drink.

April 11, 1945

Weathermen are forever complaining about unkind treatment by authorities at the posts where they're stationed; yet they themselves are usually at fault. Last night at 12:30 lights were still on in our barracks, an hour and 30 minutes after they were supposed to be off. Sooner or later, something will come up about this, and no doubt as usual, the many will be in dutch for the misdemeanor of a few.

Allan Robert Humbert

Since I worked this morning and returned to work again right after dinner, I was able to go swimming. I walked to the beach, swam awhile, and walked back, a little sunburned.

Fishing is quite good around here. Punch and some others caught over 300 pounds of fish today, ranging up to 18 pounds in weight. The fish covered a tarpaulin eight or ten feet square.

April 12, 1945

Today begins my second year overseas. A year ago, we were aboard the Ralph Izzard, wondering just where we were going, what the trip would be like, and how long it would take en route. There were all sorts of intriguing rumors and conjectures. One merchant marine fellow assured us that our ship was so provisioned that it could travel for six months without touching port. Planes as part of the cargo suggested that we might be bound for the Persian Gulf. All our shoes had leather soles, suggesting a hot climate. A few people confidently predicted that we were bound for Cairo, and they even went so far as to say this news came straight from Weather Wing Headquarters there. Regardless, the whole outfit is literally alive and well. Of the guys on the ship, one has been promoted to "buck" sergeant, many have made Pfc and corporal, and no has been promoted to staff sergeant. What would be a good slogan for the year? Stay Alive in Forty-Five?

April 13, 1945

This has been a busy day in every sense of the word—and an unlucky one for the USA. The most important event, to be sure, was the news of President Roosevelt's death. It's been interesting to observe how guys reacted to his passing. Some of my ardent Democrat acquaintances say it's the worst possible catastrophe, while the Republicans are saying that no man is indispensable and that the United States will get along as well as ever.

The chief danger that I see is that we may lose the peace by our lack of statesmen comparable to Churchill and other leaders.

WWII LETTERS TO MY GIRL BACK HOME
From Nigeria, Arabia and Turkey

Remember all the things you said about Truman? Here's hoping they don't come true. So far, nobody has a good word for him. Still, he must have at least <u>some</u> ability, and if he hasn't, there should be a few people to cover up for him.

Today Howard and I got a 63-minute pilot balloon run, a record for the present. The balloon was 38,000 feet high before I lost sight of it through the theodolite; incidentally, my feet were both asleep.

April 14, 1945

We were awakened at 0530 this morning to raise the flag. The ceremony was brief and not particularly military. We formed a column of threes, marched to the flagpole, and stood at attention while the MPs raised the flag to the top of the mast for a moment, and then lowered it to half mast. The captain in charge saluted, as did almost 2/3 of the guys in ranks, which they shouldn't have done. A minute later, a photographer shot the ceremony, and we marched to chow.

The Sultan of Oman, who owns this island, made quite a concession to us in permitting the flag to be flown. This is a neutral country, you know, and we are allowed to fly the flag only on the most special occasions. He visited the island not long ago, but I missed seeing him. Believe it or not, he's an Oxford product, is fabulously well off, and has a harem. Also, he collects a cool $20,000 per month from the Americans and British for the privilege of using his Arabian rock. For the sake of accuracy, I should add that this information is strictly hearsay.

News: Vienna is captured. Pretty soon it will be Berlin, when lots of boys are going to go home, but unfortunately, not we.

The army is begging for applicants for Engineering OCS (Officer Candidate School), apparently reaching all the way down into high school graduates for material. Why do they need more engineering officers? The answer is probably the grisly fact that the Engineers sometimes precede the Infantry. As an engineer, you try to build a bridge at one end, while the enemy tries to blow it up at the other end (or at your end). I imagine the present shortage is due

Allan Robert Humbert

either to cracking the Siegfried line or to the need for a post-war army.

A long time ago, back in pre-induction days, such an offer would have been very alluring. But I feel that the chief result of a great deal of work earlier in the army is to get kicked in the face. There is no such thing as justice in the army; the individual is nothing, and the only expedient policy is to be as ruthless with them as they are with you. Still...the bait is very tempting and it's hard to avoid nibbling a bit.

This evening we held a formal retreat, in a temperature of 100 degrees, yet we were quite comfortable because the air was dry. Tomorrow at 9:45 is another ceremony, the last of the day, I believe, and the last of the memorial.

April 15, 1945

...Time passes; the plane which was to have brought mail here, didn't. It travels under pretty low priority these days—a week must have passed since any sizeable amount came in.

News here is always scarce, and what little there is can't be written about. There are at least two dogs on the island—perhaps I should go bite one. But they're nice dogs, so why should I pick on them? Those two black-and-white canines keep morale up here more than the USO shows we receive. True, they're sleek, lazy and good-for-nothing, but so are we.

Consumption of liquids certainly rises during hot weather. So far today, I've drunk two cokes, two Toddys, a pint of orange juice, a mug of hot chocolate and lots of water, although in earlier days of cooler weather, days would pass between cokes.

Reading over the latest <u>Yank</u> magazine, I realize how fortunate we actually are here, where our woes are so few we can enumerate each one separately ...

A discussion developed in the barracks recently over the question, "Would you accept a 'bust' to private to go back to the States?" My answer was "no," if going back meant staying in North Carolina or some other place far from you. However, these alternatives aren't ours to choose from.

WWII LETTERS TO MY GIRL BACK HOME
From Nigeria, Arabia and Turkey

April 17, 1945

Bags of mail arrived today—there were letters from you, Dad, a dictionary advertisement, and photos from an English ATS lieutenant whom I met in Damascus. She had a camera, but no film, and I had a film, but no camera. So we made an agreement whereby the film was to be used in her camera, and she was to send me prints of certain ones.

As you notice, a picture of me is enclosed. It isn't too bad, although the weather was rather chilly. Nor are my feet really that big; all people entering a mosque must either remove their shoes or tie large sandals over them.

Having mail again is certainly satisfying. By now your students have probably forgotten the extra work you gave them, and you may have, too...So your brother, Verl, is in Belgium! Things are a lot livelier there than on this island.

You girls are lucky having fiancés in foreign countries. These natives are clever. They make certain that most of their gift items are for women...For your information, we are getting plenty of meat. Some form of it is served with almost every meal. I would cheerfully trade our meat for more green foods, cheese, and milk. A fellow observer here just said that he would gladly pay two dollars for a nice cold quart of milk. And so would I!

Even our subconscious mind has difficulty fulfilling its wishes. Last night I dreamed of being back home intending to see you, but the car was out of gas. So I began hitchhiking, but never got a ride. That brings events up to now, for tonight finds me far, far from you.

April 19, 1945

I've been busy all day, operating partly on the emotional steam generated by a desire to see this camp—I almost inserted adjectives in front of that word, camp—acquire some discipline. Somewhere in the line of our family clan is a marked desire to see things organized and running on schedule. And this camp is about as disorganized as they come. Every day or so, new regulations are

181

posted, regulations which are constantly, flagrantly and blithely violated.

My pet peeve is the subject of lights. Despite a post order that lights are to be out at 11:00, it is the exception rather than the rule that our barracks is dark by then. Last night, for instance, they stayed on till 12:20 p.m., while everyone in the barracks tossed and turned in an effort to sleep in spite of them. Yet each person considers that he is probably alone in desiring them out, patiently suffering the annoyance of disturbed slumber until finally some outraged soldier throws tact to the winds and says to turn the lights out before he breaks them out.

This station was inspected today, and since I hadn't a <u>thing</u> to wear, I went swimming. The beach was tops, since the water was deep and there were plenty of big green breakers to tumble us head over heels toward shore. The bigger the waves, the farther apart they are, and the more smooth water there is to swim in between waves. As the monsoon season approaches, the waves should get bigger and better.

A letter from my mother included news about Lee, who is still in the Philippines. His outfit came across a church, and Lee helped carry out the priests whom the Japs had bayoneted.

One of the worst mistakes the Nazis and Japs ever made was in getting Hollywood against them. Remote as we are from the war, such stories as we hear fill us with disgust, not only for the soldiers but also for the civilians who are fighting.

After seeing the show, "Conspirators," Swan and I talked about the motives back of the "underground" fighters. He couldn't see why an ordinary civilian with so little to gain would take such terrible risks as these people do. I believe it is a matter of emotions. If something terrible had happened to you because of the Germans and Japs, I would probably have ceased to be a person, and would have become a creature only of revenge, living only for the purpose of destroying those who had destroyed you. Fortunately for both of us, that situation should never develop.

April 20, 1945

...An Englishman just told me, "well, come on. Fill it up with x's and go to chop!" since he wants me to go eat with him. But I told him that using x's was illegal in the American army ...

April 23, 1945

The world news is fascinating these days—American troops are being cautioned about shooting at tanks lest they be Russian. And the local news is fascinating, also, but can't be written about. Nothing dangerous, of course—just intriguing rumors.

Now the barracks is discussing the subject, "Why does 19th Weather treat disciplinary cases with so much consideration?" The general idea is that guys can get away with anything short of murder, receiving exactly the same treatment as the most persevering and conscientious men in the outfit. We did not reach a conclusion. One group decided that headquarters should "throw the book" at these problem children, while the second group, mine, concluded that severe discipline would only aggravate the situation, and that these men would not only become useless to the squadron, but downright dangerous, since there are so many ways a fellow can cause trouble. As things are now, the outfit gets a certain amount of work from these guys—so I favor the present policy.

However, these questions aren't mine to solve—I have plenty of my own. Therefore I'm going to bed.

April 24, 1945

News sometimes gets to me rather late. Just today, I heard of the death of Ernie Pyle, the famous and beloved war correspondent. I had a great deal of admiration for him. His dangerous role was self-chosen, and inspired primarily by the desire to be with the boys who are fated to see war at its worst. He could have quit long ago and still have been highly respected, but chose instead to be in there till the last.

Death seems to mean so much more when one has read a lot about the person. In a way, I feel the loss of Pyle more keenly than if he were in our outfit. Perhaps it is just another casualty to be blamed on no one, or perhaps it is one more crime to blame on the Japs.

The longer the war lasts, the less patience I have with the Japanese, as an army or as a people. I favor keeping that country down after the war, extending no aid whatsoever. If they starve, then the population will be lower, and there will be less pressure on us in the future. Evidently it is either we or they.

However, I am not so foolish as to expect my policies to be followed. When the war is over, we'll start loaning them money, helping them out, sinking our ships, giving them bases, and asking them to sock us again. And years from now you and I will be wondering whether our kids will be as lucky as their parents.

April 26, 1945

The movie tonight is "Two Girls and a Sailor." I've seen it three times already, but there's no reason why it won't be good the fourth time, too.

…(Later)…I did see "Two Girls and a Sailor" again—and it was as good as ever. The music, the story, the acting, the spirit, all were superb. By the way, we had a personal appearance recently of Jose Iturbi's sister. Evidently she is the one who played in the duet in the movie.

April 28, 1945

Our PX is busy selling out all kinds of stock. We can get practically unlimited quantities of coke, Toddy, candy, native goods, etc. This morning there appeared a most delectable item: Whitman's chocolates. We are each allowed one box. The one I bought was attractively done up in spring-like pastel blue, tied with a blue ribbon, and wrapped in cellophane. It was the sort of present I would be proud to give to you.

WWII LETTERS TO MY GIRL BACK HOME
From Nigeria, Arabia and Turkey

I'm writing this in the new Rec Hall, which consists of merely another Quonset hut supplied with numerous tables and chairs. At present, there are no other occupants than myself. Very convenient. Most of these huts are covered with a heavy reed matting to keep them cool. This one doesn't, so it's quite warm. However, I'd rather put up with the extra heat and be unbothered than to have comfort and a crowd.

Two letters came from you today, both very nice. I'm currently using the envelope from one to keep my perspiration off the letter I'm writing now.

Yes, I missed the boat on that prediction about FDR. But then I'm often wrong. Certainly I wished him no bad luck.

There is a very revealing article in the <u>Saturday Evening Post</u> of a few weeks ago, explaining why General Stillwell was recalled. Briefly, the article states that a dispute arose, the question being whether lend-lease material was to be used for air bases or for equipping a land army. The Air Force won that battle, but lost the one with the Japs, and the military result was the capture of many allied air bases, and the cutting in two of China. Since "Vinegar Joe" had predicted that very defeat, he was fired.

Moreover, the article continued by saying Chiang Kai-Shek was more interested in diverting lend-lease material to combat the Chinese Communists than in using it in warfare against the Japs. The Chinese reason very astutely that America will first win the war in Europe, and then do the same in China, all without effort on the part of the Chinese. So why hurry?

The country destined to get the most from this war is Russia. She will soon be in a position to tell all Europe what to do, including England.

Nationalism is not worth the price it costs. Why should your brother be risking his life merely for the defense of names such as "France" or "democracy?" What have the Germans gained? Their country is devastated; the cream of their manpower is destroyed; they have incurred the hatred and distrust of most of the world. All this for what?

Allan Robert Humbert

April 30, 1945

Tonight Punch showed me pictures of his adorable little girl who is just 14 months old. Seeing that kid made me think of the future, and at the same time, the present. I realized that out of all this destruction and desolation, life will emerge again, stronger, perhaps, than ever, not only for our own lives, but for those of the people we know ...

May 1, 1945

...Punch knows all about President Truman. They are both from Missouri. Truman is said to have asked Pendergast for assistance in becoming a tax collector. Pendergast said he had another man whom he wanted for the job, but that he needed a US senator. And Truman, being relatively unknown and innocuous, got the job. Wonder if he was voted the "boy most likely to succeed" in his high school class.

May 3, 1945

According to BBC, Berlin has fallen, Hitler and Goebbels have both committed suicide, and all troops in northern Italy have surrendered. Moreover, the work of strategic bombing is finished in Europe, and the entire set-up is being sent to the Pacific theater. In short, the European war is just about finished.
I suppose Japan has the melancholy satisfaction of knowing she is soon to be hit with the mightiest assemblage of air power since the beginning of time. Now if only the troops committed in China by the Japs return to defend their homeland, all will shortly be over. I am still hoping that the Allies can make things so hot for the islands of Japan proper that they will ask to surrender, including the ones in China. Otherwise, we can bomb the people who want to surrender until their comrades wish to do likewise. A wog just came in to sweep the Rec Hall, so we left, thinking how nice it would be to live again in the USA where the differences between opposite parts of the population are not so vast.

WWII LETTERS TO MY GIRL BACK HOME
From Nigeria, Arabia and Turkey

The battle between my sore throat and I is almost a draw. My cold is unchanged, but my throat isn't quite as sore as it was. Disregarding the proverb, "He who treats himself has a fool for a doctor," I painted my own throat with merthiolate, producing marked improvement.

…Time hobbles on. Various things have happened. I treated my throat by gargling two more preparations: (a) Scotch whiskey, and (b) Squibb's antiseptic. At any rate it feels better still. The other news is mail. Letters came from you, Dorothy, Dad and Barbara. Also, my first copy of "<u>Time</u>" came, dated April 23.

Since there were four letters from you, I may as well answer them now…We certainly concur in wanting a home of our own, and desiring to live near a good-sized town. I don't care for a farm, either—pigs, chickens, etc. are more bother than they're worth. Still, I'd like to have a pretty extensive garden, and, if possible, a greenhouse. These would take some room, say 5-10 acres of land. I see us having a garden for vegetables, one for flowers, several fruit trees, various berry patches, not to mention a lawn, and whatever else you have in mind.

Wouldn't it be nice to sit down beforehand, laying out complete plans, rather than letting it all "just grow" like Topsy? One of our biggest problems will be to keep what we're doing from being known far and wide …

As for dogs, I think we should have one, not a yapping mite that can be killed by a pussy-cat, but a good-sized, respectable, law-abiding dog with dignity, sense and training, the sort of animal that virtually becomes part of the family.

Of course we must raise the dog from a pup, and he must have training. Therefore it will be necessary to supply at least one small boy to grow up with the dog, because each will help to educate and understand the other. Naturally, we must cooperate to the fullest extent, and to prove my good intentions, I'll meet you half way, and supply the pup …

Allan Robert Humbert

May 6, 1945

...Greetings on the last evening of my 24th year of existence. I have accomplished as little today as a human being is able to accomplish and remain alive. I am a living representative of inertia.

These hot afternoons are a nuisance because creative effort seems completely out of the question. One spends so much energy combating the heat that there is none left for work. Yet the heat isn't oppressive—its chief effect on me is sleepiness. Maybe I should just go to sleep and be done with it.

However, there's more to this mood than merely climate. It's the insidious feeling that nothing we do matters. Promotion is non-existent. There are no bonuses. There are no ways of speeding up the war, no definite indication when we'll go home. And above everything else, there is no way on earth whereby we can put in extra work, and have financial advantage of that work accrue to ourselves. We are only tenants here, co-workers in a communistic order, good-natured convicts working in a charitable and well-managed prison.

Ours is the same assurance of security, the same philosophical waiting, that prevails in a penitentiary. And we can get virtually anything we want—except out.

To a person devoid of ambition, the army is a very satisfactory organization, because it guarantees more comforts for less work on your part than any I know. But the person who has any desire to get ahead can easily go nuts here, submerged and overwhelmed in a sea of mediocrity.

This Rec Hall in which I'm writing, for instance, serves as a locale for my illustration. Originally, the place was built as a writing room, a quiet corner of the camp designed for recreation away from the barracks. But what has happened? The inevitable beer-guzzling minority has assumed control, and for the past three nights, wild parties have been held here.

I came in this morning, and found the whole Rec Hall a scene of mad confusion. Chairs were overturned—one had been smashed to splinters—the floor was littered with beer cans, peanuts, cheese, beer cases, pieces of furniture and bottle caps. The tables were piled *high with the same debris—half the cans were overturned, and big damp splotches marked the spots where cans of beer had been upset, spewing their contents on the table, chairs, floor, and soldiers.*

When I investigated, I discovered nothing could be done. The fellow I talked to was only a 2nd Lt who probably couldn't have done anything if he'd tried.

So you see how it goes. Our section of the population is outnumbered, not only here, but everywhere, by the cold laws of statistics, and our only hope is to live some day where at least enough of our equals live to form a majority in their own restricted circle, even though they are always outnumbered by people outside their own walls.

May 7, 1945

...Here's hoping that this is my last birthday in the army, and that the next one finds us happily married. This day is still too young for a play-by-play account, so let's talk politics.

Discussion in the barracks last night centered on the topic, "What are we going to do about Russia?" This was brought on by the high-handed way the Russians have behaved toward the Polish question, and their determination to set up a puppet government and move the Polish border westward.

Some of us said that Russia should be allowed to do as she pleases in Poland, for the simple reason that we can do nothing about it. Others said that we must draw the line instantly, even though it leads to war with our erstwhile ally. That brought up the question, "Could we defeat Russia?" and we agreed that to be virtually impossible, since all the industrial might of Germany failed, even at a time when she was relatively strong and Russia relatively weak.

The general attitude toward the San Francisco Conference is one of amused tolerance. It is considered to be just another League of Nations, and that when it's over, the Big Three will keep right on being the Big Three, leaving the war devoid of accomplishment.

However, this is no time to be bitter and pessimistic. I notice a marked parallel between what is being said now about the conference and what was said before our own Constitutional Convention; yet we managed to work out the difficulties then, emerging as a united nation, despite all the gloomy predictions of the people who knew it wouldn't work.

I think the basic difficulty of forming a world organization is fear. People are now afraid of Russia. This was the topic which constantly reappeared in the conversation last night. Russia has always maintained that her primary interest is within her own boundaries, and it's on the record that she made no large-scale effort to conquer Europe, her efforts before the war being the establishment of bases in Finland.

In retrospect, from the viewpoint of 2002, I think some of us overlooked the fact that Russia was not a democracy, and that a dictatorial government was perfectly capable of imposing its will on others, regardless of their desires.

VE Day
My dearest,

The date you see written is self-explanatory, and though you save this letter and read it many years from now, you and the world will know when it was written.
Naturally, the camp is celebrating, though at this early hour the parties haven't begun. I didn't hear Churchill's speech, but I did enjoy the program which immediately followed it. Somehow I caught the spirit of the celebration, and felt as happy as the exuberant Britishers themselves. Remembering back to the days of Mrs. Minniver, at a time when England's future seemed the darkest in history, I realized how far they have come.
As for that grand old warrior of theirs, Winston Churchill, he stands today in epic grandeur, like Moses of old, who led his people to the promised land. Surely such days as this are ample reward for all the heroic efforts he has exerted and commanded.
I have never heard excitement shown in more ways than on the program following Churchill's speech. Excited announcers, pealing bells, noisy crowds, were uncommon enough, but when I

heard the strange sounds of hundreds of boat whistles, I felt that the very ships themselves had come to life, and were bellowing in lusty exultation.

...Celebration in the barracks last night was convivial but orderly. Most of the fellows had gone to another barracks, leaving Swan and I alone. By and by a fellow brought over a quart of rye, presented by one of our officers, which he set beside the chair. Meanwhile, Howard and I carried on a long, interesting conversation, the sort which occurs only when two people are congenial, in the mood for talking, and unhindered by others.

About ten, two of the guys returned, one of them obviously "high" but the other reasonably sober. It turned out they were both bulging with beer, and the small drink of whiskey they drank in the barracks put them out like two lights. Five minutes after they lay down, they were both sound asleep.

Before Don dozed off, he admonished us not to wake him up "till noon—day after tomorrow!" I avoid drinking, partly from habit and partly from an aversion to destroying the inhibitions possessed by a sober person. I always know what I am doing and saying, and I'm aware how embarrassing and dangerous situations can become for people intoxicated.

Getting back to the party, things were quiet by 11:30, when we went to bed.

The next day, Swan and I decided to go on a picture-taking hike. We went over to a monument built to the passengers and crew of a boat who were massacred here in 1904, walking from there along the beach to the swimming place. Then we stopped for a very refreshing swim—I succeeded in turning 14 underwater somersaults in one breath—a record for me in that peculiar contest. We estimated that the walk back from the beach made a total of ten miles hiking, done on a sunshiny day at a temperature of 93 degrees.

One reason our talk last night was enjoyable was our thinking of people back home, namely you, and his girl. The longer we talked, the more images of our lives came into view. I remembered with deep satisfaction the long but luxurious hours we spent in the Dodge, kept apart by steaming summer weather, and sometimes snuggled close and comfortable beneath my heavy GI overcoat, emerging many hours later to find the windshield covered with thick frost, and the moon in a different part of the sky ...

May 10, 1945

At six we ate a delicious V-E supper, steak, etc. After dinner (supper), we saw the GI Technicolor film "Two Down and One to Go." It was OK, but not exceptional. You've probably read about the demobilization procedure already, how there are points being given for different qualifications: total service, foreign service, battle awards, and dependents. But the rub is that very few Air Force personnel will be released, and that any man may be declared essential and kept in regardless of the number of points he has. Frankly, dear, I am not in the least perturbed or disappointed since I never expected to get out till Japan was licked.

Mozelle, do you remember Warren Blackman? I received word that he was wounded in Europe, but there were no further details. You may recall that I sent home the picture of his brother, Howard, and Howard's wife.

There are two letters from you yet unanswered. One is rather gloomy. Somehow I never doubt that we will some day be together, and married, any more than I doubt that I will surely return.

As for the effect produced on me by such letters, it probably does no harm. In a way, people have lots of faith in each other to confide fears as well as the lighter things.

Do you remember the time you missed your engagement ring, and were worried to death for fear of losing it? I predict that your present fears will turn out to be as groundless as that one was.

May 11, 1945

Last night I wrote about the demobilization program. Point values have been announced for the Middle East Theater. To be eligible for consideration for release, a man must have at least 85 points, granted on the following basis:

WWII LETTERS TO MY GIRL BACK HOME
From Nigeria, Arabia and Turkey

A. For each month of service   1 point
B. For each month of overseas service 1 point
C. For each bronze star   5 points
D. For each child (up to three)   12 points

Since I have only 30 months service and 13 months overseas service, I have only 43 points. So it all boils down rather obviously to the fact that I'm not going home till Japan is beaten, or rather that I'll not be discharged till then. However, I may go home on rotation within a year, or the war may end.

...So I look well fed and happy! Glad you like the picture. As for being too satisfied here to desire returning, that is quite impossible. Life here at best is a poor excuse for being home with you.

...Time slowly passes, and tomorrow at 3:00 I go to work. That's quite all right with me. We will be working a shift of seven hours on and 60 off. Don't you feel sorry for me?

Life here seems unreal. We have so much time to think now that thinking becomes a burden. We're all a bunch of future-chasers pretending that the present doesn't really matter. Quip given in "WW 19," our weather publication: "Seldom have so many come so far to do so little."

Honey, do you remember the Razz Night (or play?) at Ball State when Gerhart Schwartz sat on the stage pretending to be a child, and said, "I'm waiting to be motivated." That's me—and us—waiting to be motivated ...

May 20, 1945

For over a month now, we have been able to buy unlimited quantities of coke, candy, toilet articles and beer. Today at noon there was a surprising innovation—we were served all the Coca-Cola we could drink—free.

The boys recovered quite soon from their party last night. I had guessed that all would be calm and still by 12:01 a.m., but things quieted down even sooner—before 11:30. The last thing I did

Allan Robert Humbert

before returning to the station was prop all the doors open, and clear a path straight through to the barracks.

Do you remember my mentioning the announcement of the partial demobilization system? A fellow in our barracks named Quinn had over 100 points, and received orders to return to the US. Just think, a month from now, he'll be a civilian, completely severed from the army, henceforth and forevermore! We've been calling him, "Mister," since the news came, and naturally he calls us "soldiers," complains about the way we waste his (the taxpayer's) money, and about the hardships of being a civilian these days.

Nobody begrudges him a discharge. He's been in nine years, and has been up where the fighting was in India. He represents, to a certain extent, the typical "old army" man. His rank is Master Sergeant, and a permanent rank at that.

...Eight and one half hours later...Winston Churchill's speech about blood and sweat, toil and tears would be appropriate this evening. I worked all afternoon and managed to scrape a chunk of skin from my left thumb, providing the required blood. The temperature inside the station this afternoon was 100 degrees, furnishing an abundance of the aforesaid sweat. We worked hard—hence the toil, and finally discovered mistakes along the line (higher echelon) which were enough to have produced tears. So I repeat...blood and sweat, toil and tears."

Practically all the personnel in Africa have been asked by the Army, "Do you prefer to remain in the Army after the defeat of Japan?" Notwithstanding films, propaganda, etc., all the men expressing this desire could be counted on your fingers, and not one weatherman was among them.

As for this business about military experience being valuable in civilian life, I doubt it, as Jimmy Durante would say, "very dubiously." For a small percentage of the forces, the statement is true, especially for commissioned personnel. But for most of us the army is a dull, degrading, monotonous routine, brightened by a few experiences, of course, but mostly experiences of no particular value.

When the score sheet is finally tallied, many losses must be recorded—absence from people we love—low rate of pay—loss of the most valuable years of our lives—getting out of touch with the world—becoming, in some cases, disillusioned, cynical and hard—acquiring habits that might not otherwise have developed.

All these things I've seen many people lose, and that where life is easy—no casualties, no disease, no rigorous living, and our troubles pale in contrast to those of troops in combat.

May 22, 1945

It's 5:00 p.m.—I'm busy working at the station—the temperature in here is 95—and there isn't a soul around. So I've a notion to look back over the last letters from you ...

Another letter—and the birthday one at that. Yes, I had a good time on the 7th; I'm glad some people celebrated, even though the two of us couldn't be together. I believe that since we used to enjoy ourselves in times gone by, despite the war, other people are perfectly justified in celebrating, whether the rest of the world is happy or not.

Hmm—do I notice a lipstick "V" on the back of your letter? Must be.

Incidentally, our outfit, the 19th Weather Squadron has been awarded the "Meritorious Service Unit Plaque," in case you ever heard of it. We are entitled to wear a cloth patch showing a golden wreath.

May 23, 1945

We just returned from the picture, "Going My Way." You've probably seen it already since it received an Academy Award. The final scenes were utterly superb, and the last one, best of all.

To refresh your memory, I'll explain the plot very briefly. Father O'Malley is sent to replace another old priest; he as the young father, gradually wins friends for the church, at the same time benefiting the community, helping delinquent children and adults. Events are proceeding happily until the church burns, destroying the work of 45 years, and nearly breaking the old man's

Allan Robert Humbert

heart. Moreover, the old priest's last chance to see his mother in Ireland seems ruined. But they take heart, begin a new church, and get the venerable father to preach a sermon there. He is already very happy to see the church built again, and preaches about the joys of giving. Then the choir begins singing an old Irish lullaby softly and beautifully, and the old priest's mother totters into the room. The final scene, when the priest realizes who she is, and goes over to embrace her, is something from heaven, the sort of scene you never forget. You would have thought the theater audience was leaving a church, from the unnatural and reverent quietness which prevailed.

May 25, 1945

As usual, the temperature is 100. However, a nice breeze makes it seem only about 90, so we are relatively comfortable. Also, the arrival of mail has raised our morale a few points.

Naturally we are still on Masirah, though the return address of my envelopes might lead you to think otherwise. The chances are that by the time lettters sent to APO 788 arrive in Africa, I'll be there.

May 26, 1945

...The PX gives away free cokes and beer now, Each man gets two cokes and one beer. I trade off my beer and thus get three cokes free. Good deal. The chow tonight was fine—steak, potatoes, green beans, and delicious apricot pie, as good as I hope you can make.

May 28, 1945

...Evidently another letterless interval is coming up, so if you don't hear from me for several days, you can remember, as usual, that I'm writing every day, and that it's only a question of time till all the letters reach you.

Today I sent you two more packages, one containing letters, and the other, books. Incidentally, you should eventually get a carton of

WWII LETTERS TO MY GIRL BACK HOME
From Nigeria, Arabia and Turkey

gum, since I sent one not long ago. I also sent one each to Rosemary and Helen, but am keeping it a secret until they receive it. We usually don't have gum beyond our needs. I don't see why they raised our allowance.

Last night we had blowing sand again, and this morning the stuff was all over our barracks—in our hair, in the beds, not to mention our eyes, ears, noses and mouths.

May 29, 1945

This has been another dusty day. All night long, the wind was 25 mph or more, carrying clouds of dust everywhere. The Rec Hall, where I am writing, is dustier than it would get in two weeks in the US. Just noticed: here's a fly, and even it is dusty!

Such weather as we're having now is supposed to be typical of the monsoon season. If it is, I'm doubly glad at the prospect of getting out of here. The next three months, June, July and August, are relatively hot ones over most of the area I'm likely to enter. However, there are a couple of factors in my favor, first, the fact that Masirah is considered to be an undesirable station, and second, that I've had over a year of duty in the tropics. But why think about it? I'll know soon enough.

In a week came the good news: my assignment at the air base near Ankara, Turkey. We flew first to Khartoum, en route to Ankara via Cairo.

Greetings from your loving fiancé who is writing you this afternoon from a bare room which was once a library, in the midst of a haboob. A haboob is a sort of thunderstorm without rain or thunder, the visibility restriction being dust. From a distance, the haboob looks just like a yellowish thundercloud, but it has no anvil top…Now the visibility is down to 1/8 mile.

…We weren't awakened at 3:00 a.m. after all. Instead, they got us up at 2:00 a.m. Result: We flew virtually 20 hours out of 24—entirely too many. Plane rides can be exasperating. First you roll out of bed at some insane hour, eat, wait about an hour, and climb

Allan Robert Humbert

into the steaming plane, piled high with cargo, and fully loaded with people. Then you have to adjust your parachute—a process about as cumbersome as a fat woman adjusting her corset—all on a hot day. Next you fasten your safety belt, and sit there perspiring while the plane warms up. If you're the worrying type (which I am not), you "sweat out" the takeoff. But whatever your type, your whole body is dripping wet before the confounded plane roars into the sky.

In a few minutes, you loosen the 'chute and unfasten the safety belt, enjoying temporary comfort. But the air at 10,000 feet is lots cooler than on the surface, and pretty soon you're shivering in your now cold and clammy clothes. So you put on your flight jacket (and I also put on the fur-lined gloves you gave me) and continue to sit—sit—sit until the plane is back on <u>terra firma</u> whereupon you immediately begin wishing you were at your final destination.

Chapter 18

ANKARA, TURKEY
JUNE TO SEPTEMBER 1945

Ankara, Turkey
June 27, 1945

This is just a note letting you know that I got here. Various little problems remain to be solved, but essentially the set-up is a wonderful one.

The objections are minor: taking off with no laundry other than the clothes I wore—and the possibility that a month will pass before my clothes arrive; getting three hours sleep last night, being almost broke—etc. Strictly minor matters, which will soon be cleared up.

We flew straight across the Mediterranean from Cairo to Ankara. The country between the sea and Ankara is rather mountainous, and traces of snow are to be found on the peaks. Further inland it becomes gently rolling, rather like Ohio.

It would take hours to mention all the transitions to be seen—a change of nearly 20 degrees latitude, 2500 feet altitude, going to a country where the climate is cool and invigorating, where the fields are fresh and reasonably green—not to mention trees, civilians, purple hills, different language, etc.—ad infinitum.

Later reading would reveal that modern Turkey is a republic with a small area in Europe, extending eastward into Asia Minor. It has about the same area as Texas. To the north it is bordered by the Black Sea and to the south by the Mediterranean which is connected to the Black Sea by a shipping passage extending through the Dardanelles,

Allan Robert Humbert

the Sea of Marmara and the Bosporus. To the east; Turkey is bordered by the USSR and Iran; to the south, Iraq and Syria.

Istanbul, famed Constantinople, is on the Bosporus. Ankara, the capital, is located about 225 miles east of Istanbul.

Ankara
June 28, 1945

It's 9:25 p.m.; I've just had a delicious steak supper…if only you were here …

I could write a poem about this place. Cheese as good as we have at home—splendid meals where you can only try to eat all they serve—perfectly fresh tomatoes—crisp green lettuce—cookies whose recipe I must certainly get—steak you can cut with a fork—fresh butter, eggs, and honey.

This place is nicer than Tel Aviv. The people like Americans, and we like the people, language barriers notwithstanding. Longer stay here may change some of these opinions, but I doubt it.

As yet, we're staying in hotels, and it's costing $5.00 to $6.00 of our $9.00 per diem allowance given us by the army in lieu of their furnishing us with rations and quarters. As time goes on, I believe I'll be able to cut my expenses down to $4.00 to $5.00 per day, saving about half the allowance made us.

Right now, we're staying in very nice quarters—pretty high priced, but nice. My room has hot and cold running water, and my bed, bedbugs. In fact, the whole city of Ankara wages a constant battle with the creatures. I opened the second round by putting DDT on the sheets. Last night, I thought something was biting me, but succeeded in convincing myself that it was all imaginary. Perhaps the bugs will win the third round, which is coming up in a few minutes.

I looked in vain for Turkish birthday cards—or any kind, for that matter. So…you won't receive any birthday card.

*WWII LETTERS TO MY GIRL BACK HOME
From Nigeria, Arabia and Turkey*

June 30, 1945

Tomorrow I have hopes of moving into a private house, simplifying getting to and from work, and reducing my expenses quite a lot. Incidentally, we were paid today. I drew $24.43, and Monday we'll get paid a bit more, namely, our per diem. According to reports, the first couple of weeks are the leanest financially, but once they're over, money simply rolls in.

There certainly are lots of Turkish soldiers in this town. If they left us alone, I wouldn't mind, but Turkish custom requires that each soldier salute everyone who outranks him, including members of friendly powers. So I walk down the street getting salutes right and left, which must all be returned. However, the only Turks I salute first are generals and those few officers who stare at me insistently. It certainly will be great to get out of the army, to leave this puerile rank consciousness, and this "monkey see—monkey do" business.

No sooner did I reach Ankara than a summons came for me to return to Cairo Headquarters concerning the possibility of further training in the states, which did not materialize.

Cairo
July 8, 1945

Greetings in the middle of a long and lazy summer afternoon at the Red Cross club in town. This morning I went to church, and surprisingly enough, enjoyed the sermon.

Plans continue for my trip to Ankara. After church, I visited the dispensary and obtained two ounces of ammunition for the next sortie with the Turkish bed bugs—that famous preparation DDT. My laundry and I are still separated—tomorrow will begin the second week of getting along in one set of clothes.

Here's hoping I stay in Turkey. As a matter of fact, the next three months are the critical ones in the region, because at many places the temperature reaches heights of over 115 degrees,

Allan Robert Humbert

especially at Persian Gulf stations. A safe general rule is that we go from a bad station to a good one, and vice versa, so my next stop after Ankara may quite likely be some spot such as Bahrein Island, the Persian Gulf, or Tindoof, out in the western desert. But being at Ankara for three months should practically guarantee that even if I do hit a bad station, it will be during the cooler season.

No doubt it's midsummer at home. Except during my furlough, summer is the only kind of weather I've experienced since April, 1943. However, should my stay in Turkey last into winter, it will be snowier even than home.

Cairo!
July 9, 1945

As usual, my name was scratched from the passenger list of the plane bound for Ankara. My travel priority must be slightly lower than that of a wog goat. So—I'll sweat it out here till Thursday, losing $4.00 every single day ...

It will certainly be a relief to get away from these Arab beggars and thieves—which constitute approximately 99.999999% of the Egyptian population. The first word an Egyptian learns is "baksheesh*" and he repeats it daily until the day he dies. The word "Yankee" is synonymous with "sucker," and they strengthen the concept in every deal with us.

*Webster defines it as a payment (as a tip or bribe) to expedite service.

In restrospect, I'm afraid the above paragraph is exaggerated and unfair to most of the Egyptians. Almsgiving was an accepted way of life in the Middle East, but not in Muncie, Indiana. It was easy to judge all Egyptians by the behavior of an infuriating few.

...My particular complaint is the fare charged by the ghari driver. Yesterday I paid 40 cents to travel 8 minutes—more than it would have cost in a taxi at home. That isn't a great deal of money; still I balk at the principle of paying such exorbitant rates. Do you

WWII LETTERS TO MY GIRL BACK HOME
From Nigeria, Arabia and Turkey

know of any place in Marion where a farmer gets $3.00 an hour for a team of horses and one little buggy? ...Oh, well ...

Cairo is a hot place this afternoon—meaning Payne Field, of course. Both this camp and Camp Huckstep were built when Rommel was still nearby, and the buildings were widely dispersed in case of bombing. However, none occurred, and the only inconvenience left is the long walk between buildings.

Some of the Italian prisoners around here paint excellent murals, pictures which have a great deal of depth and fine shading. The war is over for them, but they haven't any idea when they'll get to go home.

Earlier in Egypt we had stood in long outdoor chow lines and been served by the Italian prisoners of war. They would continue adding food to our tray until we said "abaste" which meant "enough." In their eagerness to glean some scrap of news from home, some of them searched the trash cans for newspapers.

Cairo
July 15, 1945

...Once again your fiancé celebrated Sunday in the traditional manner—by going to church and by loafing all afternoon. Now that I'm about to leave, the library has opened, making a tantalizing amount of reading material available after it's too late.

Strangely enough, I feel that my stay here is at an end, and that tomorrow I'll really get on my way. It's nice talking to the guys and remembering old times. One of the things which makes overseas duty not unpleasant is the circle of friends one accumulates. Probably most of us will feel a nostalgic loneliness once the outfit is broken up and we all go home.

Ankara
July 16, 1945

It's 11:00 p.m., and your weary future husband is quite ready to pile into bed, having been up since 4:30, flown over 1,000 miles,

Allan Robert Humbert

been in four countries, gone without breakfast and dinner, and moved.

Believe it or not, dear, my new room is as nice as the old one. I hope things don't change one iota till I get out of the army! I could go into rhapsodies about this lovely town and probably will. We ate steak for supper tonight.

July 17, 1945

Once again I am comfortably settled and in a new set-up even better than the first one here. The house is quite literally within a stone's throw of ATC headquarters, being just around the corner from there.

This room is on the second floor of a good-sized two story house. In it are a bed, writing table, two chairs, waste basket, reading lamp, mirror, and a large window. Along one whole side is a large wardrobe and cabinet combination furnishing more than enough space. To complete the picture, I should mention that the walls are cream colored and plain, except for a narrow maroon strip down 10 inches from the ceiling. Two doors away is a modern bathroom, very nicely tiled.

All this is mine for 125 lire per month, including breakfast and laundry. However, there is a 1½ lira charge for each pair of trousers laundered. Needless to say, I am highly pleased with the present arrangement.

And now—I'd better start answering your letters. Hmm—they smell much nicer than this Turkish cheese which I've just eaten. It has the odor of a damp cow.

...You and I heartily agree that it's foolish to work oneself to death.

The past seems very far away. Perhaps it is a good thing we can't see the future—I certainly never counted on serving three years in the army. But now, I'd cheerfully settle for that figure—or even four. Unfortunately, the years that we are losing are the best of our lives. Four years to a man of 50 mean little, but to us at least twice as much, first because this is the time we should be getting

WWII LETTERS TO MY GIRL BACK HOME
From Nigeria, Arabia and Turkey

established, and second because four years is a much higher percentage of our life up until now.

Letters go uncensored, except for spot censoring, i.e., the random censorship of a few letters. Supposedly it is a permanent practice, although only in inactive theaters such as this.

Probably all mothers worry about sons in service, although I imagine they worry less per person, the more children they have. At least my mother keeps her concern about me to herself, which is fine with me.

Supper at Madame Oktar's, wife of a Turkish official, where several of us eat, isn't served till 8:00 p.m., so we do our letter writing beforehand.

July 20, 1945

We were very busy on shift this afternoon. There is an enormous map on which we have to plot weather data from hundreds and hundreds of stations, all of them new to me. An old Turk helped me out by finding about half the stations. I can see that getting all the data written on the map is going to be my chief difficulty.

At supper we had a chicken—a whole roast chicken apiece. They were OK, I suppose, but I don't like chicken in that form. My imagination keeps reminding me of what each part of the bird's anatomy did, and I have feelings of uneasiness. Give me an honest slice of beefsteak, or cheese, or at least disassemble the chicken to make the meal a little less barbarous. Mrs. Oktar, seeing my reluctance, generously cooked another chunk of beef for me. Very nice of her! (No extra charge, either).

After supper Swan and I went up to his room (which is at Oktars') to talk. We were soon invited down, however, to be company of Mr. and Mrs. Oktar, along with Cpl Gutschick. We conversed for an hour, mostly about language differences. Mr. Oktar speaks Turkish, Mrs. Oktar, Turkish, some English, and French, Swan, English and German, and I, English and a wee bit of Turkish. Madam Oktar, by the way, was in Germany in 1939, and saw Hitler at a large public gathering. She started to take his

Allan Robert Humbert

picture and was saved from arrest only by showing that her nationality was Turkish. The Oktars are very sympathetic toward the USA.

Before we left, she had an orphan adopted by them sing a Turkish peasant song. It sounded funny, but I kept my face straight. The little boy is 10 years old, and reminds you of no one so much as "Johnny" who says, "Call for Philip Morris."

Do you realize, dear, I've been in the desert so long that I automatically brush off my feet when climbing into bed? There was always sand on the floors, even in our barracks at Masirah. Of course our tents in Egypt had no floors at all, making such precautions even more necessary.

Now there's nothing to do tonight except wind up my alarm clock, put out the light and go to bed...Do you still have those blue pajamas you were wearing that morning you let me back into the house, ages and ages ago when I was stranded and we retired to separate rooms?

July 22, 1945

Another long day is over—this one began about 4:30, even though I got up at 6:00. Bedbugs made a meal of my left arm and shoulder. The sheets had been changed and I'd forgotten to put DDT on them.

Fellow observer Jerry Davis is working on shift with me. Last night he didn't go to bed, so he was barely conscious this morning. Nevertheless, he did the most work, putting data on the big map. At 7:00 when we left for work at the airport, it was cold—52. Next time I'll wear a coat.

Every month there is a big all-American picnic here, attended primarily by the ATC, Communications and Weather detachments, along with civilian personnel of the Office of War Information, Embassy, and Military Attaché. We were at a spot named "Garden of the Gods" principally because of its trees and scenery, about 25 miles from town. As the picnic didn't get under way till 12:30, there were still plenty of refreshments left when the two communications men and I arrived at 1:30. We traveled in a flying jeep that *averaged somewhat over 45 miles per hour on roads designed for 25, passing goats, donkeys, and wagons laden with logs and hay. A civilian vehicle would never have negotiated the road which branched off the main one and led to the picnic spot, since there were no less than three deep mudholes, and a ford. But the "Mighty Willys Jeep" made it with ease.*

Refreshments consisted of ham sandwiches, boiled eggs, tomatoes, pickles, watermelons, apricots, and inevitably, beer. I casually took a bottle, downed a few sips, and slipped behind the bushes where I poured the stuff on the ground. The watermelon was good and I ate my fill of it. Then, there being no entertainment other than a couple of crap games, I crawled off into a truck, and lay down for an hour. Pretty soon a bunch of people began singing, so I joined them, singing till we were hoarse. Then it was time to go back to Ankara.

Among the animals there, was a baby jackass—black, long legged, skittish and all ears. One of the fellows picked him up and said he weighed less than 50 pounds. Really, dear, that little critter was "cute as a bug's ear."

We returned via truck—hungry again. I bought some bread and cookies and went home, but upon asking for tea (which, by the way is called "shy" over most of the world, including here) the servant brought me, also, a lot of bread and jelly. So I was, and am, very full. Then a couple minutes after I began writing you in walked a guy wanting me to have dinner with him—which I couldn't, of course.

Jerry has promised to get Howard Swan and I passes to hear the broadcast of the Turkish Symphony Orchestra Thursday. He is quite a character, and definitely a big time operator, getting away with impossible liberties with everyone, insulting them and making them like it. He lives in Ohio—probably you'll meet him some day. Jerry is partly Irish and has a vocabulary of profanity, witticisms and funny remarks that would be a hit on the radio—a natural born clown. Still, he's nobody's fool, and has a good job with Goodrich to return to after the war. No doubt you'll like him. Everybody does.

Allan Robert Humbert

July 25, 1945

...*Yesterday while going to work I got lost. I made a wrong turn, and presently found myself outside the Ankara city limits in very unfamiliar territory. I stopped and tried to talk to a policeman, but not knowing the Turkish for "airport" received nothing but puzzled looks. Then I turned around and drove back to the place where I should have turned in the first place, and again set out for the airport. I went straight ahead where I should have turned right, out to the edge of town again in a different direction, once more into unfamiliar territory, and, I believe, some kind of military zone. So there was nothing to do but make a second 180-degree turn and try asking <u>another</u> policeman—all the while feeling as silly as if I'd forgotten my own name. Turkish policemen don't speak English any more than Marion cops speak Turkish, and once again language was an impasse. Then an inspiration hit me. I drew a picture of an airplane, repeated Turkish for "where?," and received enthusiastic gesticulations. Not only that, but three seedy-looking individuals offered to ride and show me the way.*

At this point, I was prepared to seek help from anyone, not excepting the devil himself, so they climbed in, and off we went. There are two airports around here, and my jittery senses refused to recognize even familiar territory. Then I noticed a Turkish cadet of some sort, so I picked him up to talk to the Turks, not knowing what they expected of me. He wasn't quite sober, but he spoke English, bless his heart! and assured me that this really was the right road. Moreover, he said the Turks only wanted to ride to a small village on the way. When we got there, I stopped and let them off, whereupon they smiled, thanked me, shook hands, saluted and said goodbye. So about 10 till 8:00, I actually did reach the airport, though first binding my cadet to tell nobody what had happened. There sat the men I was supposed to relieve, dejected, impatient and not a little bitter. With masterful understatement, I assured them that it took a long time to find the jeep. Now—if only I can keep all this quiet! Not only that—I shall henceforth know the road to the airport perfectly.

WWII LETTERS TO MY GIRL BACK HOME
From Nigeria, Arabia and Turkey

Once I arrived, I did what little work there was to be done. About 1:30, along came Davis, with a girl, Zelma. He showed her how to take a balloon run; then we all went back to Ankara at 3:00, Sgt Anderson driving, I in the middle, and Zelma on the outside. It was an uncomfortable ride, but warmer than sitting in the back of the jeep would have been. I had to keep both elbows against the backs of the seats to keep from falling over backward.

August 5, 1945

Today I had more fun than six small boys at a picnic. The entire detachment went out in the country eight miles to a picturesque little valley surrounded by 500-ft. hills. We saw lots of beautiful scenery, and Howard and I did some mountain climbing. We were up on one about a thousand feet high, where the view was something to remember (4,000 feet above sea level.)

Guess who I dreamed about last night? You. I was driving downtown in Marion in the new Dodge when I noticed you standing by a window. You got in the car, and I promptly kissed you. Just then, you slipped and fell on the floor, making it seem that I'd put you out with one kiss—though even in the dream I realized that really you had tripped.

August 9, 1945

The war news certainly is good! Russia declaring war on Japan this morning, at the very time, according to a news report, when the Japs were trying to negotiate a peace through Russia. And the new atomic bomb is a beautifully terrible weapon; the only reports I've heard were from people who have heard the same accounts themselves as I have; but one of the bombs is said to have killed every living thing within two square miles, and to have shot a column of smoke up 40,000 feet.

Well, they asked for it. When I think of all that nation is costing us in lives, money, and time, I feel they aren't worth it, and whatever measures may shorten the war are completely justified, however savage these measures seem. You and I have been *extremely fortunate, but even we have paid by being separated and unable to marry for two years, not to mention my own loss of income totaling at least $3,000, plus the inevitable national debt to be repaid in years to come, plus three years spent doing the wrong kind of work, etc.*

The feeling of missing you is strongest during the hours of early morning when I'm on duty. The only other person in the whole big building at that time is one communications man, and he is in a different room. We turn on radios, and hear either primitive Turkish music, or the nostalgic strains of familiar tunes coming from BBC—music that makes us feel very lonely indeed. Of all the hours of the day, 4:00 a.m. is the one when I should be snuggling close beside you somewhere in Indiana, sound asleep rather than making weather observations in Turkey.

Soon, however, there is more work to be done, and I'm too busy to think. The sky slowly lightens, daylight arrives, and presently, my relief. Then comes the jeep-drive back to Ankara, dodging insane Turkish drivers and pedestrians. Once the jeep is parked, I walk around, go get a couple of cookies for breakfast, trudge upstairs, and go to bed, falling asleep in 15 minutes not to awaken till noon, when I inevitably possess an undeserved hang-over.

August 10, 1945

In response to your letters, "How do I transact business not knowing Turkish?" Well, I have a GI book containing common expressions plus a basic English book giving Turkish equivalents. My wants are mostly simple, and largely taken care of by pointing, gestures, and a very little Turkish.

My landlady herself is pleasant enough, but a mercenary old witch who would charge for the air we breathe if it were possible. Just now she has seen fit to charge us a lire (55 cents) for each bath we take. However, she generously consents to allowing us to use all the cold water we like, free! If the room weren't so satisfactory, I would raise a squawk, but as things are I accept these little injustices for the time being, along with bedbugs, mosquitoes, and poor service, simply because the room is precisely what I want.

WWII LETTERS TO MY GIRL BACK HOME
From Nigeria, Arabia and Turkey

"Granny," who stays here, seems all right, a feathery old ghost who looks ready to fall apart the first time the wind blows. The servant girl, Lela, is the best of the lot. Her pretty smile helps make up for the fact that she is broad-beamed, illiterate, and barefoot.

Mme. Oktar, the person who cooks our suppers at another house, is much different—nice, cultured, clever, witty, and a whole flock of other things. Wish I could figure a way to do her favors ...

So, in general, I like it here, though I remain always ready to exchange the whole thing for you and home the instant it's possible.

P.S. We had a very slight earthquake in Ankara yesterday. I barely felt my chair shift a little.

August 11, 1945

Shortly after writing you, I heard loud shouts and singing coming from the ATC building around the corner, and concluded the war news must be excellent. I could wait a few days until the situation has clarified, but there are so many questions and conjectures that I'll write them down now, if only to partially relieve my own excitement.

One thing is definite: Japan has made some kind of peace offer, and it must be nearly unconditional—<u>but</u> (1) China has said the terms are unacceptable, (2) the <u>whole</u> Japanese cabinet has agreed on the proposals, including, apparently, the naval and war departments, suggesting that some provision must have been made for the safety of their own necks, a safety likely to be at variance with the desires of many allies, (3) Russia hasn't said anything yet, and (4) It isn't official.

...however, excitement was keen all over Ankara last night. There were big Turkish flags on all the public buildings brought out at 5:00 p.m. when the news came out—some with lights flashing on and off. Mr. Oktar brought out various "bottled beverages" and we celebrated. After eating, Howard and I took nearly a three or four mile walk and still had energy to burn. Later we talked in my room. Even now, I'm too restless to do anything constructive, because a

dozen questions keep popping into my mind, bumping into one another and crowding out all mundane activities.

First, of course is "When do we go home?" That hinges on any number of wholly unpredictable factors. How long will weather personnel be needed here? Answer: As long as planes fly. Question: How long will planes fly? Answer: As long as there is an organization large enough to support air traffic. But what about civilian air lines? Can't they begin taking over at once? It occurs to me that GI equipment—the best in the world—is standard, and that in many cases, we can simply be replaced by civilians, with airlines or native governments buying our equipment—the Turks already own the stuff we use.

What about rotation? <u>There</u> is a significant angle. In the ATC, and supposedly in the Weather Wing (the next higher echelon above our squadron), there is an 18 months rotation policy. Formerly we were in the USAFIME (United States Armed Forces in the Middle East).

Later its name was changed to AMET, but now we are under the weather wing itself, theoretically subject to their policy. With 16 months service ...I confidently expect to be home by January 1, 1946 ...

It is my hunch that stations will soon be deactivated, first, the outlying ones, and there will be a drastic curtailment of station personnel, with elimination of much work, extension of hours among remaining members, and the lowering of station levels, i.e. making class "A" stations of Ankara into "B," "C," "D," or "E," types, without forecasters and generally reduced service. I certainly hope so.

I think demobilization is going to be a fast and furious affair. Now if <u>I</u> were doing it, the entire job of shipping stuff home would be left to civilian workers after the war. Politics will get us home sooner, too. The instant one party even hints that we be kept overseas, the other will clamor to get us back.

WWII LETTERS TO MY GIRL BACK HOME
From Nigeria, Arabia and Turkey

August 12, 1945

A lira, getting onto the subect of your letter, is $0.554, and my room and breakfast cost 125 lire per month—$69.25. Money here loses no value when exchanged, other than a fraction or so of a cent on the transaction.

In Cairo and Ankara we received practically our first ham since coming overseas. I am very fond of meat cured the way my folks fix it, with Morton's Smoked Salt. The gravy made with it is delicious, too.

It will be nice to get back to the scrupulous cleanliness of American cooking. Here, the only cleanliness is in show windows, and unappetizing items such as hairs, rocks and flies turn up intermittently in even the very best food. Americans are ingrained with the idea of cleanliness, but such attitudes are followed in Turkey (and the rest of the Middle East) only when forced upon the people. Oktars, though, are as clean as we ourselves.

Ankara, Turkey
August 15, 1945

Shortly after two a.m. this morning, we heard that the Swiss government had relayed a reply to the American government, and by 2:30 the big news broke—perhaps the greatest news in the history of mankind. We all felt as excited as if we'd won the war alone. Our information came from a Yank station, but no news of home celebration. So we listened to BBC and heard how the news hit Piccadilly.

The Japanese surrender is too big to be fully comprehended at first glance. Every now and then we think of some new ramification which changes the former situation. Guess it will take several days to get used to it.

I am writing from a new location, having moved into an apartment maintained by six other fellows at a cost far below what I'm paying now. Formerly, it cost at least 125 lire for a room, and 75 for supper, with no dinner. Here, by sharing expenses, guys live just as well as I did, and for a total of less than 175 lire. We can use the money saved—in a few months.

...I am so excited right now that straight thinking is quite impossible. So best I sign off for the evening, hoping to be a bit more coherent in the next letter ...

August 16, 1945

Another day, another dollar—and a reasonably lively and interesting day it was, too. It began about 5:30 when I started thinking about rolling out of bed, a thought which had to be translated into action by six. Then I went to work at 7:00, stayed till 2:00, when I stopped downtown briefly. By 2:15, I ate "chop"— stuffed tomatoes, chicken, and french fries, finishing with tea and cookies.

After dinner (another advantage here—I get three square meals per day), I went to Swan's and chafed impatiently while he wrote a letter to Dorothy. At last he finished, leaving us barely half an hour to work on our project—a booklet aimed to stimulate the creation of ideas by picture and word associations. By 5:00 p.m., we left to get haircuts. My barber behaved as if he were chiseling a marble statue for the ages, snipping a lock here and another there, pausing always to scrutinize his labor, and taking twice as long as the pokiest barber I ever had in the USA. I finally had to leave the place and do my own shaving.

In the evening, the American ambassador threw a big party, with several hundred guests, strictly an elite affair. All the Americans in Ankara, including even a general.

While at the party, a captain walked over, tapped another sergeant and I on the shoulder, and told us that a very drunken ATC man was just getting ready to tell the general off. So we hastened in, casually began using Dale Carnegie and adolescent psychology on him, and in a few minutes had him safely out of their company.

The ambassador's libations were plentiful and potent. Although I neglected to mention it to my fiancée, by the time I left the party, my head felt like a 16-inch gun turret which I could still turn from side to side, but only slowly.

We came home in a very crowded truck, having time to sing only "You are My Sunshine" and "Down by the Old Mill Stream." Being up front, I led.

August 18, 1945

It seems that I have blundered into another cushy job, this time as station clerk. I'll work directly under the Major, from 9:00 till 12:00, and 1:00 till 5:00 six days per week. Sleeping will thereby be simplified, and I shall have a certain degree of freedom, needing to work only when my boss is around and/or there is something to be done.

August 21, 1945

This has been a busy day and a long one. I can't seem to beat the boss to work—by 8:45 he is busy at work. We get along fine, though there is much to do. My principal job is typing.
During spare time this afternoon, I promoted a three-day pass to Istanbul for Swan and myself and suggested that he become records clerk as he was at Masirah, since the other one is leaving. Swan is good at that sort of thing—Masirah Island stood at the very top of stations the last month it was operated, and was in the upper fourth at all times.

August 22, 1945

Another hot day in Turkey—and entirely too busy a one at that. Once a month the station clerk must pull CQ— (Charge of Quarters)—going on duty at 5:30 in the evening and remaining there until 8:30 the next morning. There isn't supposed to be much to do except answer the telephone. Earlier, though, I was much too busy, struggling along not knowing Turkish, or where people were, or their telephone numbers, or names—in short, an ignorant figurehead stuck in the wrong job. The ATC delights in shoving its work off on Weather, and there is no one to prevent them.

Life seems to me to be one eternal problem of getting one routine mastered only to be stuck with another new and different. This change in jobs means much less time to myself, and a general loss of contact with the guys. Still, I have no choice in the matter. At this stage of the game, one boring job is as good as another. I'm not the only unfortunate or the only complainer. The major said today he's had only 15 days leave in four years!

Today I read the story of Mustapha Kemal's life (Attaturk). The book ended while Attaturk was still alive, and it certainly gave a full account of him as a soldier and patriot. Aside from his undisputed patriotism, he had the morals and methods of a gangster and behaved very despotically.

Istanbul, Turkey
August 27, 1945

This day was short and sweet. Up until 2:50 p.m., we were busy getting ready. I got a haircut, etc. The ride from Ankara to the Istanbul airport was quite uneventful—just a little bumpy but not enough to bother the passengers at all. Our C-47 landed some 17-18 miles from Istanbul, bounced a couple of times due to a crosswind. Aside from that, the trip was less exciting than one by an ordinary auto.

Howard and I are staying at the Hotel Tokatlian in a double room with bath, and we had a delicious steak supper a short while ago. That brings our activities up to 9:30, the time I began this letter.

We haven't made any plans for tomorrow, but we'll undoubtedly have a busy enough day, because the town is very interesting indeed. As always, I wish you were here—<u>right</u> here. Seeing the crowds of well-dressed people reminded me of you and Indianapolis.

WWII LETTERS TO MY GIRL BACK HOME
From Nigeria, Arabia and Turkey

Istanbul
August 28, 1945

Howard and I spent the whole morning exploring the street which runs past our hotel here in Istanbul. It seems to be the main one. There are stores of all descriptions, with lower prices than those of Ankara, though much higher than at home. All the merchandise was in the modern part of town, which is much like most large cities, except for narrow streets and comparatively few autos.

After noon—we skipped dinner, having eaten a late breakfast—we asked a fellow how to reach the famous bazaar section, and were offered a little tour by him. The tour began by streetcar, ending near the University of Istanbul, where we got off.

The bazaars were most interesting, consisting of a labyrinth of tunnels or roofed-over streets, whose sides were lined with every kind of store—furniture, silk, china, watches—all pretty nice stuff. I bought a bonnet for David, my new baby brother, and nothing else.

Our path took us in and out of the bazaars a few times, and one stop was in an antique shop. There were exquisitely beautiful Turkish rugs, all costing upwards of $100. The proprietor had only three small ones, one of which I purchased for us, paying $15 for it. Ours is 1½ by 3½ feet, with a Turkish design of red trimmed in buff and blue. It is quite new looking, but deceptively so, its actual age being about 60 years. The only evidence of age is a silver sheen caused by long usage.

Later, we visited the large mosque near the bazaar, while services were going on. This is the month of Ramadan—Mohammedan Christmas. About the only other items of note were trees approximately 400 years old. The mosque we visited was built in 1480.

So, honey, you can see we're having a good time on what I hope will be my very last pass in the army ...

Allan Robert Humbert

Istanbul
August 29, 1945

Today we were off on a tour of the city by 1:00, under the expert guidance of M. Baha Yurtbay, who spoke excellent English and was willing to take only the two of us.

For the sake of simplicity, Mr. Yurtbay began in the oldest part of the city. We saw first the Kora church, so named because it was once outside the city walls, built 1280-1320. It contained samples of Byzantine mosaics decorating the ceilings of two corridors, one representing the life of Christ, and the inner one, the life of Mary. Also, there was an ancient passage leading to the church of St. Sophia, six miles away, blocked by the earthquake of 1894.

Nearby was the Roman wall of Theodosius, a formidable obstacle which held till 1453 when it was treacherously and forcibly opened by the Turks.

Next we visited the beautiful mosque known as the Mirimah, a marvelously ornamented structure with intricately interwoven porcelain designs too complicated to believe. The dome was over 120 feet high.

Another mosque followed, that of Suleiman I the Magnificent. It was big but rather moldy-looking inside, and not very pretty.

The Church of St. Sophia was next. It was unbelievably huge, and quite new-looking, despite its origin of 532 to 537 AD. At present it is a museum, and we were alone there until ready to leave. You can imagine how we felt, standing in a building that was over 900 years old before Columbus set out for America! Not only that; parts of the building were older still, being taken from the Temple of Ephesus; I hope you and I can go there some time.

Last of the mosques was the Blue Mosque, one lined with porcelain not unlike blue china. The whole roof is supported by four massive columns, each 30 feet thick. We even got to see a Moslem church service—the bowing, salaaming and praying. Quite an experience.

Finally, we saw the Hippodrome, once the center of the Ottoman Empire, but later plundered. We looked at obelisks standing since the

6th century AD. They were impressive, to be sure, but the amazing thing to me was a spiral column which looked just like an old, short, spiral post made of bronze. However, it was constructed by the Greeks in 400 BC from the arms of the defeated Persians!

To us, having a comparatively brief national history, that of Istanbul—ancient Constantinople—seemed overwhelming. Once called Byzantium till renamed in 330 AD by the emperor Constantine, the city stood as the capital of the Roman empire till it finally fell to the Turks in 1453.

Later, as people in the region grew stronger, the Ottoman Empire became the most powerful in Europe, and ruler of the Mediterranean. Constantinople became a city renowned in art, literature and culture. Growing fears of Ottoman expansion led various nations such as Poland, Spain and Persia to oppose the Turks and the empire was gradually lost. In World War I, Turkey sided with Germany and was defeated, together with the other Central Powers.

Mustapha Kemal Pasha became the first president of the Turkish republic in 1923 and proceeded to modernize the country. The office of sultan was abolished. A civil code replaced the Koran as law. Men were forbidden to wear the fez, symbol of the Mohammedan religion; the language was changed from the Arabic alphabet to the Roman one and industrialization was vigorously pursued. He was succeeded by President Inonu who was still in office during my stay in Turkey.

Throughout the Middle East, Islam is the predominant religion. To us, some of their worship activities seemed bizarre, but to the Mohammedan they were (and are) dead serious. To orthodox believers, we were infidels, whereas true Moslems everywhere were brothers.

Islam, established by the Arabian prophet Mohammed who died in Medina in 623 AD, is unlike Christianity in that it prevails not only in spiritual areas but in secular ones as well. To the true Moslem, his religion is a way of life that not only dictates beliefs and worship, but also economic, social and cultural activities. This attitude causes some Islamic religious leaders to be at odds with those who favor modernization, although no one can fault such basic Islamic tenets as almsgiving, monotheism and brotherhood.

Allan Robert Humbert

Ramadan, 9th month of the Mohammedan calendar, is supposed to be the month in which Mohammed received his divine revelation. It is a month of solemn observance by the faithful. Between daylight and dusk, the true believer abstains from all eating, drinking and smoking, devoting himself to prayer and reading the Koran. The fast ends at nightfall, a time of feasting and joyous celebration which lasts until morning when solemn observance is again the rule.

As soldiers in the Middle East, we were warned to be especially careful not to offend Mohammedans during their holy days. For instance, one never offers a Moslem anything using the left hand, nor does one offer him pork. Some of our guys made a great hit with Turks by learning a few Turkish religious phrases and repeating them to people they met. When Ken Gutschick conferred with a Turk, he would often say, "Il hum d'Allah! which means "Praise be to God!" which was sure to bring a smile and a nod of agreement from the Moslem to whom he spoke.

Istanbul
August 30, 1945

Today's plans didn't go so well. We intended to visit the Black Sea, but decided to check on our plane reservations first. It turned out that we weren't even scheduled on the plane, and we had to fool around signing up in the afternoon when we should have been getting on the boat. Therefore, we made the best of a bad situation and visited the bazaars again.

I bought two articles, the first being a pretty doily about 10" in diameter, and the second a brilliantly-colored silk scarf which you can either use as a babushka or as a tablecloth as you choose. For myself, I purchased two ancient Greek coins which I'll send to you later for safekeeping. One is of Antioch the 7th, dating back to 280 BC, and the other was issued by Alexander the Great around 350 BC. Both are in fine condition, and I have a bill of sale for them, as well as for the rug I bought earlier. The coins are pure silver dating back to pre-Roman days and were most reasonable, costing about $4.00 apiece. Howard also bought a pair of them.

WWII LETTERS TO MY GIRL BACK HOME
From Nigeria, Arabia and Turkey

So you see, dear, our house will contain some pretty old objects, coins that were 2,000 years old before either of us were born. Having seen the old mosques in Istanbul, I thought it particularly fitting to take away something older even than those.

This was Turkish Independence Day. People here are prouder of their liberator, Mustapha Kemal, than we are of George Washington—but then of course their liberation took place only 20 years ago.

Ankara, Turkey
August 31, 1945

I returned to Ankara to find a shocking bit of news—the death of Howard Blackman, "Blackie" as we called him, in a fighter plane crash. Somehow I felt all along that he wouldn't survive the war, and that all the plans he and Helen were making would be in vain. Only a little while ago she wrote that they were expecting another baby, a child which will never see its father.

It is not just the person who dies who is to be mourned, but also the ones he leaves behind. Poor Helen! She waited for Blackie all through high school, and college, cherishing their every moment together. Yet on the very day she last wrote me, they had only a few brief weeks left. What will she do now?

I recalled the time before his enlistment when he and I had visited the neglected graveyard near Kendallville and had seen the broken tombstone of the Union soldier who had died in the Civil War and our thoughts at the time.

If I were qualified, I should write an epitaph, not so much for him alone, as for the thousands like him, the real heroes of the war whom the GI Bill of Rights can never benefit, the greatest of all losers in this game which no one can win.

I hope you won't feel sorry for me, for I will be somewhat reconciled by the time you get this letter. I'm not even divulging the news to the fellows at the house, since it will do no good to spread the gloom that much further. Read the Gettysburg Address again. It says so eloquently what I mean.

Having devoted these sombre lines to the subject of death, mention of love seems incongruous, but it should serve to remind us that love is to be enjoyed every hour as though it were the last, since no one can tell when that may be ...

September 2, 1945

Might as well start a letter to you while waiting to attend church...Church is over. We had communion, and with it some kind of potent wine which left people feeling warm inside. Good way to encourage church attendance.

Before going to bed last night, I wrapped the silk scarf and doily for you. Just what you can do with that brilliantly colored scarf puzzles me; it's pretty loud.

This is certainly a beautiful day. I wish you and I were spending it together somewhere. Before long, fall will arrive, the prettiest season of all. It seems like years since I've really had the opportunity to pay attention to the season.

We keep hearing all sorts of exciting rumors, and every now and then a big list of surplus personnel comes out.

September 3, 1945

Another busy day has ended. The chief items were the afternoon mail call and a formation at 5:30 at which we were congratulated by the General for winning the war. Also, news announced that points for demobilization are reduced to 80, and age to 35. The present pile of letters from you totals eleven, so best I skip some of the news and begin answering them ...

WWII LETTERS TO MY GIRL BACK HOME
From Nigeria, Arabia and Turkey

Wish I were home now, and the last few days. Dad wrote that with gas rationing now ended, 100 cars went past our house in 30 minutes the other night. I'd like to climb into the Dodge with you tonight and drive right to the Pacific Ocean.

September 4, 1945

Another day, another dollar, or to be technical, another $10 or so. The Major is leaving, being replaced by Captain Richardson. All day we have been taking inventory, which is required whenever there is a change of weather officers.

You and I seem to agree that America is the greatest country of all—I've thought so for a long time, and the more I see of this beat-up world, the greater I think America is.

My sympathies are more with the enlisted men than with the officers. Anybody who thinks people are going to accept this distinction in rank after the war will be surprised ...

Today I am on KP again; the cook we have now leaves after preparing supper, and makes it necessary that two guys clean up the dishes. Our KPs range from corporals up to and including a first lieutenant.

September 5, 1945

Our new officer, Capt Richardson, is much too eager—it is apparent that I'm going to be plenty busy during these remaining months. Our only other officer, Lt O'Bert, mixes very well with us and isn't all GI.

September 6, 1945

Today I sent home a check for $150, representing the net profit from per diem up until now. As near as I can figure, I have about $938 at home, more or less.

Mail was very scarce this afternoon—my share of three letters was a generous one. Sgt A. F. Cohen, my advertising course instructor, wrote quite a nice letter, even suggesting that I look him up after the war *(For me, dear, the war isn't over till I am a civilian).* Cohen has 74 points and is looking forward to getting out soon.

Days are rather alike here in Ankara. I get up at 7:45, cook breakfast, go to work at nine, leave at 11:45, eat and return at 1:30, work till 5:00 and go home. The next six hours are occupied by writing you, eating and reading a little. By eleven, I'm either in bed or on the way. You'd be surprised how time flies.

...the whole topic of conversation in the army these days is, "When do I go home?" We are impatient and eager to be on the way, to get home to our wives, sweethearts and children. House construction, loans, education, and planning are our chief interests.

September 7, 1945

This day was practically wasted. There is a code book which must be revised every month, and I spent the whole day copying in little notes which will never be looked at again—an example of the infantile sort of work which is keeping us in the army a long time.

According to rumor, I am going to Istanbul next Thursday to copy some maps—even though there are already suitable ones on hand at the station. The fact is that the army is not at all anxious to let people out; those in authority know that the loss of each soldier reduces their power by a certain amount.

Last night I had the pleasant dream of being in a large store simply crammed with fine jewelry and books. I saw a pin I thought you'd like and asked the price. It was 19.50, so I asked 19.50 what—rials, rupees, lire...The clerk had never heard of anything but dollars, and the dream ended while I still attempted to explain to her what I meant.

September 8, 1945

I'm currently enjoying the luxury of solitude while serving as CQ. So far, there hasn't been much activity, and if nothing is doing by eleven o'clock, I shall go to bed here, as is the custom.

WWII LETTERS TO MY GIRL BACK HOME
From Nigeria, Arabia and Turkey

Webster defines CQ (charge of quarters) as "an enlisted man designated to handle administrative matters in his unit, especially after duty hours." Frequently the job entailed being responsible for problems having nothing to do with your normal activity—not a very efficient arrangement.

Last night was quite cold. We shall soon have to start buying coal for the house. Only a month ago, when I had this job, the night was very hot, and the bugs were as thick as could be, but now I"m wearing a flight jacket and all the doors are closed.

September 10, 1945

I've just come off CQ, and am just sleepy enough to be useless for work, though not quite sleepy enough to be able to sleep.
After I wrote you last night, events followed a pattern characteristic of this, the most disorganized base in my experience. About eleven o'clock, a fellow brought his pal over in a jeep with instructions from the flight surgeon that the guy be given some sulfaguanadine tablets from the first aid room. On looking for the key, I found it was missing. The building was practically without lights, so I continued the search by candle, there being no flashlight either. No good—the key could not be found. There was no record of the medic's name—nor address—and the flight surgeon neither knew his name nor address, despite the fact that there is only one medic! By and by, the captain (surgeon) came around, and looked for the key. Of course he couldn't find it, so he dramatically smashed the lock to the door with three resounding kicks, and dispensed pills among the splinters. I went to bed.
About 2:00 a.m., Swan woke me up calling me for transportation, for a distance requiring less than a five-minute walk. I again went to bed. At 4:00 a.m., some captain called for transportation, so I rolled out again, and once more retired. Another awakening at 7:00 completely finished my sleep, so I got up. By 8:30, the whole job was done—thank the Lord.
This time next week I shall be in Istanbul for another brief loafing spell—not my idea, but reasonably agreeable to me. My

chief objection is spending your and my money while you are being so frugal. However, the actual expense isn't likely to be over $15 more than it would cost to live in Ankara. Maybe I can do some Christmas shopping.

Since breakfast, I have had six cups of tea. It is delicious on these chilly mornings. Mecheff, our Chinese cook, is back, and as usual is eager to serve us at any and all times of the day. His gratitude for our payment of his hospital bill is worth more than any mere money it cost.

Mecheff was like a father to us. We understood that he had been in the merchant marine in a vessel that had been torpedoed and that he bore a ten-inch scar across his abdomen. His beaming smile and gentle manners made him a favorite. Speaking in broken English, he would refer to us as "Missa Gootch," never by our first name. He enjoyed conferring with the group regarding a proposed menu, discussing gravely the merits of dishes such as "Russ salade." It was said that food sellers believed he was cook for the Chinese embassy, and that Mecheff did nothing to dispel their impression. On days when he prepared boiled cabbage, you could smell it the instant you opened the door.

On Sunday evening, his "day off," he always baked a cake for us which was my job to cut. Later, when I managed the household accounts, each month we would offer to increase his salary, and each month he would refuse to accept the increase.

In addition to a Chinese cook, we had a Russian washerwoman. Since there were no washtubs, she would just put the clothes into the bathtub, add soap and water, remove her shoes, draw up her skirt, climb into the tub and trudge up and down, manipulating the clothes with her bare feet until they were clean.

September 11, 1945

Bit by bit, news about demobilization keeps coming in—the latest is that people in the Indiana area will be discharged at Camp Atterbury, Indiana. As you know, a long time will pass before I get to go home, but will you please send me telephone numbers of your home, the place where you'll stay, and the school at LaFontaine? I just happened to realize that I've forgotten all the telephone numbers, and it would be awkward not knowing yours, since I'll want to call and meet you before anyone else.

Now I might as well comment on your latest letters. The reason I never told you about the floating dry dock at Lagos was that the information wasn't supposed to be divulged. As far as packages I've sent, the only one you are missing is the nylon stockings. <u>Time</u> magazine predicts that nylons will be common by Christmas, so I'm not buying any more for gifts ...

Nearly time for supper, dear. Mecheff is cooking wonderfully these days—best food I ever had in my life.

September 13, 1945

It's evening and I'm still in Ankara. Tomorrow, maybe we'll get going again. First we went to the airport at 2:00, where we were told that the plane wouldn't arrive until 5:00, then we went back to Ankara. At 5:00 we drove out again, only to learn that the plane had stopped at Lydda for the night without notifying us. The captain wasn't very happy about the turn of affairs, but it suits me fine, because it will mean one less night's hotel bill to pay.

Evidently Congress is really putting the screws down on the Army and Navy demobilization program. I expected as much to happen, regardless of how sincere was the Army's effort to let us out quickly. Today appeared also a bit of news which seemed highly significant to me. The Queen Mary and her sister ship will cease carrying troops December 31. I'll bet a dime that means the great majority of troops will be out of here by the 31st, including, let's hope, yours truly.

Istanbul
September 14, 1945

Greetings from Istanbul again. I am staying at the Hotel Tokatlian, high up in a little dingy little room crowded with *furniture and dimly lit by two ancient bulbs. However, the place costs only 5 lire per night, so it's good enough for me.*

We flew here through cloudiness, traveling first between a low cloud deck at 5,000 ft. and an upper overcast at around 8,000. Halfway here, though, the pilot climbed to a spot just above the overcast, and we flew over an unbroken sea of dazzling silver clouds, so bright they made our eyes uncomfortable even within the plane. Toward the last, the pilot spotted a hole in them, and soon we were out of the too-bright world above and back down where the same sky appeared leaden and dull.

8:00 p.m., and I have just eaten supper (ham and eggs, with hot chocolate), and seen a Frankenstein picture which was not particularly heavy.

Our job at Istanbul was to hand-copy an intricately detailed map showing the location of all weather stations. It took many hours to complete but we were left with a couple of days for sightseeing. En route to the airport, we drove under a Roman aqueduct which still carried water, although built in the 4th century.

Istanbul
September 16, 1945

Another kaleidoscopic day leaves me in bewilderment. As you know, I decided a long time ago to go up the Bosporus and view the Black Sea. After dinner, three of us went to the boat station, bought tickets, and climbed into the same boat with a large crowd of people. It had hardly begun moving before we realized it was the wrong boat. However, a pleasant diversion arose in the form of a pretty Italian girl named Amelia, who had made the wrong connections and boarded our boat instead of the one which was to take her to a party for British sailors. Karlinsky got acquainted with her, so all four of us headed for the party, where we tried to get her to go with us, while she tried to get us to go with her. Finally, when we came in sight of the party grounds, she met the girl with whom she'd intended to go, and we said goodbye, returning via tram and boat to the bridge where we had boarded in the first place.

WWII LETTERS TO MY GIRL BACK HOME
From Nigeria, Arabia and Turkey

By this time the other guys' desire for making the trip to the Black Sea had cooled off considerably, especially since none of us spoke enough Turkish to find the pier or say what we wanted. I managed to find a Turk who offered to take us to the boats, which offer we accepted. Furthermore, he wanted to be our guide, but the fellows objected to the 5 lire he asked for the work. So I asked how much he would charge for me only, and was told only three lire. Thus began the trip of the old man (60) and I.

The cruise was very enjoyable, and Mr. Birum's assistance made things much clearer. We sailed 12 miles close along the European side, noticing many fine buildings, resort hotels and outdoor cafeterias. Near the end of the trip (going) I could see the entrance to the Black Sea, between two slopes, one surmounted by an old Byzantine fortress.

Returning, we sat inside, facing a group of people who talked constantly. There were two married couples, both Greek, and America was the continual topic of conversation—where had I been?—was I in the fighting?—etc.—etc.—etc.

When that detachment got off, another quickly formed—did I have any sisters?—ha-ha—<u>six</u>?—I must have a young mother and a strong father! But they were all good natured, and sincerely friendly—very nice people.

Istanbul
September 17, 1945

This time tomorrow I'll be back in Ankara, having left Istanbul. Today I visited the bazaars again, but bought next to nothing.

I trust you folks at home are clamoring for Congress to get us out of the Army. The hotter you make things for the big shots, the sooner we'll be out. True, we won't be in forever, but something tells me that the high ranking officers of the Army have gotten so used to telling people what to do that they've forgotten their responsibility to the people. Remind them of it!

Allan Robert Humbert

Ankara
September 19, 1945

At this table sit two very lucky guys from our shipment, Staff Sgt Don Sibel and Sgt Joe Graczkowski, both having 60 points and children. Today they received orders to Payne Field, Cairo, from where they will go to the States, according to all reports.

Also, Pan American Airways will move in October 1st. What effect this will have on us is not stated, but it's a step in the right direction…For the time being, I shall have to do Sibel's work in addition to my own, so I'll be pretty busy.

September 21, 1945

The end of another busy day. Last night Captain Richardson came over to the house announcing that he didn't feel like making the trip to Adana, and that Lt O'Bert will have to go. It has since developed that Richardson has malaria. Result: I'm running the office alone.

Graczkowski and Sibel left today; rumors say the boat leaves October 1st, so by the time you get this letter, they'll be on the way home.

September 22, 1945

The first day of autumn ends while we sit comfortably around the well-lighted table in our apartment listening to the radio and writing letters.

There is more to do at the office than I can manage, with additional work piling up every hour. To tell the truth, I did very little even considering the time I had. At Captain Richardson's request, I took the afternoon off. Tomorrow being Sunday, I'll have that free, too, for a picnic. So when Monday comes, I'll be swamped. However, it doesn't matter.

Richardson didn't show up all morning, so I went to his house to see that he'd not become worse. No answer came when I buzzed his room, so I returned an hour later. This time he heard me, and asked that some food be sent up. Therefore I bought him some soup and a couple of rolls.

After dinner, five of us got the idea of visiting the dam near Ankara. It is a beautiful spot, carefully landscaped and kept up, lying in a valley between two rather large and rocky hills. Attaturk had the reservoir made in the shape of the Sea of Marmara, to impress people with Turkey.

The "Hit Parade" is on now—"Sentimental Journey" is the number two tune, while the number one spot is occupied by "Dream"—a song with the lazy restful sort of melody you and I like.

I'll bet that more dreaming has gone on during the past four years than in any four since the Civil War, because so many, many couples have been separated so long with only such intangible things as dreams to bind them together. But in the long run, perhaps dreams are strongest of all, since they exist without being affected by time and material changes.

September 23, 1945

Sunday evening again, and we're seated around the table listening to the radio and writing letters. The American station at Foggia, Italy, is coming in quite clearly.

US personnel in Turkey attended a picnic lasting all day; it differed only slightly from the last one we attended, being held in the same valley. Refreshments consisted of hot dogs, boiled eggs, and the usual accompaniments.

It was necessary to make a trip to the airport for the purpose of getting some chemicals out of the warehouse there, so we drove there from town, Swan, Farber, and myself. I was at the wheel for a change, and enjoyed it. Having a few guys in a jeep is fun, buzzing over the countryside in beautiful weather, with nothing to do and all day to do it in. You would have liked the road and the ride, up and down hills which required second gear, besides several places where the jeep could have gone tumbling off the road. Naturally it didn't.

Being sleepy after eating, I lay down on a blanket beside a ball game, too lazy even to watch it. Instead, I had Swan describe what was happening while I lay relaxed in perfect repose.

Allan Robert Humbert

Soft strains of "Clair de Lune" are floating through the air just now. Despite the months which must pass before we can be together, I feel that the whole show is over, and that only a small percentage of time continues to separate us. All around us is an attitude of expectancy, expectancy of virtually anything. Back on Masirah, we were settled down to a long period of waiting, but here we expect to leave at any time, perhaps within the next month. Actually, we make plans as if we were to be here for the winter, but psychologically we don't accept it.

September 29, 1945

This day has been livelier than most. Despite the fact that Weather is greatly reduced in personnel, the ATC is still trying to stick me with CQ, and succeeding admirably. Today I took the trouble to show my orders to Captain Bartley, the adjutant, orders which clearly state that we are here for weather duty only. Bartley became very angry and told me we'd either "pull CQ" or move out into the street." You being a lady, I can't very well describe him to you in adequate terms.

Since our own CO (Comanding Officer), Captain Richardson, is in Cairo, we don't dare do anything (Lt O'Bert and myself). But if Capt Richardson returns Monday and is willing to back me up, we'll write Headquarters and put the finish to this business once and for all. Whether Bartley knows it or not, he is violating an Army Regulation signed by five-star General Marshall. Perhaps we shouldn't make an issue of it, but since they won't listen to reason, the higher the matter goes, the better I'll like it.

We just finished some delicious cocoa—another one of my favorite drinks, especially during cool weather. As usual, it's eleven o'clock, and I'm still not in bed. The house is much like a fraternity, one of the pleasantest and most congenial set-ups I've ever seen. It isn't merely good food and comfort, but something more, the comradeship of a very fine bunch of guys who would do nearly anything for one another, where rank means nothing and cheerfulness is the keynote.

WWII LETTERS TO MY GIRL BACK HOME
From Nigeria, Arabia and Turkey

In short, sweetheart, this is the final pleasant lap of the journey which will end when you and I are together. These days, I can actually feel the time slipping away, and any temporary impatience is quickly overcome by the certain knowledge that the current of life is bringing us together as inevitably as it once parted us.

September 30, 1945

Your fiancé celebrated this beautiful day by working right up till 5:30. ATC is behaving with characteristic and versatile inefficiency. By grapevine I discovered I was scheduled to work all day instead of all night. Then they all took off for a picnic, leaving me two vehicles, a car known as a "carry-all" and the colonel's big shiny Buick. So when the carry-all failed to work, I dispatched the Buick, much to the pleasant surprise of the GIs who expected to ride the usual clumsy trucks. The colonel may not be happy about the situation, but if the jerks insist on shoving unwanted responsibility into my lap, I'll discharge it as I see fit. I would have dispatched a tank or a battleship with equal abandon.

…Now the day is over. We've eaten supper, done the dishes and played fan-tan, while listening to the radio. Earlier, we played a set of Strauss waltzes, all favorites of everyone, including, of course, yourself.

Strangely enough, a few moments after we begin playing cards, my hands become ice cold and remain that way as long as I am losing. But upon winning, they become warmer, and when we cease playing, they return to normal.

Speaking of cold, Lt O'Bert says that after a fellow is married, he simply becomes a big radiator for his wife, who, on chilly nights, warms her icy feet against her husband. Still, I doubt whether your feet get cold—mine don't. I enjoy being curled up in the blankets, having them tucked tightly all around. The final pleasant touch is achieved by curling up my toes and sleeping with them furled.

In a few months, you and I will be working on such attractive problems as the most comfortable way to enjoy our nocturnal leisure. Of course we must insure our health by getting plenty of sleep, so best we go to bed early and rise late…

Chapter 19

ANKARA, TURKEY AS WWII WINDS DOWN

Ankara
October 1, 1945

Outside a storm is brewing and it seems much colder.

We received lots of news today. Captain Richardson returned from Cairo with information that the station was to begin 12-hour operation immediately, reduced from the 24-hour operation, and that 50% of our personnel were going to ship out this month. The fellows who are leaving naturally feel very glad, and we are tickled that they can go. Soon it will be my turn.

Our personal budget is doing all right lately. Tomorrow I shall send home $125. That, plus the usual $50 will swell my cash to over $1100. Per diem is very nice!

October 3, 1945

I almost got caught up with the work today, Captain Richardson and I get along as well as he gets along with anyone. He is definitely the "eager" type, but essentially he is all right and has the interests of the fellows at heart. Since Staff Sgt Sibel left, I've been NCOIC (Non-commissioned officer in charge), and have thereby acquired the additional nicknames of "boss" and "adjutant."

WWII LETTERS TO MY GIRL BACK HOME
From Nigeria, Arabia and Turkey

October 4, 1945

This day began with a telephone call before I had even shaved, saying that two guys, Hefley and Wheat, were to ship out immediately. Since then, I have dashed around madly all day long—taking the Communications jeep to notify the boys one hour, then supervising a Turk who helped me move the office into our new building, next a dash off to dinner, followed by a brief pause. Once at work there was a new work schedule to type, climatology percentages to be computed, records to be checked, and mail to be sorted.

October 9, 1945

As usual, I've been having a pretty good time, and working a little, spending the morning in town conducting some business and getting a haircut. The business was delivering a message from Grenko to his girl in an antique shop and checking on my camera and film. By and by, I'll send some photos from Masirah. The negatives don't look very promising, but the pictures should at least be recognizable.

Tomorrow morning, we get the coal—45 lire per ton—about $20. Actually, the stuff is coke, so the price isn't quite as high as it sounds. Coal and coke are rationed in Turkey, and we've had no end of trouble obtaining permission to buy it. Hoping to be gone before all of it is used, we've ordered only one ton.

You know, dear, receiving my civilian glasses again makes me feel like a civilian all over. Reconversion from situations such as Ankara will be easy, because we're nearly on civilian status already. At noon we were joking about the hard life here. We were seated at a dining table in a warm room, eating Mecheff's superb Chinese cooking, while listening to Strauss waltzes on the phonograph—that while drawing $9.00 a day. A cushy set-up if there ever was one.

A long time ago, I decided to take life as it comes, whether good or bad. This is a lot easier to take than the sands of Arabia. Still, I don't feel guilty about it.

Allan Robert Humbert

October 12, 1945

Tomorrow, I'll try to mail you a package of books to be kept. Later, when orders come to leave here, I'll send home nearly all my personal possessions—tools, letters—everything which isn't government property.

October 13, 1945

This has been a lively day, and the evening promises to be livelier still, since most of us are going out around eight-thirty or nine. Frankly, I'm not terribly anxious to go, but since it is to celebrate O'Bert's going home Thursday, I feel obligated to.
A rather pleasing surprise was my opportunity to see the quarterly sheets which are used by Headquarters to compare and rate personnel at each station. There is an individual sheet for each person covering most job performance topics. The pleasant surprise was seeing myself rated above everyone else in the station. By and by I'll surreptitiously make a copy of the evaluation and send it home for the purpose of raising my morale when I'm discouraged. Hmm—maybe the reason I was given the high rating was that they knew I'd quit working if they didn't...Seriously, I feel a sense of accomplishment, a rare feeling these days. Also, as a side issue, I was recommended for promotion to staff sergeant. Of course it won't do any good, but I enjoy knowing I'd be promoted if people had their way.
So often I hover on the verge of telling somebody off, feeling that all my work is useless and unappreciated by someone, only to have that same person do me a favor.

October 14, 1945

It's four o'clock on this drowsy Sunday afternoon; the radio is playing, "How Sweet You Are" and I have plenty of time to write you a nice long letter.
...You should have been with us last night. We seven inhabitants of 99 Bayindar Sokak went out to give a farewell party

for Lt O'Bert. We filed into Serge's, a rather crowded but nice place and sat in a circle around a small table, eating potato chips and pistachio nuts. The guys of course ordered various drinks—I settled for a mild sherry wine—good, too. Somehow the conversation got around to champagne, so we decided to order some—the first that four of us had ever tasted.

The bottle was brought out in true Hollywood fashion, wrapped in a towel, with a small bucket of ice to cool it. Champagne is very good. It tastes a lot like 7-Up, being made from white grapes, and is clear and sparkling. Altogether, we had three glasses each. The only ones who noticed any after-effects were the fellows who had preceded it with vodka and scotch.

I felt a little sad when the circle broke up, realizing that we would never again reassemble together. The army is like that—time and time again you make friendships, only to be separated in a few months, apparently for good.

Shall we have champagne for our wedding? Or maybe just later. The stuff is rather expensive over here. We might at least think about it.

A pleasant thought occurred to me before falling asleep last night. Six months ago, I was on Masirah with practically no expectation of going home. But six months from now, I'll be home, and we'll be married, living happily ever after ...

October 15, 1945

More nice letters came today—the sort which make me tingle all over and long more than ever to be home.

I have just taken over another duty, namely that of keeping the accounts for our house expenditures, collecting money, paying bills, etc. I'll be responsible for somewhere over $500 per month. But who knows—it might be good experience. Anyway, the harder I work, the faster time flies, and the faster it goes, the sooner I'll be home to you.

Tomorrow Lt O'Bert and Cpl Tice will leave, O'Bert for home, and Tice for Bahrein Island.

Allan Robert Humbert

October 16, 1945

O'Bert and Tice are in Cairo by now, and the house has that gloomy, deserted atmosphere which always appears when someone we like leaves. Captain Richardson wrote a personal note to Major Warner asking that Tice be left here, but to no avail. Being the oldest man from the time spent at Ankara, he was the logical fellow to send out.

O'Bert was certainly anxious to go. He is one of those guys for whom you would do anything—maybe you and I will meet him some day. However, I don't believe there will be an "alumni association" for the simple reason that some fellows not in our group have done things which they don't want their wives and families to find out.

October 17, 1945

Greetings again from Ankara where your sneezing correspondent grows lonelier every minute. This has been an uneventful but busy day.

Evidently Richardson is still happy about my doing the work, because he again gave me a "Superior" rating and recommended me for Staff. As you know, nobody has ever yet made staff sgt in the 19th Weather region; still, it's gratifying to know that if anybody were to be promoted, I should.

We could use a few more guys here in our house. Unless a large house has enough people to fill it, it seems empty and forlorn. You'd be surprised to learn how many supposedly solitude-loving people have moved into apartments with others merely to have someone to talk to.

In a few minutes it will be time for another of Mecheff's famous meals. I now weigh, complete with shoes, flight jacket, etc., 140 pounds. So I must have gained 5-10 pounds here. But everyone does so at this place—, food, food, and more food, with Mecheff forever insisting we take more. You should see him smile when you ask him for seconds. I'll really hate to leave him when orders arrive, because he is so lovable a character ...

WWII LETTERS TO MY GIRL BACK HOME
From Nigeria, Arabia and Turkey

October 18, 1945

Now that the colonel has a new Buick (the one of CQ fame), the Chevrolet sedan is available for use by weather and communication departments. So I got to drive it out to the field today—the first time I've driven a sedan since the very morning I kissed you goodbye, February 14, 1943. I didn't hit anything. The Chevrolet is just like the one Lee's folks have.

At present we are listening to a silly but funny radio program after playing fan-tan. Sometimes I enjoy that game—have you ever played it? If not, you can learn it in five minutes.

Sometimes on a Sunday afternoon, the guys would invite girls from the US Foreign Service to play cards, usually fan-tan, for a nickel a point. After one of them had ended the day with a loss of $4.15, she remarked, "I wonder who would ever believe that I spent all afternoon with a group of American soldiers and left with less money than I had when I came!"

October 20, 1945

Last night came the exciting news that Ankara is to be cut to a staff of five observers, which definitely means that all the "old" men and either Cpl Gutschick or myself can expect to leave shortly. Actually, I don't especially care. Even if I were to be sent to the worst station in the region, it wouldn't be for over a month. The show is just about ready to wind up ...

Newly installed in our room is a cute little stove which is throwing out enough heat to chase me out into the main part of the house.

Beginning Monday, Swan is coming into the office to help me catch up. There isn't enough work for two men, but he'll keep me company.

Where shall I spend Christmas? The possibilities are exciting and widely different. Here? Cairo? Bahrein Island? On the ocean? In Muncie? Good arguments could be advanced for each and every possibility—Which would you guess?

Allan Robert Humbert

October 21, 1945

This was census day in Turkey. Everyone, Americans included, had to remain at home until mid-afternoon under threat of a 25 lire fine. The censors rolled us out of bed at 8:15 a.m.

The boys bought the cutest little Angora or Persian kitten—yellow hair, blue eyes, fuzzy and fat. We fed it veal cutlets and condensed milk from the table, much to its delight. After supper, I deloused it with bug powder and brushed its fur while it purred in contentment.

All cats have certain characteristics in common. Earlier, in passing through Cairo, I met a sergeant who had brought a pet young leopard to camp there. He bought it in Khartoum, and transported it in his gym bag on the plane. Its paws were as big as my hand, and it enjoyed being petted. When the leopard purred, its throat vibrated like that of any cat, only at a much slower rate. A low-IQ dog tried to pick a fight with it, and escaped with no more than a bad mauling because the boys pulled off the leopard in time.

October 26, 1945

Another lively day has passed, complete with one earthquake. This afternoon at 3:40, Lt Goodman, Capt Richardson, Swan and I were all upstairs in the corner of the ATC office. Goodman was sitting on my table; suddenly, I thought he'd begun shaking it back and forth. He thought I was responsible, but Richardson, leaning against the wall, realized that only an earthquake could move him, because he was there alone. We continued working as usual.

S/Sgt Schroeder is visiting us from Istanbul, and he told us of their misfortunes. The Turks steal everything they can lay hands on, especially flashlights, pencils, and other portable items. To stop thefts once and for all, the boys bought a watch dog. Did that stop them? No; the Turks kept right on stealing, and finally stole the dog!

WWII LETTERS TO MY GIRL BACK HOME
From Nigeria, Arabia and Turkey

October 27, 1945

Did I tell you the latest rumors from Headquarters? Don Tice, who departed recently for Bahrein Island, stopped into HQ to see how many points we have, and when we might head for home. According to them, I have 51 points and can expect orders about December 1st.

Not many minutes ago, there was nice music playing. Needless to say, I enjoy it, but it isn't good for my morale, because a perfectly innocent tune may be responsible for the beginning of a sad mood. A couple of nights ago, two of the fellows had girls up for dinner and to play bridge. When Swan and I went to our room, we could hear Andre Kostelanetz playing "Beautiful Ohio," a song with all kinds of romantic memories. Lying on my bed, with two shots in my arm, thousands of miles from you, I felt downright sorry for myself despite per diem and our life of ease. Yet only the minute before I had been cheerful. Just when I was deep in gloom, came the insistent ring of the telephone, and I was forced out of my lethargy to listen to Istanbul weather reports. By then the mood was gone.

You should be at our table during some of our noon and evening discussions. Of course, if ladies were present, the topics of conversation would be altered somewhat—indeed, it's marvelous to behold how discreet and proper our conversation becomes when guests are present. Among other things, at supper, we talked about weddings and wedding nights. There was a story of a couple who, after the reception, retired to their bedroom. What happened next? He sat on one side of the bed; she sat far over on the other side, and they both bawled as if their hearts would break. Something for H. Allen Smith.

October 30, 1945

Tomorrow being Halloween, Swan and I decided to make a jack-o-lantern. We couldn't find any pumpkins, so we bought a watermelon for 50 kurus, and made a pumpkin-face of that. Mecheff was quite pleased, since jack-o-lanterns are an old custom in China, the same as in the States.

Allan Robert Humbert

Halloween, 1945

Another day, another gob of money. I distributed it as follows: one war bond: $18.75, one check sent to my account at home: $100.00; money sent to my sister Vera, to do my Christmas shopping: $50.00. Of course there was the usual automatic $50.00 deduction from my pay for the allotment. Therefore my (or our) cash at home is about $1263, exclusive of bonds and insurance. Naturally I'm curious about your section of the treasury, too.

Now I'd better look at your letters...Binoculars—they're dirt cheap here. I'd be lucky to get $15 for the ones I brought over from the US. All the refugee stuff ended up here, since optical goods are easy to ship. Also, Germany poured lots of stuff into Turkey, trying to persuade them to join their side. While on that subject, I should pass on a rumor about the snazzy new Turkish buses. It is said they were made in Germany for the occupation of Russia, but after Stalingrad the Germans sold them to the Turks.

November 1, 1945

Today Swan received orders making him a sergeant, after more than three years in the army. In fact, he was a corporal before I ever got in. Another fellow, Cpl Force, also made it. I'm glad to see them make the grade. Soon we'll all be out, but it's good to have the rank on your record. Noted somewhere: It's been said that there are three kinds of veterans: the dead, the disabled, and the lucky.

Life around here is very hectic lately. We run to and fro—or I do, at any rate—trying to be six places at once. This evening, for instance, I had six different phone calls in fifteen minutes—all of them after my working day is over.

November 3, 1945

Four lucky people received orders to go home today. They were Cpls Thomas and Richard, and Sgts McGreen and Swan. Swan left the states on March 20th, 1943 less than a month before I did.

There are rumors that 51-point boys (including me) will be on the boat early in December.

I hope our boat hits terrific storms all the way across the Atlantic, so long as it doesn't break in two... Ships are very crowded on these return trips, and we probably won't travel as comfortably as we did on the inbound trip.

By this time, we were getting into specifics concerning civilian life. Topics such as family, transportation, and life after the army became more frequent.

I still can't help wondering whether Dad would be interested in selling the Dodge ...

I think our best bet is to give him an idea of what sort of car we want, and allow him to shop around until the proper bargain appears.

Now that going home is so close, it's fun to allow yourself the luxury of imagining what things are going to be like. No doubt my sisters will be changed from what I knew earlier, though in many cases, they may have simply have moved up a notch, so Rosemary, who is younger than Barbara, may well seem more as I remembered Barbara. I expect my folks to appear definitely older, although at the same time hoping that they won't. Curiously enough, I don't think your folks will have changed much, because they are both at an age when several years make little or no difference.

Did I tell you that I now weigh 140 pounds? If my entire life had been under the influence of Mecheff's cooking, I'd probably weigh a hundred pounds more than that. Nobody ever eats enough to please him, and between the combined attraction of his persuasion and his delicious food, overeating is the rule rather than the exception.

Swan and I disagree on the subject of how our girls will seem to us when we return. He has the theory that we will both feel awkward and out of touch with each other, and that it will be necessary to get to know one another all over again. I think, however, that we'll get reacquainted in very short time because we've never been far apart so far as sentiment and affection go. Not only that; we are engaged and would have been married long ago but for the war.

November 4, 1945

Sunday passed much like any other day of the week—I worked all day long. Rich and I had some reports which just had to go out, so we worked at the office all morning.

We paid the rent today—or rather I paid it for us. Cost: 265 lire; cost for Mecheff: 122.52 lire, and for a telephone bill yesterday, 60 lire. Total amount spent today and yesterday: over $248.

Can you imagine my paying one of our allies to keep another of our allies out of her country? Turkey is our ally and so is Russia. Yet Turkey is afraid of Russia, and maintains a relatively large army. To support the army, there are high taxes—we paid 40% tax on the telephone. QED.

Swan and I were on KP tonight—a minor job but one that takes time. Speaking of jobs, Weather is continuing to escape CQ, thanks to the determination of Richardson.

November 5, 1945

Today we had to take tests for Turkish drivers licenses. Seven of us rode in the jeep, only one person drove, but all of us will receive licenses. The test, plus having photos for the licenses taken, took all morning.

I received lots of mail today—eight letters from you, besides others. Here's hoping mail is finally coming through to you again. You are right about my not making any effort to surprise you. The day I receive orders, I'll write, and as soon as I get to Cairo on the way back, I'll wire from there, giving all possible news. You may even receive the news before our boat leaves Cairo.

It appears that I got my sight-seeing done just in the nick of time. Palestine has been closed for some time as a furlough center, leaving only Cairo and Alexandria available. Due to the recent trouble there, both these places have been placed off limits, too.

WWII LETTERS TO MY GIRL BACK HOME
From Nigeria, Arabia and Turkey

The news these days is too disturbing to think about—peace conferences breaking down—American troops taking part in Chinese civil war—strikes everywhere—and Shirley Temple getting divorced. Grr!

The thing to do is go back to Indiana and let the rest of the world fight it out. At least we can get some order in our own lives, if not in those of others.

November 6, 1945

Greetings from your overworked, overfed, overeager and overpaid fiancé. As usual, we have worked like mad all day long. Surprisingly enough, Capt Richardson did a little work. I sure pity the guy who gets stuck with my job, for as the British say, he will have "ad it."

Some of my dad's letters mention nothing but work. Speaking of dads, I frequently quote your father. When we are deeply engrossed making a meteorological report and are dealing with some hair-splitting technicality, I recall what he used to say when working on a tax report: "This isn't hard; it's just a little confusing."

November 8, 1945

Honey, you and I don't see eye to eye on the subject of an automobile. Despite all the inconveniences of having a car, we can hardly do without one. The particular make we get is not too important, but I don't see how we can do without a car of some sort.

Having driven since the age of 16, I never realized what doing without one is like until entering the army. There is something degrading about having to stand in a crowd of people waiting for a bus. Life becomes a waste of time, and you develop an inferiority complex having to scurry about meeting the bus company's schedules.

But with a car, it's different. You go where you wish to go, with the passengers you choose, and at your own pace. You are king of your section of the road, and lord of all you survey.

If we rely on Dad's judgment, I'm sure we can count on economical transportation, whatever we pay. So let's see what he has to say ...

The weather here this evening must be like a November night back home—cool, crisp, with the smell of leaves in the air. It's like many of those nights a couple of years ago when we sat in snug contentment in a world of our own. Time was flying then—flying to separate us for a long period. It's flying now, too, but every tick of the clock brings us nearer the moment when we'll be together for keeps.

The letters you wrote from Ohio are arriving now—I hope you returned to find a stack of mail from me. Mail should be reaching you now in record time, because some of it flies all the way here from New York, arriving in four days.

Let's not cease writing to one another till we actually meet again. First of all, there is always the possibility, however remote, that I may not go home even after I receive orders and everything seems definite. I want to cross the ocean knowing that your thoughts are being recorded for reading in future days. Needless to say, I'll write every day until I see you again.

November 9, 1945

Swan is scheduled to leave for home from a boat which is to pull out of Port Said, Egypt, on November 27.

Our little yellow tom cat (as inspection verified it to be) is very dirty, and since it won't wash the coal dust off itself, I shall give it a bath Sunday morning. I anticipate quite a struggle, and plan therefore to take a bath myself at the same time, since I'll get wet, anyhow. The kitten promises to become an immense cat—I can see it lengthen every day.

Last night we saw "Meet Me in St. Louis," which you've seen previously. It was the best family picture I've seen in ages.

WWII LETTERS TO MY GIRL BACK HOME
From Nigeria, Arabia and Turkey

November 14, 1945

Greetings from my lonely room where I sit hoarse and forlorn. Four of the guys left today, two from this house. House morale drops a few points whenever anyone leaves. In a few days it rises, but there is always that gloomy interlude. Nor does knowing that ATC received orders to send home anyone having either 50 points or 15 months overseas, both of which I have, make me any merrier...

November 15, 1945

About the only news of interest was the acquisition of two new fellows, Sgts Stoia and Haynes. Haynes will be my roommate. Now back to your letters...You mentioned staying alone at night. About a month ago, I stayed home while everyone else went to the show. By and by the doorbell rang, and I was confronted by the apparition known as the albino. She is a horrible looking creature having white hair, very pale skin, and pink eyes. She ekes out her income as a cook somewhere by obtaining special-purpose dates for a half dozen Turkish members of women's oldest profession. Naturally I slammed the door in her face, since we'd had trouble before this. Sitting there alone, I couldn't help realizing that she is quite unbalanced, and that sooner or later may snap with dangerous consequences to whomever is around. Then what did Richardson do, but enter from outside and creep quietly upstairs? Just as I stood beside the door, it popped open, startling me so much that I jumped perceptibly. I'm not usually frightened, but there's something about people who are a little off that scares me.
    Here's a little story of army rank. The division commanding officer, a colonel, visited Istanbul yesterday, and planned to fly on to Athens and Naples this morning. He called for a forecast, which Richardson begrudgingly supplied, although it meant working till 8:00 p.m. last night and rolling out of bed at 5:00 a.m. today; so before he, the colonel, retired, he left orders for an Istanbul captain to pick him up at a certain time. For one reason or another, the captain was 40 minutes late—characteristically late, so the boys

Allan Robert Humbert

said. All the way from the city to the airfield, the colonel said nothing. But just as he stepped into his plane, he remarked, "Captain, you've got just one hour to catch the returning plane. You're all washed up in Turkey." So ...the captain leaves Turkey, with all his books in disorder. Moral: Don't keep the Colonels Waiting.

November 18, 1945

Another chilly day at the office has ended, with not much done. Due to transportation difficulties, my working day lasted from 10:00 to 11:00 and 3:00 to 5:00. The temperature last night fell to 2.7 degrees F.

Poor Rich has had it. Headquarters has sought and obtained permission to hold all officers for 60 days beyond the date they are eligible for discharge. This means he won't get started for home till March 1st instead of the first of January.

Darling, you amuse me. The mere idea that your landlord could say anything likely to embarrass me is downright funny. Three years of army life have about completed my education in that respect, and I just don't become embarrassed. I imagine that his frequent lapses into rather plain language regarding sex are due to his wife's unfortunate physical condition, and I heartily sympathize with him. Has she ever consulted a specialist?

November 23, 1945

...Your picture sets right in front of me, looking young and sweet. You are wearing that charming expression of naive innocence which is so appealing. Seeing your photo, I feel as if you were reading my mind and silently watching all I do. Perhaps the feeling of silence is the lifelikeness of the portrait. You appear quite able to speak.

At long last some woolen clothes arrived at ATC. I am now comfortably attired in warm winter clothing for the first time since my furlough to Palestine. Also, I have a new pair of GI shoes, the first ones in 20 months.

WWII LETTERS TO MY GIRL BACK HOME
From Nigeria, Arabia and Turkey

Thanksgiving, 1945

This has been a perfect holiday. Mecheff put out the best meal ever—turkey, dressing, carrots and peas, french fried potatoes, spinach, ham, Russian salad, pickles, two kinds of wine, and two big cakes. We had a couple of guests over, Selma Young and Eleanor Bergman. After eating, we played bridge and fan-tan, the party lasting till twelve.

You and I probably have more to be thankful for than at any such occasion previously. The end of the war and the immediate prospect of my return makes this Thanksgiving especially appropriate.

November 24, 1945

Our kitty isn't at all bright. On Thanksgiving day, I was holding him on my shoulder, while standing beside the stove in our room. All at once, the little cat sprang onto the stove, landing on all four feet. In a split second there was an agonizing yowl, as the kitten bounced to the floor below, and began trying to lick all of its feet at once. For a few seconds it cried a little, but the maid put olive oil on its feet and it became quiet. Half an hour later, the kit was as frisky as ever.

November 25, 1945

Christmas is a month from today—not very far away. From the looks of things, I won't be home by then. We haven't received a bit of information since the other boys left.

Just for the sake of convenience, I intend to save $100 to $200 and keep it on my person, so that there is plenty of cash for tickets, etc. I imagine the Army takes care of such expenses, but there's no use taking chances.

This day has certainly been a lazy one. I got up at 10:00, worked on some papers, then stretched out on the sofa to play with the cat. By 1:00 it was time to eat. Richardson had invited Eleanor

Bergman over for dinner, so we ate a little late. The suggestion was made that we play a few hands of fan-tan—a half hour or so. We began a little after two, and were still playing after 6:30. By then it was time for supper, and Eleanor stayed for that. After supper, we <u>again</u> played fan-tan, quitting around 8:30 only so they could play bridge and I could write letters.

We enjoyed Eleanor's company. Captain Richardson needed someone to accompany him at the many social functions he had to attend. She supplied a good feminine touch at the house, which we all appreciated.

November 26, 1945

Six letters from you, one from Swan and another from my folks comprised the day's mail. Swan's letter was downright discouraging. He reports rumors to the effect tht men with <u>55</u> points won't be going home until late in January. However, he wrote this information before the War Department announced the 50-point deadline as of January 1st. So it's the same old story—rumors—rumors, and more rumors. HQ, 19th Weather Squadron waits on orders from the next higher echelon—Weather Wing. Weather Wing awaits orders from HQ, Army Air Forces. HQ Army Air Forces awaits orders from the General Staff. The General Staff awaits orders from the Secretary of War. The Secretary of War awaits orders from the President. Harry awaits the decision of the people. Is it any wonder things take so long?

November 27, 1945

This has been a busy if unorthodox day. It began with a telephone call from Ray Force, who announced that a driver had run their car into a tree en route to work. The roads are very slippery when wet—in fact, the same spot was the scene of an accident two weeks ago. Rich and I didn't work until after 9:30, since we wanted to hear about the accident. Ray received the only injury, a cut on his forehead.

WWII LETTERS TO MY GIRL BACK HOME
From Nigeria, Arabia and Turkey

After dinner, we sat down for a few games of fan-tan—and quit slightly after 4:00 p.m. Rich went to the office for a few minutes—I didn't go at all.

Next, Gutch and I decided to wash the kitten. The maid heated water; I put on old clothes and gloves, and we proceeded to carry the kit into the bathroom—Gutschick, Goodman, and myself. The poor little creature yowled in terror even before the water got on it. Soon it was soaking wet, looking ridiculously fragile and naked, shivering with a mixture of fear and cold. We used shampoo on it, rinsed the kitty, and carried the dripping little mite into the front room beside the fire. For a change, the kitten began licking itself, and was dry an hour later. I combed its hair, rubbed it with DDT, and finished with some sweet-smelling powder. Result: kitty was as clean and fluffy as a pastel powder puff.

...Now the conversation here has turned to airplane crashes. From the tales you hear, an airplane is about the most dangerous piece of transportation there is. Plenty of guys say they'll never ride in one.

November 28, 1945

This has been a dreary day—showers and drizzle all afternoon. However, I got lots of work done. Also, I found time for a much-needed haircut, complete with lemon-extract tonic. Anyway, the hair is cut.

We invited a couple of lieutenants over for supper, and then played fan-tan, the game lasting until after 10—a few minutes ago. In a few minutes more, I intend to be fast asleep... might as well glance over your unanswered letters...your information about my folks' courting was news to me...I knew Dad was a good student, having seen his report cards, and as for my mother, she had the reputation of being the brightest kid in her school.

November 29, 1945

Outside there is the steady patter of an all-night rain. The house is warm and cozy, though, and I have arisen from the sofa to write you. I was reclining on my back, while our purring kitten slept on my chest. Naturally I closed my eyes and wished that you and the kitty had changed places.

Got quite a bit done today, considering a late start, quitting early, and attending an enlisted men's council meeting.

We received our Turkish drivers licenses. The license is a small red book that looks very official. It will make a nice souvenir.

Contrary to expectations, the Cairo plane was unable to get through to us today, and was forced to turn back an hour out of Cairo. Another plane is already stranded here, which will make the delay of outgoing mail even longer.

We received a new weather officer for the region, a full colonel named Heinlein. Ordinarily, such news would suggest that the region will enlarge, although it may be that personnel reductions have thrown the colonel out of work, so to speak. Hope he wants to get the boys home. Sweetheart, there's hardly a guy overseas but wants to go home to his girl.

Getting there is our chief interest, and our job is secondary, no matter what it is.

November 30, 1945

This morning we received a radiogram to the effect that 55-pointers were going home right away. As you know, they are eligible for discharge tomorrow. Since I'll be eligible January 1st, I should be on orders in 31 days, too. Here's hoping.

Ankara received the first snowfall this morning, wet, slushy stuff which later turned to rain. Part of it is still on the surrounding hills. The ATC building is cold as usual. The present heating hold-up is stove pipe.

The big shots around here aren't very happy today. Due to hazardous landing conditions, C-54s will no longer stop here on eastbound and westbound flights. Furthermore, fewer C-47s will fly here than formerly. All this means that the base at Ankara will dwindle in importance, creating a possible surplus of one general, one colonel, and one lieutenant colonel. Therefore, these people are excited, and are doing their best to keep as much business as possible in Turkey. Colonel Nelson is thought to be responsible for the curtailment, and isn't very popular with them.

December 7, 1945

Remember this date? You should; it took a long time to be avenged—four long years, three of them taken from the two of us.

There was boku mail today, two packages from you (one of which I partially inventoried, indeed partially ate), a <u>Time</u> magazine, the <u>Readers Digest</u>, and at least 18 letters. I raced through them all, discovered that life at home seems OK, and decided to answer them later since I have to attend a meeting.

A group of us are going to sing carols at Christmas time and the first rehearsal was held at 8:30. It felt so darn good being in a group singing again—I thought of the many happy hours I've spent in similar groups in the days before the war.

You'd be surprised how much I look forward to returning to church. There is something about the atmosphere of quiet reverence which gives you perspective and makes you realize your proper place in the world. As you sit listening to good music, you realize how petty are the things which trouble us most.

We ate part of the delicious roll of candy. As usual, everyone from Mecheff to Rich was raving over it. The fruit cake we put aside for a later day, and the second package I left unopened.

December 8, 1945

Today I mailed you a Christmas present in an envelope about ten inches square and bearing 24 cents postage. The wrapping as you will undoubtedly notice is second-hand, and not too artistic. Hope you like the gift.

This being Saturday, we had the afternoon off. I wrapped your package and finished some 60 algebra problems. Might as well get in the habit of studying again, since there is plenty of it ahead.

December 9, 1945

Allan Robert Humbert

Would I be jealous if you went out with someone else several times? Yes. In general, it's a rather bad idea for this to happen, since it leads to all sorts of complications—jealousy, suspicion, worry, retaliation.

You mentioned champagne. Actually, most liquor has a rather bad taste, and why people drink the stuff is beyond me. Like other indulgences, drinking does the most harm among the lower classes. If it weren't so highly propagandized by brewers and distillers on the one hand and the WCTU on the other, its use might drop to the nominal figure resulting from the actual desire for it by the public. According to my Materia Medica (which see), slight amounts have a beneficial effect on a person, and total abstainers from alcohol do not live longer than those who drink. I suppose the drinking we do will be mostly for the novelty of doing something which not everyone would approve of. Still, best we keep drinking to ourselves, lest our reputations be shattered by LaFontaine's wagging tongues.

December 10, 1945

Events of the day: mail, study, work. Another letter from Swan saying the Sea Porpoise, which carries 55-60 pointers home won't reach New York till Dec. 23rd. The colonel at Payne Field is very GI—about like old General Brady at Seymour Johnson. A few days ago, some of the guys—not weathermen—climbed the giant pyramid at Giza. One fell off, hit his head and was killed.

How should our finances be handled? Considering our "high" prospective income of $75 per month, we'll about have to keep a budget, because the one thing we don't want to be is broke in a year or two. Our $2,000+ savings is more than many couples have for years after they're married; if we're wise, we can have a new house long before most people do.

December 11, 1945

This afternoon I heard an exciting rumor. Two ships, each with a capacity of 400-500 men, have already left New York and are on the high seas bound for Port Said in Egypt. If you hear a steady grunting sound, you'll know it's me trying to speed the boats up by sheer will power. Doggone it, honey, there's something epic about the knowledge that those ships are getting nearer hour by hour, and one of them will certainly carry me home!

In front of me sits a tube of Burma Shave, purchased from our new PX located on the third floor of the ATC building, above our office. Now we will have plenty of gum, cigarettes, toothpaste, etc. My own personal supplies have nearly run out—all except razor blades. I must still have a full year's supply left.

...Supper is, and Eleanor was, over. Our table conversation is really funny—everybody cutting up at once, telling jokes, making bright remarks, etc. The occasional lapses into improper language are cause for great merriment. One of the funnier errors is that which occurs when a guy starts to use any common but vulgar expression which is universal in the army, but hesitates on the very verge of the hateful word, suddenly inserting a pale little substitute which gelds the expression and is more noticeable than the familiar usage.

That reminds me of a bit of advice which all nice girls should follow: never repeat a joke unless you know thoroughly its point— because it may have some peculiar twist which isn't very nice.

December 12, 1945

Another rainy day with barely a peep of sunshine. However, I got quite a bit done, a couple days' records and most of an inventory.

Our kitty leads a rough life, but always comes back for more. One of the fellows, Gutschick, got a bottle of champagne, so we gave the kit some, to its spitting dismay. Then I took a balloon and blew it up, scaring the kit somewhat. Next, I placed the balloon on the floor and balanced the kitten on top. Naturally he immediately sank his claws into the balloon, which burst with a loud pop. Kitty went flying to a distant place, unable to figure out what had happened. He and the dog are great pals now, although he's a little undersized

Allan Robert Humbert

for the scrapping which takes place between them. The kitten never runs, but gives the pup as much as it takes.

December 13, 1945

Snow was falling before I got up this morning, and it has continued intermittently right up to the present moment—nearly 10:30 p.m. The ground is white and the streets are slippery. Personally, I enjoy the snow from the viewpoints of beauty, walking, and driving. Coming home from work, I had lots of fun sliding the length of the sidewalk—wish there were ice skating in Ankara.

Rich didn't get to work till late this morning, having been to a party. I myself did lots of little jobs, finding time nevertheless to play (and lose) a couple of ping-pong games, eat candy, play with the kitty, and repair Richardson's cigarette lighter, not to mention working a lot of algebra problems. Two jewelers had declared themselves unable to repair that lighter, but I finished the job in about 15 minutes, much to Rich's surprise. Confidentially, dear, little feats such as that don't do one's reputation any harm.

December 15, 1945

Saturday night and here the three of us are, sitting around a table writing letters, while in my lap reposes our stupid little cat.

This afternoon Rich, Eleanor, Force and I went about 30 minutes out of Ankara to ski. Eleanor had her own skis and we had one additional pair among the three of us, as Rich didn't ski at all. It was fun, except the fruits of ten minutes hard climbing are used up in one whoosh. Naturally I fell down once, upon attempting a rather steep slope. Some day, honey, you and I must go skiing.

We took Butch, the dog, along, and he shivered and cried as the damp snow froze on his hair. So I bundled him up in my overcoat, where he continued to shiver.

Today Cpl Gutschick who came to Ankara when I did, received orders sending him to station LGH-3, a mobile unit away out in the corner of Iraq. Also leaving Turkey is Sgt Geib, with 46 points, bound for the same forlorn place. This time next week, as even

Rich believes, orders for me should be in, for there's a boat leaving, according to rumor on December 25. If that's true, and I'm aboard, you can bet I'll have a <u>very</u> merry Christmas. Wonder where that boat is tonight.

December 17, 1945

The time is only 4:15 p.m., but my day's work is done. Despite definite rumors that the base will close about January 31st, work on the ATC building continues with incessant clatter.

Today I sent home $200, increasing our cash at home (in my department) to about $1478. No doubt you and I will find plenty of use for those two hundred dollars, and for many more like them. If this saving continues, folks might accuse us of marrying one another for the money—however we know that isn't true, since at the time we decided to get married neither of us had enough to count.

At noon I mailed Dad the leather kit containing all my tools. I only intend to take on the boat my GI equipment and what few books and personal effects are likely to be needed…Now, dear, this is station ARH signing off …

December 19, 1945

Last night the temperature was below zero, and since our bedroom has no heat, I found my washcloth frozen solid. Brr! We ordered additional coal this afternoon, after much red tape.

The personnel reports went in today, and I had the pleasure of typing a very nice recommendation. Gutschick and I were rated equal, both above everyone else. Not that I believe in ratings, but still, it's gratifying to know you're at the top of a list, because it suggests that some day one's reward may be a bit more tangible than mere satisfaction is.

Virtue sometimes pays, I guess. When we came overseas, there was wide variation in people's abilities and attitudes; yet for a long time no distinction seemed to be made between those who were conscientious and those who weren't. I shouldn't wonder that a good many "Turkey candidates" lost out because of their attitudes.

December 20, 1945

...Your mention of the barn makes me think of the situation in my family. Dad and Mom decided to build a barn before constructing their new house, but by the time it was finished, the Depression had hit us, and we couldn't afford the house. So we stayed in the old one, a hardship which cost us plenty in sickness, uncomfortable living conditions, social standing and morale. Of course what they did was their own business, though I would have planned on considerably fewer children, and would have concentrated at least some effort on making the old house larger and more livable.

Once I get finished with grad school and we get settled somewhere, we ought to get the house built quickly. By starting the process early, it should be possible to quit work for a year and concentrate on the house while living on savings. But if we wait till family expenses are high to start, we may be trapped in the same old rut of earning at a low rate but paying money out for construction a a high rate, and the house may never be built.

Could I take charge of the building? I believe I could. Dad is building theirs, even in wartime, and is acquainted with many men in the building business who could supply any needed expertise.

Aside from the savings, building the house would be fun. We'd plan it like a military campaign, and when the time came to start, I'd work around the clock till the stones fairly flew, while you kept the books, urged us on to greater efforts and supplied lemonade in the summer and hot chocolate in the winter. We could have the time of our lives.

Christmas, 1945

Merry Christmas, Darling.

WWII LETTERS TO MY GIRL BACK HOME
From Nigeria, Arabia and Turkey

I opened the remaining package promptly, and was very well satisfied with the contents, which I began using immediately—comb, talcum powder, and all.

Last night all Americans in Ankara attended the party given by the ambassador, and we had a good time. Most cocktail parties are dull, but this one was lively and interesting. The crowd joined in singing carols led by us, and the effect was fine. Our choir ranged in rank from Pfc to full colonel, but no rank-consciousness seemed to exist. I got home at 10 pm., and awoke (without hangover) at 6:30.

Unknown to me, the guys decided to get rid of the kitten, much to my sorrow.

The carolers left the American Embassy at noon, on a lorry containing the organ. We sang old-time songs en route to the British Embassy; once there, we got out and sang before a group of 50 or so. Afterwards, they gave us sherry and cookies. The next stop was the Swiss Embassy, but with muscatel and cake. Finally, we took in the beautiful French Embassy, an elegant building with spacious halls, sparkling chandeliers and tapestries that looked brand new. They gave us cream puffs, orangeade, and more cookies. By then it was 2:00, so we broke up the party "till next year."

In an hour or so occurs our Christmas dinner. I'm really not at all hungry; I still feel sorry for that poor little kitten, wandering out alone somewhere, forlorn and lost, getting used to going hungry, while we daily throw away ten times what it ate. Darling, it isn't any wonder there are wars, crime and misery. Just so long as men show their contempt for the principles of right and justice—yes, even to a fragile little cat—these things will continue to exist, propaganda notwithstanding.

I hope that when we are again together, we shall not content ourselves with kindness only to humans, but will extend the same sympathy and understanding to the animals we possess, applying the golden rule to them as well as to anyone else. But you already have that natural refinement of character which makes acts of kindness natural.

Allan Robert Humbert

December 26, 1945

Here it is 11:00 p.m. already. Since morning, I've done seven days' records, a two months balance sheet, a drawing or two, a trip to town and engaged in various conversations.

Lou Stoia's girl, Renata Ebert, was over for supper. She is very tall, pretty, 19 and quite American. She told us the story of her name "Renata." It seems that her mother had such a difficult time at the birth that the doctor told her father it was impossible to save both the woman and the child, and that he must choose between the two. Her father said he was sorry, but of course the baby must be sacrificed. So it was assumed that she would die, but strangely enough, she didn't. So they named her Renata, which means "reborn."

We were telling her what a wonderful land the USA is, and meaning every word of it. We talked for over an hour, extolling the merits of such topics as drug stores, installment buying, freedom of speech, building privileges, freedom of travel, department stores, modern kitchens, bathrooms, the opportunity to get ahead and many other things.

She and Lou are going to be married—they'll make a fine couple. And so will we.

During the past 70 days, I have handled 3,334 Turkish lire for the house, over $1800. The books balanced within 50 kurus, so I pocketed the surplus and felt very well pleased. Upon checking the totals, however, I was shocked to find us 700 lire short, but an investigation revealed that our temperamental adding machine was printing one amount and adding a different one. By checking each page at least twice, I got the books to balance within 25 cents—or one part in 6,000. Good enough?

WWII LETTERS TO MY GIRL BACK HOME
From Nigeria, Arabia and Turkey

December 27, 1945

Tomorrow Richardson is going to wire Cairo and see why my orders haven't come. So I'll be patient for a while longer.

Mere saving of money is such a dreary and monotonous activity; there is no tangible evidence of your work. But a house would grow month by month, and each day's work would be plain to see.

As you say, a five-room house with fireplace costs $7,500. The two of us have only been able to save a little over one third that amount in three years, and much longer time must pass before we save enough to have it built. All that time, we'll be paying rent when we could be living in the unfinished structure, and having it help us.

Did I tell you one personal reason for wishing to build in this way? It's simply that three long years in the army have made me too accustomed to taking orders and have created a feeling of personal insignificance. Building a house would restore my morale.

What I wish is a real battle-royal, the sort of struggle into which you can throw mind, body, spirit, and money for a tangible reward. I want to work 12 hours a day, battle mud, flies, rain and whatever, making the job an epic adventure.

December 28, 1945

Today Rich sent the radiogram inquiring why S. Sgt Swing and I haven't received orders. No doubt he'll soon receive a snappy reply to the effect that he should mind his own business and wait till they are ready to issue them.

That is one significant difference between Rich and some other officers. He is never afraid to go to bat for you, even at the risk of being censured himself. Some guys were so afraid of criticism that they wouldn't say "Boo." Strangely enough, they were the officers whom Headquarters had little use for, while Rich can get away with murder.

Allan Robert Humbert

December 29, 1945

Grr! Today we received a degrading bawling out by the officious Lt Colonel who is our new CO. How long, Oh Lord?

December 31, 1945

Hello again on the last day of the year. The guys have persuaded me to attend the arrival of the new one, although I'm not particularly eager to. Fact is, without coaxing, I wouldn't.
Mail arrived, but no letters from you. I assumed they were traveling by ship. If they are, I could be a civilian before receiving them.
19th Weather surely does believe in squeezing the last bit of work from us. Officially, I have enough points to be discharged. But does Headquarters know or care? Evidently not.
We were paid today. I received the usual wad of per diem, plus my meagre regular pay. However, since this will surely be my last pay in Ankara, I intend to hang onto it until such time as it is certain the money won't be needed for expenses on the way home. The customary $50 went home, no doubt raising my estimated cash at that happy place to $1528. Perhaps we should take a final fond gaze at our capital, for years must pass before it is again so high.
Best I end this letter on the cheerful note of ultimately returning to you. Here's hoping "ultimately" means January, and that we're married long before any birthdays arrive.

Ankara, Turkey
January 1, 1946

...Yippee!
About ten minutes ago, Rich called from the field with the words, "I've got good news for you, boy." Then he proceeded to read the radiogram which orders Swing and I into Cairo bound for the USA.
As you can imagine, I'm pretty excited, since this surely means getting home in January. A plane leaves Ankara tomorrow, but

there is too much work to make catching it practical, so I'll probably get out in three or four days.

January 2, 1946

Last night your fiancé was higher than a kite.

After receiving the orders, I knew it would be necessary to work, holiday or not, so I went to the ATC. But about 3:00 p.m., in buzzed Rich, telling me to skip the work, that we were having a party. It was the first cocktail party I've ever helped put on, and I learned just how simple it was—a table in one corner of the room with drinks, and the buffet covered with candies, fruitcake (yours, honey), etc. For a while I zealously played the part of host, but as time went on, I found standing increasingly difficult, and therefore remained seated as much as possible. Meanwhile, Rich set out deliberately to make things worse, and he succeeded. After a time, things became funnier, and I found that remarks which were completely unspontaneous would cause gales of laughter from our corner of the room. So I plied people left and right with compliments, jokes and quotations. By and by we sang—and I became even happier.

Then came supper. Champagne began the meal, and the cork hit the ceiling just as in the movies. Mecheff, of course, did splendidly, though I ate little, having filled up on candy. After supper came another bottle of champagne—and nothing would do but I must be given a whole glass of it. That was enough.

In all seriousness, Lou Stoia, Haynes and I were bubbling over at the wonders of America. It was wasted energy, for both Renata and her sister, Chris, are already sold on the States. We read a stirring poem, "America for Me."

Then Lou and Renata began to kiss. I promptly condemned their hesitancy, and explained that <u>my</u> girl hardly counted a kiss that lasted less than a minute. Thus inspired, they produced a very superior performance, one that made my blood tingle with anticipation of our own. There really wasn't a lot else to the party—at 10:00 I retired, buttoning my coat on the hanger and behaving quite soberly.

Allan Robert Humbert

January 3, 1946

By 7:15 a.m. the next morning, I was awake and worked like the dickens till 5:00 p.m., when I packed with equal ardor. Surprisingly, I had no hangover at all.

10:30 p.m. finds me packed and ready to head for the airport at 9:00 a.m. tomorrow. All day long, I've been doing things "for the very last time," and gloating between gaps in a final furious working spree. The records are off two days ahead of schedule, though I know they are lousy with errors. Can't do everything, though, much as I would like to. The fact is, I didn't have to work, on this, my last day as an observer. However, one guy has been sick, and people are going to have a rough enough time working shorthanded as it is.

What a fantastic set-up this has been! Everything I could ask for except home and you. Let's see, now, when I am paid tomorrow, I'll have over $200 in pocket money, $100 of which will go home. That will mean a net rise in actual cash at home from $640 to $1628, over $988. But there have been many other gains here that I'm too sleepy to name.

Honey, I am dog-tired. For the past 48 hours I have been pouring out energy on countless tasks of all descriptions. I desire nothing so much as to crawl off into a corner and go to sleep.

Last night it occurred to me that most of us have more good will toward our fellow men than we realize. We tell ourselves how we hate people, but immediately begin making exceptions, and by and by we realize that we do indeed love one another.

January 4, 1946

The plane remained grounded today because of low ceilings and low visibility due to snow. Since there was no way we could learn that it wouldn't take off, we had to be weighed in at 9:00 a.m. as scheduled. For some reason I felt rather sick, so I went back to bed at 11:00 and stayed there. The time now is only 8:00 p.m., but I intend to go back to bed upon writing this.

Mecheff took one glance at the sky this morning and told us the plane wouldn't take off. You know the saying about the cleverness of the Chinese.

Darling, you can imagine how little there is to write about, since I haven't done a thing since last night's letter but sleep.

Evidently most of even Weather's 50-pointers have been called to Cairo ahead of us. From the length of the list, it seems probable we shall return to the states by boat.

News reports tonight mentioned several troop transports having difficulty with stormy seas. Perhaps my wish for a rough crossing will be granted.

...this is the beginning of a hectic time, especially for the next month or so. We will no doubt be pushed around here, taking the usual stupid orders from permanent party members, eating in mess halls, etc. However, it's worth it.

Allan Robert Humbert

Chapter 20

HOMEWARD BOUND

Cairo, Egypt
January 5, 1946

Greetings from your plane-weary fiancé, who still doesn't feel well, and who plans to go to bed at the earliest opportunity.
There are vastly fewer people at Payne Field than there were in July. The place has an air of utter lifelessness which is intensified by the cessation of the roaring motors of the C-47 plane on which I flew. Now we have an abundance of room in every building, and Payne always was a monster place.
...Time out while I get some coffee and pretzel sticks. The way my digestion is the last couple of days, surely nothing can make it worse.
...Might as well acquaint you with the latest information, wise or otherwise. Fact No. 1: Today a shipload of Egyptian students and soldiers' wives left for the US. Fact No. 2: Ankara received a radiogram suspending all applications of civilians for transportation to the States, due to military requirements. Thought No. 1: Rich optimistically predicted that I'll be home by the 20th of January. Rumor No. 1: A ship leaves here on Jan. 15. Rumor No. 2: The next one doesn't leave till February 5th, so you may take your choice.
Despite only a few hours in this little paradise, I have succeeded in losing three pieces of equipment—my pistol belt, canteen and first aid pouch. Hope I don't have to buy the darn junk.

A wog is walking nervously about as if he wishes to close this room. For that matter, it's almost time to begin the long pedestrian journey back to the barracks. Therefore, I hope you won't feel bad if I say good night ...

January 6, 1946

Sunday finds me well and nearly normal again. I have rested most of the day. My first two meals were good. If the chow remains so from now on, there will be little reason for complaint.
  After a shower and a trip to the dispensary where I was given a glassful of chalky liquid, I went to Headquarters to sign in. There I met Major Warner. We talked about Ankara and I brought before him certain matters at the request of Rich. You already know how much I think of Major Warner—he's the sort of fellow you're proud to work under.
  Following a good roast beef dinner, I read in the library. Ankara was rather short on books, and it's nice to have plenty for a change.
  Since over a year has passed since seeing many of the guys in our shipment overseas, many have changed perceptibly. In general, the more excitable ones have done the changing, while such stable personalities as Tice and Spear remain unaffected. One acquaintance has become rather bitter, and argues more than ever. He has too much of the crusading spirit. Instead of applying it to his work, he uses it in fault-finding, which seems to get him in dutch with his officers, causing low efficiency ratings, etc. Still another fellow has drunk quite a lot and run around too much, while he and many others have indulged in black marketing.
  One virtue which I constantly admire in our romance is our complete sincerity. I read your letters knowing they say just what you mean, and realizing that no note of falseness enters. Without boasting, the same can be said for my letters. It's nice going home to the girl you love, knowing that you've been true to one another and that you have nothing to hide.
  It just occurred to me that I may have left the wrong impression about the cost of the champagne which we drank as if it were pop.

Allan Robert Humbert

Ordinarily the stuff is expensive, but somebody worked out an arrangement whereby one bottle was exchanged for a carton of cigarettes. Since these cost us only 60 cents per carton and at least 6 people shared the champagne, the cost was about ten cents per glass.

Tomorrow I hope to begin a buying spree which will stock our larder with as much PX material as can reasonably be used—shoes, handkerchiefs, etc. Even after sending home the $100 raising our cash to $1628, I still had left over $140. Profitable place, Ankara.

Major Warner said a boat is leaving the 18th of this month, the one we shall probably board. At a guess, we should be home by Jan. 30th.

Strangely enough, I feel rather patient lately. Knowing that perhaps not even a month separates us, there seems little need to get excited. Not only that; I enjoy the temporary ease which is ours. In my Ankara job there was a constant feeling of responsibility, even when I wasn't working. Here there is next to none.

Cairo, Egypt
January 8, 1946

Civilian reconversion note: Today I bought a good pair of low-cut shoes for $6.28 at the Huckstep PX. They are Allen Edmonds brand, a good one, according to their advertisement. Also, I purchased a chocolate malt and a sundae. Both were good; however, PX ice cream has a characteristically artificial taste which rather spoils it.

Last night after writing you, I went to the dispensary again, discovered that I had a fever with a temperature of 99 or so, and was therefore given sulfaguanadine pills to be consumed at the alarming rate of 42 per day—seven every four hours. Apparently they fixed me up all right, because the only adverse effects I noted today were due to the pills themselves. The doctor said the 9:00 a.m. dose should be sufficient, so on that one I quit. Since he told me to take things easy, I returned to bed at 12:00 a.m. and slept till 3:30 p.m. The bed was so comfortable that I was tempted to remain there, but didn't want to spoil the night's sleep. While we're on the

WWII LETTERS TO MY GIRL BACK HOME
From Nigeria, Arabia and Turkey

hypochondriac subject of my physical profile, perhaps I should add the remaining boring details, that I have a slight fever and headache now, and that a dental appointment has been made Friday to have my only cavity filled.

January 9, 1946

Today I feel perfect for the first time in days. Didn't get much done, but had a reasonably good time. Just added a new item to my civilian wardrobe—a pair of pajamas. No doubt you'll be seeing them (and me) soon.

Last night a movie called "The Three Caballeros" played. It was a sparkling combination of Technicolor, Donald Duck, Latin America and music—a sort of popularized "Fantasia." Tonight, "The Bells of St. Mary's" is being shown; in fact, I'm sitting in the theater right now waiting for it to begin.

A letter from home informed me today that I received a life subscription to the <u>Reader's Digest</u> for Christmas. Needless to say, I'd planned to buy the subscription myself if the folks hadn't. I had wondered why they delayed sending the money order for it I'd requested for so long.

Camp Huckstep really is crowded now. Although the movie doesn't begin till 7:30—it's 7:00 now—the theater is almost full. Bet our boat will be heavily laden.

Wish I were a prophet. Every article I pick up stresses raising teachers' wages. If I thought the pay would go up, I'd be tempted to stay in the field. It's the old shell game again, guessing, guessing.

January 10, 1946

Greetings from the capital of wog-land, which I intend to revisit in only 150 years. Yes, I'm in Cairo, and I haven't had a very good time. Old King Ibn Saud had to visit the place today, so all truck transportation stopped, making it difficult to get here in the first place, and stopping our proposed tour. Not only that, the museum was closed. In short," I've 'ad it."

Allan Robert Humbert

Are you impatient just now? I am. Aside from wanting to be married, I feel the pressure of a thousand problems, and the desire to get going in a routine which will solve a few of them. But here I am in the Red Cross Club, sitting in an upholstered chair and watching two guys play checkers. This isn't my fault, but it might as well be insofar as results are concerned. This isn't a new theme, to be sure, but it's surely an important one.

January 11, 1946

Two items of going-home concern occurred this morning, a clothing check and a dental appointment. The dentist put in one new filling, without any pain to speak of.

After dinner, I bought and mailed a couple of other things for our house. First was a little silver filigree knick-knack tray which had been marked down from $2.20 to only 40 cents. The second was a pair of ivory candlesticks which cost $4.00.

Originally there was a pair in the PX which someone had chipped so as to mar the trimming at the base of the candle cup. These were priced at $4.00, having been reduced from $12.00 by virtue of the chipped cup. In an effort to get a nice-looking set, I exchanged the cups on this set with another $12.00 set, explaining to the native clerk what I was doing and why. Liking the new combination, I decided to buy it, and said, "with the exchanged top, the price will be three pounds ($12.00)." To my surprise, he stuck with the old price, and I departed paying only $4.00 for a set worth three times that. I still haven't figured why he reduced the price, but I'll not argue. I sent them home first class, wrapped in a cigar box tied with heavy string. Even as I bought them, I thought, "sooner or later one of the kids we haven't had yet will knock these off and break them."

Getting back to your last three letters, should I tell you shady jokes? I don't think so. At least not in letters, anyway. Fact is, dear, there are quite a few good ones that I know which really ought to be on file. However, there is a time and a place for everything, and this is neither.

WWII LETTERS TO MY GIRL BACK HOME
From Nigeria, Arabia and Turkey

January 12, 1946

Just 21 months ago today, we left the USA, not knowing when we'd return. But here we are ready to go back, little the worse for our experiences. I imagine that 21 months from now the army will seem like a distant and unimportant interlude.

Those mass meetings protesting men being kept overseas illustrate one point which has long been apparent to me. Army discipline, for all its severity and rank-consciousness lies only skin deep with us. Our obedience is obtained pretty largely by the fear of consequences, and little else. Now that the war is over, we realize the chief personal trait of most officers is luck, having the necessary credits at the right time, etc. So when people wish to hold a mass meeting, they hold it.

This morning I purchased another pair of items for you. One is a mother-of-pearl butterfly brooch (wingspread 1 7/8 inches), and the other is a tan leather purse bearing Egyptian designs on both sides. It features several compartments, one of them with a zipper, a mirror and a small coin purse, and is about 8 x 11 inches in size. Hope you like it.

January 13, 1946

A week from today we should be at sea. Here's hoping. I spent the day quietly enough, went to church at 11:00, took a walk with Tice during the afternoon to see some C-46 planes being wrecked, and spent the evening repacking before our departure tomorrow for Huckstep.

You should see what they're doing to those C-46s. Only the motors and the tires are being saved; the rest is being junked. The instruments were in flying condition, but the wreckers deliberately break in the face of every dial in the pilot's compartment, ruining thousands of dollars worth of your war bonds' purchases—in order to keep them off the market so manufacturers can sell more.

The evening is still young, so I'll answer some of your letters. Speaking, as you did, of dates, Europeans never write "1946." They omit the "1" and write "946"... By the time we meet all the people to be met, it will be the 4th of July...You must be quite a snow-shoveler. Fact is, dear, I like people who don't sit by helplessly when there's work to be done. Between the two of us, we should have lots of energy for most any job.

Can we design and build our own house in two years for $2600? I'll bet we do. I doubt whether many people could. But we <u>aren't</u> many people. We are <u>us</u>, two distinct and separate individuals, the only combination on earth of its kind, now or ever. Of course people will say it cannot be done, to which I reply, "wait and see."

I am sick and tired of competing in a friendly little game where nobody may work over eight hours because it isn't "nice," where each person's life is dedicated to the pursuit of futility and the escape from reality. We humans were designed to function as were other animals, and there is nothing like a real battle to bring out our hidden reserves and make living worthwhile. I therefore propose to declare war on some 9600 cubic feet of earth and a good quantity of wood and stone. With you as my loyal ally, we shall speedily bring the enemy to terms, and spend the rest of our lives walking on him!

See there, honey, enough energy wasted to have dug out 20 or 30 cubic feet of earth, and nothing to show for it but a letter. That's the sort of waste that goes on these days.

This morning we moved from Payne Field to nearby Camp Russell B. Huckstep, where we will remain until ready to board the boat. It took all morning to get settled in the tents and after dinner a tough major told us what's happening.

Our ship is the Santa Margarita, to the best of his knowledge. About 22 officers and 201 enlisted men will make up the passenger list. She docks at Alexandria on the 17th or 18th, and we go there by truck on the 19th or 20th, boarding the ship the same day.

Since there aren't enough places for everyone, some of the guys having less than 51 points were placed on the air backlog and will fly back. Which category of soldiers will get home first is uncertain. The guys are saying we shall be in the USA during the first few days of February.

Since travel arrangements are now definite, I'll send a couple of cables tomorrow.

WWII LETTERS TO MY GIRL BACK HOME
From Nigeria, Arabia and Turkey

About mail, darling, it still isn't definite where we shall go from New York. Our orders foolishly send us to Oklahoma City, a mistake, because we are all eligible for discharge. Local headquarters is trying to have us go straight to our reception centers from the boat, which would be Fort Harrison in my case. Since things are undecided, our orderly room is going to send all mail to our home address. So honey, best you discontinue sending letters to me at any address. I would still like you to write them, but merely refrain from mailing them to me. Chances are I'll pick them up in person. Of course I shall do the same for you, and our faithful correspondence will thereby be continued till the very last. Some folks would consider this foolish, but we won't.

Sweetheart, if you like fireplaces, you should be here. I am sitting in front of a huge stone one jutting out four feet from the wall and measuring at least 12 feet from one side to the other. The mantel is so high I can't touch it on tip toe. Inside is a cozy fire, leaving plenty of room for anyone so minded to sit right beside the coals themselves. Quite a big service club they have here.

Well, dear, events are happening fast. Long before you get this letter, we shall be at sea; battling our way across the Atlantic. Do you know, honey, I shall miss writing you once we are together? The closest I ever get to home is while writing you or reading one of the letters you've sent.

January 16, 1946

Another day, another dollar, and I feel interested in life again.

My eagerness to get started isn't because I can't wait to have certain things, but rather because I am afraid of slipping backward, or reverting to a habit of postponement which will keep us from ever getting a house. Our combined $2900, if conserved, will go most of the way toward that, provided we don't use it for other things. Having seen my folks get stuck in a hopeless rut for years and years, reminds me that such misfortunes can happen to the best of us.

Really, dear, I don't want an easy life. I only want the struggle to be against matters worthy of our attention. There is something degrading about having to fix fires, scrub constantly and work your fingers to the bone. Aside from that, every hour spent on such profitless tasks is an hour lost to creative work.

I hope our life together can be something more than an apology or excuse, that we can take pride in not only the little things but in the larger ones, too. I despise excuses—my own more than those of anyone else. I'd rather be considered flatly wrong or be misunderstood than to weasel out with some lame and ineffectual excuse.

Soon we shall be married, and the realization of that dream ought to keep us happy awhile in itself. It will be part of your job to see we keep on an even keel, since you're the more level-headed of our partnership. I, on the other hand, will constantly surprise you with new and strange ideas, some of which I am going to make work, or bust…Time to go to bed, so good night, and be good.

January 17, 1946

Surely this pen will go dry tonight. It hasn't been filled since I left Ankara. There's no more black ink to be had, either.

I've had a hectic day. First came the two-hour wait in line before we received our smallpox vaccination, then dinner and a trip to Payne Field. Tice and I went together, he to buy himsef a ring and get a haircut, and I to get a haircut and collect the last few dollars per diem. The money wasn't ready, so I was told to return at 4:20 when the girl expected to have it taken care of. Don and I separated, and I stepped in briefly to the AACS warehouse to see whether any radios had been declared surplus.

Sure enough, several had been, and there was a sizable group of guys looking the radios over and buying them as fast as possible. I found one, of the model known as "Super-Pro," the very same radios which have carried weather messages throughout the war. After brief inspection and testing by the radio lab, they declared it was a good buy, so I purchased it for $18. That, honey, is less than 10% of the cost price during wartime. Moreover, they very generously replaced several bad tubes with brand new ones. By 4:50 p.m. the radio was boxed and hauled to Huckstep. To be sure, I missed supper, but I got the radio.

WWII LETTERS TO MY GIRL BACK HOME
From Nigeria, Arabia and Turkey

Just how well it will stand the trip is questionable, but at least it plays all right now. It does not have the regular broadcast band but possesses the shortwave ones. I intend to use it in preparing weather maps for our own use, such as I did at Ball State.

There may be some difficulty in getting it home due to its weight, but we'll see. There is a 70-pound limit.

Two letters came today, one of them bearing the exciting announcement that you got the last letter. I trust you won't form any false impressions of my arrival date. I think you can definitely expect to hear from me within two weeks from the last letter you receive. According to the first sergeant, even though our orders direct us to Tinker Field, Oklahoma, the practice is for the port authorities to disregard them and send us direct to separation centers.

Sweetheart, there's a full moon out tonight, and it makes my heart beat quickly to know that before the moon is full once again, we'll be together at long last, ready to begin our life side by side, where we shall be during many years to come. Rather than tantalize myself imagining the luxuries of being married, I shall simply repeat, I love you, and wait just a little longer.

Yours forever,

January 18, 1946

Hi, again...That box weighed exactly 87 pounds—17 pounds too much. So, I had to get rid of 17 pounds. First I uncrated the darn thing and tried to remove some of the heavier parts. No luck, because the set was too complicated and the heavy pieces were soldered together. Finding that the box alone weighed 30 pounds, I set out to find one lighter in weight. This, plus repacking took all afternoon, and the evening to boot, since I finished at 9:20. My fingers are blistered, my feet ache, and I had only sandwiches for supper, <u>but</u> the radio is packed and I think it will make the trip OK. Nothing remains but to carry it to the post office.

Speaking of trips, we are restricted to the post tomorrow. Sunday afternoon we board the Santa Margarita, and at 4:00 p.m.

Allan Robert Humbert

she weighs anchor and heads for home. Tomorrow's letter is the last you'll receive until you're ready to receive me also.

The pleasure taken in having that radio ready to go, together with the satisfaction of going home—not to mention my genuine enjoyment hearing a bunch of hillbilly songs rendered by some guys near me—these things make me very happy.

Cairo, Egypt
January 19, 1946

...Your letters...Sure we had water in Turkey. Fact is, that's what we drank 99% of the time...Our house plans...well, let's wait and see. Things may have changed plenty in two years' absence, especially prices. I believe school on the GI bill must be attended within two years—not sure. Wonder how the school treasurer's books you kept turned out. Hope you didn't give them an excessive amount of medicine. Mine were OK, thank goodness. Handling money is a thankless job, yet at times a dangerous one. Heating a home with oil vs. hot water. Temperature is much more steady with hot water.

...About the radio; it weighed only 66 pounds, and seems likely to arrive in good condition...Now to wrap two packages and get a few money orders.

...Done, and the time is 5:30 p.m. I'm busy packing all my stuff, preparing to leave in the morning. About the pocketbook, when it arrives, better get it resewn because the threads look weak.

As usual, there seem to be things to do right up to the last minute. Must take a bath, too. For the past several mornings, I have got up late (7:15 a.m.), after debating whether or not to take one. It's cold in the tent, and I'm always sleepy, so up till now the battle has always resulted in my doing without.

The two chief things I intend to do on the boat are to exercise and study math.

Guess what I'm doing with dirty socks these days? Having a surplus of old ones which weren't any good, I wear each pair till dirty, and then throw them away. The army will only discard them if I don't.

WWII LETTERS TO MY GIRL BACK HOME
From Nigeria, Arabia and Turkey

Well, honey, there's a lot to be done between now and bedtime, so best I cut this short until next time. We'll have fun reading each other's letters; indeed, perhaps I'll read some of yours in your presence. That would be fun, you know, having my arms around you while opening and reading your own letter ...

Camp Kilmer, New Jersey
February 4, 1946

From the ship's newspaper, "The G.I. Finale":
"SS Margarita departed Alexandria 20 January 1946. Traveling a total of 5458 miles, the ship docked in New York City on 3 February 1946."

This is the first letter of today. By the time my calls got through, it was too late to write.
    I thought the peak of satisfaction had been reached when we steamed up the Hudson past the Statue of Liberty, but darling, when I actually talked to you last night, I was happier still. It would take a book to say everything you mean to me—perhaps I'd better not try.
    Strong head winds delayed our arrival yesterday until we were several hours late. The SS Santa Margarita passed the Statue of Liberty at 2:50, and docked at Pier 84 an hour or so later. The bay narrows as one goes upstream. There were dozens of ships of all sizes, and as we passed or met each one, they gave us three greeting toots, which we answered with another three. Of course the SS Santa Margarita had flags flying from bow to stern, indicating that it was a troop ship, and the whistles were for us, as were numerous signs along the piers. Most of them read, "Welcome Home—Well Done."
    In case your geography is as hazy as mine, New Jersey and the statue are on the left of our course, and the piers on the right—number one being toward Coney Island, and the higher ones, inland. Frankly, our welcome at the pier didn't amount to much—a dozen or so Red Cross girls, a couple of records over the PA system, and a cameraman or two. But then New York is getting ten troop

ships daily, and the weather was hardly conducive to being outdoors. We did get all the doughnuts and milk we wanted—delicious, too.

A group of steelworkers are telling some wild tales about guys falling into molten steel, etc. Evidently when someone falls into the stuff, all they do is bury one ingot as a symbol.

Last night we boarded GI buses at the pier, went down the Speedway, through the Holland Tunnel, and out a fancy road system known as the Pulaski Skyway, in New Jersey. Once inside Camp Kilmer, we had a brief lecture, were billeted, and went to chow.

There we received a truly epic meal—peas, corn, mashed potatoes, salad, rolls, one pint of milk, coffee, and a monster piece of perfect beefsteak so heavy it made the tray unbalanced. We couldn't begin to eat it all—I left some of every dish—but it was sure fun trying. There are subtle differences in flavor that instantly mark all home products as superior. Ice cream is better, potatoes are better, and likewise for the rest. I thought my taste for milk might have changed, but no such occurrence—it was good as ever.

After supper, most of us went to the Telephone Building, where a battery of 30 phones were handling nationwide calls. Long lines extended everywhere, and the call I placed at 8:35 EST took over two hours to go through. However, once we got a booth, service took only five minutes. Originally, I asked that your call precede the folks', but the phone company got them on the line before you. I could hear you much more clearly than they.

This morning I slept late, arising finally to eat an orange, visit the PX, and wait in a long line for haircut, shampoo and tonic, and returned here afterward.

Honey, at this particular instant, I am so excited, so much in love with you, and so eager to be home that I'm almost jumping up and down.

February 4, 1946

There still isn't much news as to where we'll go, though my guess is Atterbury, Indiana. At any rate, we are supposed to get out of here some time tomorrow.

Chow continues to be very good, especially the bread, which seems to be served almost as soon as it is baked. Bread on the boat was hardly fit to eat. It was baked at intervals of several days and stored in the refrigerator, where it acquired the miscellaneous flavors found there. In general, the ship was not nearly so well run as the Ralph Izzard, although it had better facilities.

When I talked to Dad last night, he said they hadn't known I was coming; yet I mailed the letter to them at the same time as I did yours. Wonder what happened to it.

Since my bunk is warm and comfortable, I spent most of the afternoon in it working algebra. Since starting at Ankara, I have completed 105 pages of a 233 total. Let's see, I completed two lessons out of ten in a few years. At that rate, it will be 1972 before I'm done.

The United States of America... am I really here, or is it a dream? A song comes to the rescue: "Are the stars out tonight? I don't know if it's cloudy or bright 'cause I only have eyes for you..." Darling, the food was good this evening, but my head is in the clouds, and if they had handed me a moldy dog biscuit, I would have smiled and eaten it. I am coming home to you and that's all that matters.

DEMOBILIZATION—FEBRUARY 1946

Soon we were on the bus bound for Camp Atterbury, Indiana. We turned in all the government property we had except for clothing being worn and were counselled by an interviewer who gave us official documents summarizing our military experience for the benefit of future civilian employers.

In contrast to the tense atmosphere which had prevailed at Ft. Harrison where we had been inducted ages ago in 1942, mood at Camp Atterbury was laid-back and cheerful. The captain who was in

Allan Robert Humbert

charge of our pre-discharge physical exam told us, "You men will go through this line, and we'll have your chest X-rayed. If you want to reenlist, we'll have your head X-rayed."

Less than a week after first setting foot on US soil, we were given the lapel button that signified our status as "veterans," along with our honorable discharge, and the first $100 of our $300 mustering-out pay.

We were soldiers no more.

Epilogue 2002

The years following the war unfolded for us much the same as they did for countless other couples. Like families of most veterans, we were so glad the conflict was over that we wasted little time seeking special considerations, but plunged eagerly into our new life, determined to make up for lost time.

We got married in March, barely one month after I was discharged. Graduate school at Ball State followed, thanks to the newly-created GI Bill of Rights which paid my tuition and a modest stipend for living expenses. Mozelle worked in a professor's office while I attended classes.

Our son, Richard, was born in 1950 and our daughter, Kathryn, in 1952. After a few years living in a house trailer which I built, we moved to Marion, Indiana, my wife's home town. Conditions seemed right for constructing the home we had always wanted.

Working summer and weekends, I did indeed complete it, doing most of the work myself. The house took years to build, but in 1959 we finally moved in. We live there to this day.

For years we were teachers, both working in the same school. Retired since the early 80's, our lives continue busy as ever with church activities, family gatherings, gardens and hobbies.

Allan Robert Humbert

About the Author

Robert Humbert was born in Muncie, Indiana. He earned B.S. and M.A. degrees from Ball State Teachers College. After serving as a weather observer in World War II, he became a teacher in the fields of science, mathematics and English. His wife, Mozelle, was also a teacher. They are now retired.

He has served as the president of various organizations including the Indiana Inventors Association and holds a US patent. He is an amateur radio operator with a General class license. His hobbies are gardening, photography, travel and the design of new products. He and his wife have a son, Richard, and a daughter, Kathryn. They reside in Marion, Indiana, in a home of their own design and construction.